A Venture in Africa

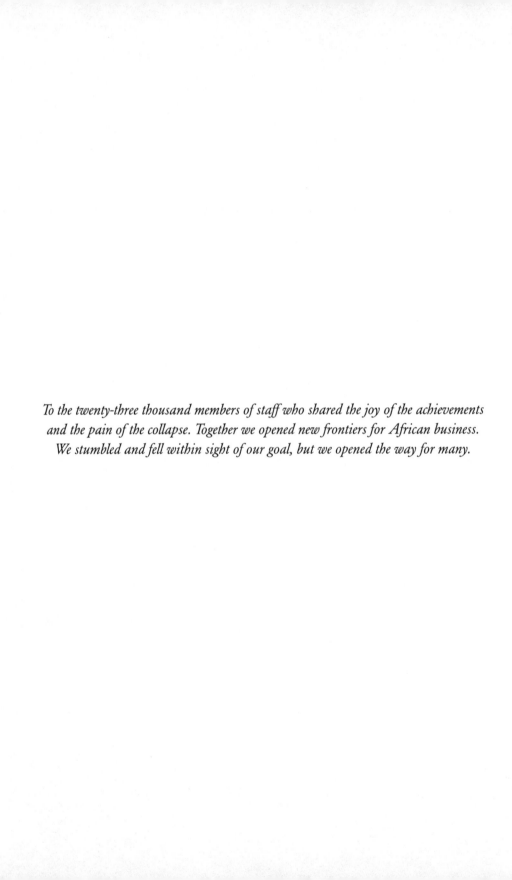

To the twenty-three thousand members of staff who shared the joy of the achievements and the pain of the collapse. Together we opened new frontiers for African business. We stumbled and fell within sight of our goal, but we opened the way for many.

A Venture in Africa

The Challenges of African Business

Andrew Sardanis

I.B. TAURIS

LONDON · NEW YORK

Published in 2007 by I.B.Tauris & Co Ltd
6 Salem Road, London W2 4BU
175 Fifth Avenue, New York NY 10010
www.ibtauris.com

In the United States and Canada distributed by Palgrave Macmillan,
a division of St. Martin's Press, 175 Fifth Avenue, New York NY 10010

ISBN: 978 1 84511 288 2 (hardback)
      978 1 84511 513 5 (paperback)

A full CIP record for this book is available from the British Library
A full CIP record for this book is available from the Library of Congress
Library of Congress catalog card: available

Typeset in Garamond by Dexter Haven Associates Ltd, London
Printed and bound in Great Britain by T.J. International Ltd, Padstow, Cornwall.

CONTENTS

LIST OF ILLUSTRATIONS

ACKNOWLEDGEMENTS

My thanks first go to Danae for her unwavering support and encouragement. And for her courage to relive all over again through the medium of this painful book the trials and tribulations, the breakthroughs and the setbacks, the joys and the sorrows and all the other challenges we experienced doing business in so many English-, French- and Portuguese-speaking African countries and learning to cope with their ethnic, cultural and linguistic diversity and the legacies of their former colonial masters.

Also to my sons Stelios and Harry, who read the manuscript and helped me fill up gaps that had been pushed deep into my subconscious because they hurt so much to remember.

'Παπαῖ Μαρδόνιε, κοίους ἐπ' ἄνδρας
ἤγαγες μαχησομένους ἡμέας, οἳ οὐ περὶ χρημάτων
τὸν ἀγῶνα ποιεῦνται ἀλλὰ περὶ ἀρετῆς.'

Zounds, Mardonius, what manner of men are these that you have brought us to fight withal? 'tis not for money they contend but for glory of achievement.

(Translation from the Loeb Classical Library Edition
of Herodotus 'The Persian Wars' Book VIII)

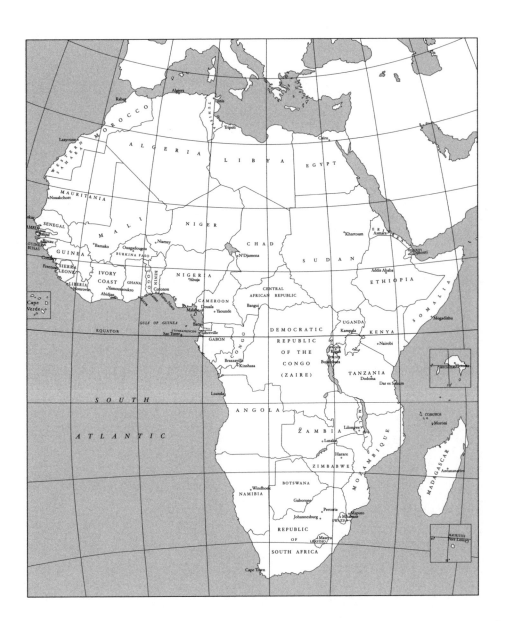

INTRODUCTION

Everybody has been meddling in Africa. And everybody has a formula for its salvation. In the old days salvation was the promised 'protection' of one European empire or another and the Christian gospel. Nowadays it is more of the same, but for European empires read 'Western democracies' and for the Christian gospel read free markets.

Imperial protection and Christianity brought colonialism and exploitation. But with it came advancement that culminated in independence. The Gospel of the Free Markets according to the Western Democracies is expected to bring Foreign Direct Investment, which will cure all the present-day ills of Africa and propel it to the economic levels of the Asian tigers. African countries are, obligingly, following the commandments of the free market, either out of conviction or in order to reach one divined goal or another and obtain the promised rewards.

So, they opened their markets to foreign goods and they have been very accommodating to the demands of foreign direct investment. Sometimes these are exorbitant, such as the foreign investment in the Zambian mining industry that managed to secure virtually tax-free status for a couple of decades and left the citizens wondering when they are likely to enjoy any advantages from such investments. But such are the privileges that go with big investors or, as some might say, the new colonisers.

At lower levels foreign direct investment comes in many guises: white South African companies (the new voortrekkers, not running away from the British this time but piggybacking on their black government instead) spreading into the black north; Rhodesian farmers fleeing the land redistribution in Zimbabwe and looking for new land as far north as Nigeria; but the most common appears to be in the form of new immigrants, from the Middle East, from South Asia, from China, etc. They engage in trading and small and medium enterprises that provide some useful addition to the industrial foundation of small African countries. But such immigrant 'investors' with

1

greater access to finance are likely to displace the locals who occupy these levels of enterprise at the moment.

Ideally, foreign investment should come as an adjunct to local enterprise. But this is not possible, because in most African countries local enterprise has not developed sufficiently to generate projects and expansion that would attract foreign investment. So, in the near term, foreign investment, like the colonial regimes of old, will continue to pursue its own goals on its own terms and remain a caste apart. And, like the old colonial regimes, it will delay the emergence of local enterprise.

Free markets carry a different risk. They destroy nascent local enterprises, which cannot compete with imported products because of their size and the mediocre skills of their workers. But substituting local products with cheaper imported ones is considered the cornerstone of free markets, even though Africans may think that this condemns them to remaining producers of raw materials for ever.

And the apostles of the free markets do not practise what they preach. So far, they have merely promised that, if Africa does join the Free Market Church, they may, some day after the year 2013, begin dismantling the economic barriers they set in order to protect their own agriculture against competition from African and other Third World produce.

Africa's defences are limited. Very few countries, most prominent amongst them Nigeria and Ghana, have attained the levels of sophistication that enable them to stand up to these pressures and protect their own interests. South Africa is equally capable of making up its own mind, but its problems are domestic. Its economy is dominated by huge, long-established white-owned businesses whose interests and viewpoint are at variance with those of the majority of the population. Most other countries do not have sufficient experience and self-confidence to determine the suitability of the economic advice they receive, so they go along with it, sometimes because it is easier to acquiesce than resist, and in any case there is always the hope of a promised land at the end of the tunnel.

When is this going to change? When countries have firm opinions on what is in their best interests and are in a position to stand up to the conflicting pressures placed on them. Financial sophistication is necessary, and like the Nigerians and Ghanaians before them, Africans from many other countries are now working internationally gaining that extra experience. But the most important ingredient of economic emancipation is the development of African business. It is only when local enterprise becomes big enough and sophisticated enough to prime it that foreign investment will become meaningful and part of the national scene.

A Venture in Africa is the story of the rise and fall of an African conglomerate I founded in 1971 and led for the next 25 years. Its industrial arm, the ITM group, spawned a financial arm out of the sheer necessity to finance supplies to Africa during the dark decades of the 1970s and 1980s. This evolved into Meridien BIAO, the most extensive African banking network.

Over the years we had operations of one kind or another in some 30 anglophone, francophone and lusophone African countries, and in the process we became familiar with their idiosyncrasies and problems, some of them of their own making, others resulting from their colonial history and yet others from superpower rivalry and the cold war. For example, the United States is as much responsible for the rise of Mobutu and his iron grip on and plunder of Zaire (now the Democratic Republic of Congo) as Belgium, the colonial power that ruled the country until 1960 and then engineered the breakaway of its richest province, Katanga.

I have tried to give a flavour of all the challenges we met, adding short historical and other details, especially where I thought that they were a factor in shaping later events, such as political developments, civil wars, military dictatorships and economic collapse. In my travels, I always kept an open mind and tried to understand the roots of problems and make an informed interpretation of events. Telling the story after the passage of years makes me see the funny side of many an unmitigated disaster that at the time I thought we would never be able to overcome.

The group collapsed in 1995 and I describe the events that led to its destruction. Even though it was the most painful chapter of my life, I have tried not to be emotional and not to lose my sense of humour.

I have tried to tell the story with honesty and frankness without holding anything back and without embellishment, so that the reader can get a true picture of the challenges we faced, as well as a genuine flavour of Africa in the 1970s, the 1980s and early 1990s.

Part 1

The Vision and the Journey

1. THE FIRST STEPS

'I need BIAO like a hole in the head,' I said to the London manager of the Banque Internationale pour l'Afrique Occidentale when he approached me suggesting that I take it over. He made the suggestion during a conference in Paris on the subject of 'Growth of Private Enterprise in Africa – Opportunities for International Investment', organised by the *International Herald Tribune* and the African Development Bank on 23 and 24 March 1990, at which I was one of the speakers. I did not follow my own counsel, and I would come to regret it five years later.

BIAO started life in Senegal in the middle of the nineteenth century as the Central Bank of West Africa. It carried on this role until after the dissolution of the French colonial 'empire' in 1960, when it converted to a commercial bank. It had been in difficulties for some years and the French government wanted to merge it with Banque Nationale de Paris (BNP), one of the major French banks, but the African countries in which BIAO had subsidiaries were wary of the French monopoly of the banking sector in francophone Africa and were looking for an African solution. The French, unlike the British, had kept a firm grip over their colonies after independence.

At the time I was the chief executive of ITM (Investment Trade and Management) International, a trading group, whose operations spread over some 20 African countries and which had a banking subsidiary, the Meridien International Bank (MIBL). ITM was the successor of Sardanis Associates Ltd, a conglomerate I had set up in 1971 in association with the British merchant bank Fraser Ansbacher, a Zambian friend and some associates with whom I had worked in the Industrial Development Corporation (Indeco) of Zambia in the 1960s. They were mainly British, some of them of East African Indian origin, expecting their positions in Indeco to be 'Zambianised', and they joined me as they completed their contracts.

Sardanis Associates had phenomenal growth. Its initial equity was small, but it used the formula I had devised for the Indeco acquisitions in 1968 and 1969 (paying the vendors out of future profits) in order to grow. Successful settler businessmen wanted to cash out of Africa. But buyers were few because not many had faith in the future of the new Africa. So when we came along and made an offer we were able to negotiate extended payment terms. My successful career in Indeco and my international exposure provided the comfort that the purchase price would be paid. Local banks helped with some down payments and working capital. Banks in those days were ready to extend facilities on an entrepreneur's reputation and their confidence in his abilities. And, as I have already said, my associates and I had proved ourselves in Indeco and, as time went by, in the successful and efficient management and the profitability of our group.

The development picture in Africa looked very rosy to our eyes in those days and we determined to build the group around Africa's development needs – in other words, heavy equipment, machinery and construction. Our first acquisition was the Caterpillar Tractor dealership in Zambia, the biggest supplier of heavy equipment to the Zambian mines, which were thriving at the time. This was followed by a construction company and other industrial equipment suppliers. A pharmaceutical business was added as one of the associates' capital contribution to the group. We rationalised this deviation from our original philosophy on the basis that pharmaceuticals were another of Africa's major needs. I wrote extensively on the history of our Zambian business ventures in my book *Africa: Another Side of the Coin* but I shall give a short summary here for the new reader.

After an exciting and intellectually very rewarding career in Zambia's first administration from 1965 to 1971, I joined Tiny Rowland's Lonrho, a trading conglomerate that straddled white and black Africa with some operations in England and parts of Europe. A very succinct synopsis of my sojourn with Tiny appeared in the *New Africa* magazine in the middle of 1971, a couple of months after I left him in May of that year. It says:

Andrew Sardanis is back in Lusaka after a brief unhappy association with Lonrho. He had been invited to join the London conglomerate earlier this year but left, quietly and without fuss, when his terms were not met. Sardanis has had ideas about reorganising Lonrho, which is hot on enterprise, rather weak on administration. Among other things, Sardanis wanted the company's wide ranging interests controlled by subject, not location. For example African and Mauritian sugar estates would be administered as a division where they are now the responsibility of the regions. But Sardanis and managing director Tiny Rowland did not see eye to eye. They exchanged words, then a golden handshake... The wider implication of all this is that Lonrho is pigeonholing its plans to separate its white and black African interests. Last December it was announced that Sardanis was to become joint managing director with Rowland of the new African Industrial and Finance Corporation – 'Black' Lonrho. President Kaunda then gave Sardanis his personal blessing. Now, presumably, he has been welcomed back with open presidential arms. Not least perhaps because his services as company doctor are urgently needed for the ailing Indeco. From the start Sardanis was extremely uncertain about how things would pan out with Lonrho. He retained his Zambian citizenship and his seat on the boards of Mindeco and the mining companies. Lusaka will doubtless be delighted to see 'Mr. 51%' [*a soubriquet given to me by the* Newsweek *magazine a couple of years earlier*] in circulation again.

I did not exactly get the open arms welcome that *New Africa* was predicting. I found that people had mixed feelings about me. The politicians felt that I had abandoned them and treated me a little like a deserter, and my colleagues in the civil service saw the commercial success of Sardanis Associates and some of them treated me with disdain. There were mutterings about our acquisition of the Caterpillar dealership in Zambia. 'It was a big company; why had Sardanis not taken control of it for the government in 1968, as he did with most other big companies? Obviously he kept it for himself,' people said. I wish I were that far-sighted and it was not true, anyway. The companies taken over, three years previously, were all dealing in products that affected everyday lives, and suppliers of equipment to the mines were not considered, because in 1968 we had not as yet decided to take control of the mines. That was done almost as an after-thought in August 1969, as I describe in *Africa: Another Side of the Coin*.

Sardanis Associates had its admirers and it had its detractors. Some admired our aggressive training and localisation policies (rare in those days), which had been the hallmark of my business life, ever since I set foot in the North Western Province of Northern Rhodesia in 1951. Others criticised our expansion and made sour comments about it. The most notable was a comment from a politician when we made a few experimental exports of Zambian mangoes to the UK: 'Is Andrew not satisfied with the millions he is making from Mazembe [the Caterpillar dealership] and he wants to take the food out of our mouths too?' In those days the price of copper was still very high and 'non-traditional exports' had not yet entered the Zambian vocabulary. And the mango experiment was not a success.

By 1973 we had achieved considerable expansion in Zambia. We had the Caterpillar business, which we operated under the name Mazembe; we bought controlling interest in Roberts Construction, the biggest construction company in Zambia, at the time owned by the eponymous South African Group; we bought another engineering company that specialised in smaller mining equipment; we had a pharmaceutical and cosmetics company; farms, etc. In view of the economic and political climate in Zambia at the time we decided that we would be tempting fate to expand any further within, so for further expansion we started looking outside.

***

Why we chose Botswana as our first country for expansion, I do not quite remember – I guess because it was the only independent country south of Zambia and it was very close. It had been granted independence a couple of years after Zambia and much later than the rest of Africa. But its evolution as an independent nation was extremely slow. It was extremely poor, its main product was beef and its export was entirely dependent on European Economic Community quotas. The new capital, Gaborone (Botswana had been administered from the South African city of Mafeking during the colonial days), was developing slowly and it was a 'two-street town' at the time. The biggest city, Francistown, had been built around the railway hub, and also served as the commercial city for the not far-off Selebi Pikwe mine, a singularly unsuccessful copper mining venture and a monument to how wrong mining projects can go even if they are promoted by the world's biggest mining groups.

For an independent African country Botswana looked and felt like a colony – and a South African colony to boot. It seemed to have provided refuge to retreating colonial administrators from as far away as Kenya and Tanzania, and of course Zambia. Its civil service was reminiscent of Northern Rhodesia's, with white district commissioners in charge of the administration. The commercial sector was South African. Botswana was part of the South African Customs Union and South African companies had free access to its market. The South African contribution in lieu of customs duties was a very big source of revenue for the government at the time, and created a dependence that seemed to have a paralysing effect.

A small government organisation operating along the lines of the Industrial Development Corporation of Zambia and managed by some well-meaning and bright Americans and Britons was attempting to promote local enterprise, without much success because of the constricting influence of the South African industrial Goliath next door. It never seemed to occur to the Botswana government of the day that in order to promote local enterprise it had to loosen the bonds of the South African Customs Union. Some of the younger members of the government talked about breaking away, but the fear of jeopardising the South African contribution held them back. The customs

Pupils of Maru-a-Pula school receiving technical training in agricultural equipment from Kalahari Ford, one of the ITM companies in Botswana.

contribution amounted to some SA Rand 120 million per annum at the time, and the then Permanent Secretary of the Ministry of Finance (he later became President) was persuaded that it was very generous and that the government would not have the capacity to collect the equivalent in customs revenue.

Botswana was a difficult country to do business in. For a start, there were no direct air services with Zambia. To get to Gaborone one had to fly via Johannesburg, but as I was not allowed into South Africa I had to charter a plane every time I needed to visit. Air charter flights in that part of the world were cowboy operations. They used single- or two-engine propeller planes and their pilots, some very experienced, did not care much about aviation rules. Bill, the pilot I used most often, would always have a couple of beers with lunch before we proceeded to the airport for the return flight to Lusaka. One of the planes he was using was a trainer and, as I was sitting next to him, he often passed the controls to me. One day, he did it immediately after take-off. I was concentrating on gaining height when Bill asked me to look left. Somehow the earth had risen and it was standing like a mountain outside. I had not realised that I turned the plane on its side. Bill roared with laughter, but after that I gave up my attempts at learning to fly and preferred to sit back and have a drink instead. In any case, a couple of years later we bought a 50% share in a Learjet and such escapades became impossible.

Our flights to Gaborone became faster and more comfortable for a while, but as the Zimbabwe liberation war intensified different problems emerged. Flying from Gaborone to Lusaka one has to fly over Zimbabwe, but when sanctions were imposed the then Rhodesian government closed its airspace to all Zambian private flights. The result was that we had to fly over South Africa to Mozambique and get to Lusaka from the east. The flight was beyond the Lear's range so we had to refuel at Lanceria airport, and as I was not allowed in South Africa I would remain in the plane during the stopover.

The rigidity and narrow-mindedness of the apartheid bureaucracy manifested itself in a comic incident when my wife, Danae, and our sons Stelios and Harry, 11 and nine at the time, were travelling with me. The Lear was a small plane and the toilet facilities on board were rudimentary so Danae decided to use the airport facilities instead. The pilot asked a guard (they were all white in those days) and he obligingly called a lady, who escorted Danae to the airport loo and back. But children are unpredictable. A few minutes later they also wanted to go. We approached the same guard. He was outraged: 'Man, just because we were good enough to the lady you want to take advantage of us; they cannot go,' he pronounced in his Afrikaans-accented English. I tried to persuade the boys to do it on the tarmac instead, in full view of the guard, but they were too shy.

Economic conditions in Botswana improved with the discovery of diamonds, which made the country one of the most prosperous in Africa. Despite its wealth, the country remained very conservative and seemed disinclined to spend any of its riches for development, particularly the development of its people. Secondary schools remained few and the University did not open its doors until 1982, 16 years after independence. (Zambia opened its first university two years after it became independent.) Botswana is now sub-Saharan Africa's 'diamond sheikhdom' and is much praised for its $9 billion in foreign reserves, held in various Western banks and financial institutions. I wonder how much better off the country would have been if it had spent more for the development of its people early on, at the expense of its reserves. Skilled jobs still need to be done by foreigners from South Africa, other parts of Africa and elsewhere, a source of grievance and resentment for the local population.

As our operations in Botswana increased in the late 1970s and 1980s, we had to use more and more Zambians in senior positions because locals were not available. And, even though it is the only African country that can afford expensive anti-HIV/AIDS campaigns and free anti-retroviral (ARV) medication for the infected, Botswana remained the last to start, and in 2005 it had the distinction of the highest infection rate per head in Africa. Yet the people do not protest, and Botswana is one of the most stable countries in Africa, much praised by the Western countries for its conservative governance.

Over the years we did a lot of business in Botswana, starting with builders' hardware and pharmaceuticals, and later on adding construction, motor vehicle franchises, tractors and machinery to our range. But we always had to contend with competition from South African firms, which did not have any investment in Botswana but could collect large orders by sending their salesmen in and out and delivering with their own trucks, as if Gaborone was a suburb of Pretoria.

And the Botswana government did restrain itself from giving wholehearted support to the African National Congress that was fighting the apartheid regime in South Africa, an attitude I found very strange. I occasionally gave a lift on the Lear to ANC officials who wanted to visit Gaborone and I witnessed the difficulties they had with the immigration officers before they were allowed in for a day or two. In the late 1940s, while I was still a journalist working for the *New Cyprus Guardian* I had translated some articles written by Ruth Williams (later Lady Khama) on the upheaval her marriage to the Bamangwato Chief Seretse Khama had caused, culminating in his exile from Botswana until he renounced his chieftainship, and I was outraged. But in the 1970s the same British-deposed chief, but by then knighted by Queen Elizabeth as Sir Seretse Khama, was the President of Botswana and mindful of the problems that open support of the South African freedom fighters would bring on him and his country he held back. Knighthood for Botswana's Presidents became routine, a phenomenon not seen anywhere else in Africa. Ketumile Masire who followed Seretse Khama was also knighted. And he carried the title of President Sir Ketumile Masire for the rest of his term. It never seemed to worry him that a British knighthood alongside his position of first citizen might be demeaning to his country.

***

Malawi followed Botswana as our next business destination with the acquisition of the Caterpillar dealership from its South African owners, who wanted to withdraw from black Africa. Dr Kamuzu Banda, the President-for-life of Malawi at the time, was the only African leader with close ties to the South African apartheid regime and the Portuguese dictatorship in Lisbon – both shunned by the rest of Africa at the time. But this did not provide enough comfort for the owners of the Malawi Caterpillar dealership, who opted for retreating to the white world of South Africa and Rhodesia.

Dr Banda, who had been born in Nyasaland in the 1890s, had studied medicine in the United States and Britain, where he practised until 1953, when he moved to Ghana. In 1958, when the Nyasaland African Congress was looking for an important personality to lead the struggle for independence, he was persuaded to return to his native land. Nyasaland achieved majority rule within the Federation of Rhodesia and Nyasaland in 1961 with Banda as its Prime Minister, and independence (as Malawi) in 1964, after the dissolution of the Federation the previous year. Banda became President in 1966 and in 1971 he declared himself President-for-life. In the process he grew increasingly authoritarian, treating his lieutenants (he called them 'my boys') with condescension, making it quite clear that he considered them inferior, much to their dismay. On their part, they became progressively embarrassed with his courting of the apartheid regime of South Africa (he declared himself President-for-life after an official visit to South Africa) and the Portuguese government, which had been fighting the independence movements in Mozambique and Angola since the early 1960s.[1]

As the rest of Africa was unequivocal in its support of the independence movements in the south (South Africa, Namibia, Rhodesia, Mozambique and Angola – the unliberated part of the continent at the time), Banda's familiarity with those regimes became intolerable to his lieutenants. They agitated for change and they even attempted to mobilise the rural masses in support – but in the end he defeated them. Many had to flee into exile, mainly in Zambia and Tanzania.

One of the most prominent amongst them, Orton Chirwa, who had handed over the leadership of the Congress to him and had been Banda's Attorney-General, ended up in Zambia with his wife Vera, also a lawyer. But Banda, a vengeful person, never stopped pursuing the exiles. During Christmas 1981, when the Chirwas were visiting Chipata, a Zambian town a few miles from the Malawi border, they were abducted and taken back to Malawi. They were tried for treason by the Southern Regional Traditional Court in Blantyre – an infamous branch of the judicial system devised by Banda in order to take care of his enemies without due process. They were sentenced to death and the verdict was later confirmed by the National Traditional Court of Appeal, but Banda had to commute the death penalty to life imprisonment as a result of the international protests that followed. Orton Chirwa died in jail in 1992 and Vera was pardoned a few weeks later, again because of international pressure.

The bus is a vital link in Africa, transporting people and merchandise between villages and towns and its arrival and departure creates scenes of vibrant activity. The bus in the picture was manufactured by PEW, one of the ITM companies, in Blantyre, Malawi.

Banda remained authoritarian, eccentric and capricious throughout his life. In the late 1960s he issued a decree banning blue jeans, miniskirts and long hair. There were hilarious scenes at the Blantyre airport when international visitors were forced to have a haircut and change clothes. But Banda took no notice. Amongst his many other follies was the Kamuzu Academy, a boarding school for boys that was modelled after Haileybury College, a British public school, and included Greek and Latin in its curriculum. As Malawi is one of the poorest countries of Africa he used £10 million of his own money for the project, Banda would repeatedly boast, never bothering to explain how a President of a poor country could come by such a large fortune.

But while other African countries were introducing their brand of social and economic policies in the 1960s, nationalising or partly nationalising various businesses, Dr Banda's formula was simple. He was doing the same thing on behalf of the Malawi Congress Party. And since he was the President-for-life of both the party and the country he assumed that the income was his and he knew best what to do with it. He did not declare himself Emperor of Malawi, as Bokassa did in the Central African Republic, but he sure behaved like one. He moved the capital of the country from Blantyre to Lilongwe, which was financed, designed and built by his South African friends. And he decided to construct a new presidential palace there, whose slow progress became legend. Whenever Banda travelled outside the country and saw something he fancied, he wanted it copied and added to his palace, which was getting bigger and bigger and was never quite finished during his lifetime.

Some of his original lieutenants who did not flee the country and kept their positions in government ended up in jail or died in unexplained motor accidents. But discontent eventually caught up with him with widespread anti-government demonstrations and rioting in 1993, which forced him to abandon the one-party system and call elections in 1994, which he lost. In 1995 he was charged with the assassination of four political opponents, but by that time he was senile and he was acquitted. Banda was over 100 years old when he died in 1997 even though officially he was ten years younger. During his lifetime it was a punishable offence to discuss his age.

For us, Malawi was like home. Its people are much the same as the people of the eastern districts of Zambia and speak the same languages. As it had been part of the Federation of Rhodesia and Nyasaland many Malawians had worked on the Zambian mines, and their children were educated in Zambian schools. Despite its poverty, Malawi had more educated and skilled people than Botswana, and we were able to recruit and implement a localisation programme that had become the hallmark of our group. We expanded substantially in various directions, including builders' hardware, paint, engineering and construction. Our Wade Adams group undertook many important engineering projects, one of the most prominent being the construction of a timber products factory and township for Viply Plywood and Allied Industries Ltd.

***

In no time we became a successful regional group, with an office in London that procured supplies and organised finance for our companies and our customers who wanted to purchase heavy equipment fleets. On the family side, we had a house in London and our sons Stelios and Harry at Cranleigh, a public (read private boarding) school in Surrey. Danae spent most of her time in London and I would come and go. The future looked great and we were looking forward to more expansion in the region when a bolt struck from the blue.

On 17 November 1973 the Bank of Zambia instructed Barclays, our main bank, to freeze the accounts of all our Zambian companies. As I explained in *Africa: Another Side of the Coin*, this was the consequence of the abrogation of the mining agreements that I had negotiated on behalf of the Zambian government and the Cabinet and Parliament had approved in 1969/70. I had applied my usual formula of paying out of future profits and the government had issued bonds (the Zimco bonds) to the two mining groups that had owned them, repayable over eight and 12 years with interest at 6%. Tiny Rowland, my erstwhile boss in Lonrho, persuaded the government to abrogate the agreements and repay the Zimco bonds at par when the bonds were trading on the market at 48%. Rowland bought bonds before the redemption and, with a small number of Zambian accomplices, he made a fortune. I had smelt the rat and informed the President of Zambia. Even though he took no notice, his subordinates decided that I had to be kept under pressure in case I spilled the beans, and they embarked upon a vicious campaign of persecution. I covered the events in great detail in *Africa: Another Side of the Coin* so I do not intend to repeat them here. But the next three years were spent on protecting business, family and self from the never-ending twists and turns of investigations and attacks. The problem was resolved in 1976. By that time the government had negotiated a new deal with the foreign shareholders of the mines, which created the Zambian Consolidated Copper Mines Ltd (ZCCM), in which it took absolute control (66%). That set the mining industry on a gradual course of self-destruction which would occur before the end of the twentieth century.

The three-year period from the end of 1973 to 1976 was, for me sad and demoralising. Many a time I was tempted to give up, but it is not in my make-up to succumb to intimidation. So, I had to devise an alternative strategy. It dawned on me that if I wanted an international business career it should no longer carry my name, as Sardanis Associates did, and should be domiciled outside Zambia. I had to resort to the anonymity of Luxembourg, where ITM International was set up.

2. LIBERIA: A BLACK RHODESIA

'Liberia is another Rhodesia but the world has not noticed because the "Rhodesians" of Liberia are black,' I told Kenneth Kaunda, the President of Zambia, in 1976 after I returned from my first trip there. He roared with laughter and narrated his own experience with the Americo-Liberians. He had been at the airport when Tubman, Liberia's President from 1943 to 1971, arrived to attend the Tanganyika independence celebrations. As is customary in Africa, foreign dignitaries are entertained on arrival by local dancing troupes. Watching the Tanganyikan troupe, Mrs Tubman turned to her husband: 'Look, darling, the boys here dance like the boys at home,' she said – a telling comment that summed up the 'Rhodesian'-style attitudes of supremacy and remoteness the Americo-Liberians held towards the indigenous people of their country.

I had gone to Liberia to investigate the Caterpillar dealership there, which was owned by an Italian-American who wanted to retire. By that time we were running the dealerships in Zambia and Malawi very successfully and his approach to us had the blessings of the Caterpillar Tractor Company's office in Geneva, which supervised Africa and the Middle East.

Liberia, the oldest republic on the continent, was one of the three independent countries that existed in Africa before the collapse of colonialism created 50 more out of the large tracts of the colonial empires of Britain, France, Belgium and Portugal and the mandated territories that had belonged to Germany before the First World War. It was created in the 1820s by the American Colonization Society which acquired land from the local chiefs and started settling a large number of freed slaves from America and the Caribbean. Resettling African-Americans back 'home' may have appeared a good idea at the time but in reality Liberia was not their home. The new residents were not aware of their roots and in spite of their African origin they remained a caste apart. They treated the indigenous people like most other settlers did in Africa and the world did not notice.

Monrovia, Liberia's capital, named after the American President Monroe when the then Governor declared its independence in 1847, was reminiscent of the American South, with grand solid buildings dotted around the town and churches on every corner. It seemed to have the biggest number of churches per head of population I had seen anywhere. It also had a university, which had started as a college in the nineteenth century. Amongst the impressive stone buildings were the Masonic temple and the grand headquarters of the True Whig Party, standing next to each other on top of a hill overlooking the harbour. (In later years these magnificent buildings were occupied by squatters and civil war

The size of logs from Liberia's tropical hardwood forests is awesome and can only be handled by huge machines, like the one above. The loggers relied on Libtraco, the ITM company in Monrovia, for their supplies and product support.

refugees.) The True Whig was the Americo-Liberian Party and had been running the country for ever, as far as I could gather. They represented less than 10% of the population but they dominated the government until 1980, when President Tolbert was assassinated by Master Sergeant Samuel Doe, who then took over.

Tolbert was highly regarded overseas and his brother Steve, who was his Minister of Finance, was a big businessman with fingers in many business pies, one of the many signs of corruption in the country. The Liberian business community, mainly foreign (European, American, Lebanese and Asian), seemed very content with this set-up and thought that it would carry on for ever. Or so they tried to make me believe.

The Liberian Tractor Co. (Libtraco) we were proposing to buy was managed by a team of American and European expatriates, but its chairman was local. Rudolph Grimes was an Americo-Liberian Harvard-trained lawyer. A nice man, he had been President Tubman's Secretary of State and his house was full of memorabilia of his glory days. Pictures with President Kennedy, Dag Hammarskjöld and many other international dignitaries at various international conferences adorned the walls of his house. His circle was entirely Americo-Liberian and in the few days I stayed I realised that, though small in numbers, their influence in the country was pervasive, while the local population was relegated to the level of second-class citizenry.

Liberia was a small but prosperous country, nevertheless. It had big iron ore mines owned and operated by very reputable international companies; rubber plantations, the biggest of which, not far out of Monrovia, had belonged to the American Firestone company since the 1920s; and many timber concessions – all very big users of heavy tractors and other industrial machines, which made Libtraco a very profitable business. Other Liberian products included diamonds, coffee and cocoa, palm oil and sugar cane, all of which generated substantial exports. Citibank and Chase, the two prominent American international banks then and now, were the main banks in the country.

We concluded the deal and reaped good profits from Libtraco for a few years. But the inevitable had to happen. The discontent of the local people encouraged Doe's coup, which was followed by atrocities, including many executions of prominent citizens on the beach, near the barracks of Monrovia. Yet gradually life in the country settled down again and many Americo-Liberians cooperated and accepted important Cabinet positions in Doe's administration, though some had to flee the country afterwards, in fear for their lives. But the economy kept deteriorating, until civil war broke out – that would be in the 1990s.

***

In the meantime our group was moving from strength to strength. We were running a very efficient business and did not confine our activities to the Caterpillar dealerships. As time went by we redefined our aims and expanded our range of goods and services. Our first group brochure in 1978 describes the development scene of the time:

> The developing countries have a constant and growing demand for a wide range of goods and services. Depending on individual development programmes such demand is usually linked to the spread of education, health and social services, the exploitation of raw materials or the development of agriculture, transport, communications and housing.

Apart from the Caterpillar franchises we put together a group of other franchises of motor vehicles and parts, farm machinery, light industrial equipment, tools and hardware, building materials and construction, mechanical and electrical engineering and industrial chemicals and pharmaceuticals. Our companies would either import or produce locally depending on the local market and the product.

By the latter part of the 1970s we were employing 6000 people in 19 countries, mainly in Africa, and our annual sales had risen to over $200 million. Our management philosophy was to give employment priority to local people and for this purpose we operated very extensive training programmes. We employed expatriates in jobs where there was no local expertise. Occasionally we had to deviate from this rule when the main clients were foreign companies, which in those days did not take African executives seriously, as was the case with the mining companies of Zambia, even after the Zambian mines came under government control. Localisation had been my philosophy all along and I was at pains to explain to my associates that it was not starry-eyed. It was based on the common-sense point of view that local people have an intuitive knowledge of their market place, which foreigners need decades to absorb, because of their different cultural background and because expatriate life is insulated from local realities. My other point was that when you give local people responsibility and authority they respond to it and try harder than expatriates. This view was not commonly held at the time; in fact, the view that 'you cannot trust Africans – they are lazy and incompetent and dishonest' prevailed. And some competitors viewed our policy with derision; but our many years of successful operations have proved that it was sound.

Of course, Zambian executives viewed their expatriate counterparts with the same jaundiced eye – 'They are extravagant, they are here for the good life and they really are not any better than us.' I remember the comments of a Zambian friend and partner since 1958 who was in charge of our Zambian operations in the 1970s when I proposed to transfer the manager of Mazembe to supervise all the Caterpillar dealerships out of New York. 'Good luck,' he said. 'Take him, but watch him. He is a big spender. He changes motor cars like he changes shirts.' I often agreed with the Zambians' view of some expatriates, an attitude that my deputy in London considered 'disgusting' and said so to me many times. The mentality of 'you must not let the side down' if you had a white skin transcended fairness, business principles and common sense.

We had many hard-working and dedicated expatriates over the years, who not only cared about performance and results but also paid serious attention to training. But we had other varieties too. Some of them, especially some older Britons who stayed on, still lived in the past and had an exaggerated idea of their importance, while they undervalued the abilities of black employees. Some paid more attention to the golf club and their social life and persuaded themselves that these were important tools in business promotion. Others fancied themselves as business geniuses of international calibre and often flew at tangents completely unrelated to the business at hand. Most would have loved to be out of Africa, but were trapped in the perks of the expatriate contracts, such as overseas education for their children paid for by the company, and marked time dreaming of the day when their children would finish high school and they would be free to go home. But by that time they would have fallen into the trap of the expatriate life and become permanent roving expatriates, a little like the 'Flying Dutchman', I often thought.

To service the needs of our African businesses we opened offices in London, New York, Munich and Toronto. These offices had direct liaison with some of our major suppliers and procured goods for our African companies, but, more importantly, secured finance for both our companies and other customers in the countries where we operated. The choice of London, New York, Munich and Toronto was made in order to tap the Export Credit Guarantee Department of the UK, the Foreign Credit Insurance Association and Export Import Bank of the United States, the Hermes Kreditversicherungs of West Germany and the Export Development Corporation of Canada, which at the time provided generous cover for the financing of their countries' exports to Africa. That became more and more necessary as the recession resulting from the oil price explosion of the mid-1970s set in.

Over the years we gained the reputation not only of being a very efficient group but also of having in-depth knowledge of Africa and the ability to operate anywhere, regardless of political, social and economic problems. Even the Caterpillar Tractor Company must have thought along these lines when they asked us to go to Angola.

3. ANGOLA: DIAMONDS AND ... THREATS

'Bon dias, Camarada.' I found the greeting of the receptionist of the Hotel Tropico, in Luanda, unnerving. I travelled in many parts of the world, but I had never, before or since, been addressed as 'comrade' by hotel staff.

We had arrived in Luanda, the capital of Angola, in the middle of the night, after a repeatedly delayed flight from Lisbon. Going through Angolan immigration and customs was an exhausting process. The forms were long and detailed and in Portuguese, and there were only a couple of officers on duty, who did not speak English and who were suspicious of all foreigners. It was lunch time by the time we arrived at the Hotel Tropico in the centre of Luanda.

It must have been a beautiful city in its prime. It had obviously been a Portuguese colonists' town, with beautiful villas and gardens, but as the colonists had departed en masse before independence it looked abandoned and neglected. The shops in the town centre had been looted and the shop fronts were either boarded or had gaping holes for shop windows. Refuse had not been collected for months and was lying all over the place, rotting in the tropical heat. The stench was unbearable. In the hotel, nothing worked. The elevators and air-conditioning were not functioning. It was hot, but you could not open the window of your room because of the stench from the street. Electric bulbs were few and far between, placed sparingly to give a little light in the public areas and the corridors. The rooms had one each. The restaurant was on the eighth floor and as the elevators did not work one had to climb eight flights of stairs in the stifling heat. There were only two items on the menu: meat stew and rice or fish stew and rice. And the hotel staff addressed you as 'comrade' but were not inclined to help you. I guess they thought that comrades should share the workload.

I had gone to Luanda in August 1976 with a group from our finance and Caterpillar divisions at the request of the Caterpillar Tractor Company to investigate what could be done with Sorrel, the distributor of its earth-moving equipment in Angola. The Portuguese owner, like most Portuguese, had left the country before independence and decided that it was not safe for him or members of his family to return. I understood that before his departure he had cleverly managed to ship most of his inventory out of the country, and he was afraid that he might be arrested for economic sabotage if he went back.

Sorrel's operations gave an insight into the Portuguese governance of Angola, where the literacy rate before independence was just 10%. Sorrel's labour force had been 50% Portuguese and 50% local (the expatriates in our Zambian operations at the time were less than 5%), an indication that the Portuguese were performing not only the skilled jobs but unskilled ones as well. As they had now left the country and the Angolan labour force was completely untrained the company could not function. Yet it had been very profitable and had been very important to Diamang, the diamond mining company that owned about 1200 earth-moving machines, most of them lying idle in various diamond fields up-country and in urgent need of repairs. The government was very anxious to resuscitate diamond mining, a major earner of hard currency, and making the machines operational was imperative – but impossible without skilled workers.

Angola's independence war had been one of the messiest in Africa. It had been fought against Portugal since 1960 by three different liberation movements representing the dominant ethnic and linguistic groups in three different parts of the country: FNLA (Frente Nacional de Libertação de Angola – National Front for the Liberation of Angola), representing the Bacongo in the north-west; MPLA (Movimento Popular de Libertação de Angola – Popular Movement for the Liberation of Angola), the oldest of the groups, representing the Mpundu in the north as well as the intellectuals of the Luanda region; and UNITA (União Nacional para Independência Total de Angola – National Union for the Total Independence of Angola), representing the Ovimbundu and related tribes in the south and east. But independence did not come about from the struggles of these movements. It came about as a result of the military coup that ousted the dictatorship in Portugal in April 1974 and decided some months later to grant independence to its African colonies. This acted as a signal to the three liberation movements to start fighting each other for domination.

The Bacongo of FNLA, a small group representing some 15% of the population of Angola, centred on the provinces of Cabinda, Zaire and Uige, turned to Mobutu for support because they considered the country of Zaire (now the Democratic Republic of the Congo) as their spiritual home. MPLA, representing a third of the population, whose stronghold was Luanda and was dominated by left-wing intellectuals, African, mulatto and white, turned to the Soviet Union and Cuba. UNITA, representing the Ovimbundu tribes that comprise some 40% of the population, spread on the central plateau provinces of Benguela, Bie and Huambo, as well as the Luena along the borders of Zambia, turned to the South Africans, who administered neighbouring Namibia. In view of the Soviet–Cuban influence on MPLA, the Americans inevitably got involved too. They assisted FNLA through Mobutu but, more seriously, they assisted Jonas Savimbi, the UNITA leader, through the South Africans. Together they hatched a plan to split Angola in two along the 11th parallel (the northern end of the Ovimbundu tribal area) and thus give control of some two-thirds of the land area of the country to Savimbi. I remember an officer of the American embassy (presumably the CIA agent) expounding the merits of such division at the Lusaka Flying Club, on the grounds of the old airport.

An interim government under Portuguese High Commissioner Cardoso and with the participation of all three movements was established in January 1975 and independence was set for 11 November of that year, but this did not stop the civil war. Eventually MPLA, with the assistance of the Soviets and the Cubans, prevailed. Cardoso duly departed on 10 November and independence was declared on 11 November 1975, with the Soviet Union being the only country to recognise the new nation. In January 1976 the South Africans, who had invaded Angola in order to carry out the partition plan, departed and UNITA withdrew to its tribal areas, as FNLA had done some months earlier. After a lot of hand-wringing, with Zambia's Kenneth Kaunda holding it evenly split between MPLA and UNITA, the Organisation of African Unity (OAU) recognised MPLA as the government of Angola in February 1976.

Having prevailed over the other two liberation movements, the MPLA government was anxious to get the country back to some semblance of normality – a near-impossible task, as it had no access to many parts of the country that were under the control of the rival movements. Getting Diamang back into production and earning hard currency from diamonds would be a major step forward. To achieve it they needed to rehabilitate the earth-moving machines, and they wanted us to agree to do so as soon as possible. We visited various ministries and the central bank in order to familiarise ourselves with the government's thinking before we made the decision to take on the task of running Sorrel. The sheer optimism, bordering on wishful thinking, that prevailed was touching.

One young man at the central bank was bullish about the prospects of the economy, which was based mainly on agriculture and diamonds before the discovery of oil. 'But how can agriculture run, without the participation of the Portuguese owners who fled the civil war?' I asked. He explained with great enthusiasm the MPLA plan to organise volunteers from nearby towns to work on the coffee plantations. He was taking part, he said, and he and his family would be spending their weekends working on the plantations. I did not have the heart to tell him that weekending bankers and picnicking government functionaries could not possibly keep the plantations going. The plan worked

Working in remote areas, where logistical support was paramount, became the hallmark of ITM, as we proved with our Angolan diamond mining operations. And river bed mining first required diversion of the river Cuango by the construction of large dykes and dams.

surprisingly well, though, for about a year, but the enthusiasm could not last and inevitably the industry was destroyed.

We did agree to run Sorrel under contract with the Angolan government, which had nationalised it together with every other business and property in Angola. But Caterpillar felt that we had to pay $2 million to the departed Portuguese owner – a courtesy it would not repeat in relation to our own departure many years later.

I do not remember who suggested recruiting Filipinos as mechanics for our Angolan operations, but it was a brilliant idea. It solved our skilled labour problems and turned Sorrel into an efficient Caterpillar Tractor dealer. We offered 12-month contracts (nine months in Angola and three months' home leave) and within a few months we had over 200 Filipinos of various skills operating in various parts of the country. They were efficient, but, more importantly, they were tough. They did not mind the lack of personal comforts. Initially they worked and slept in partitioned freight containers, but as time went by we improved the living conditions and organised well-tended compounds, messes and clinics, with Filipino doctors, nurses and cooks. Most of the workers were happy to renew their contracts time and again. And they ignored the hostilities around the diamond mining areas, and the UNITA raids which kept increasing in frequency, because UNITA was determined to take control of the diamond mines, which were located in and around its own tribal areas, and use the income to finance its military operations. We operated in many mining areas which were spread over a large part of the country. As time went by our Filipino force grew to a few hundred. Apart from Caterpillar mechanics, we recruited long-distance drivers, motor mechanics, miners, clerks, doctors, nurses, cooks and many others. They played a vital role in transporting supplies to the mining areas some 700 miles east of Luanda. Without those supplies neither the mines nor our camps could function. And the runs from the port of Luanda to the mines were not easy. They were long military convoys with many trucks, trailers, troop carriers and military escort vehicles, which frequently came under fire from UNITA.

My own 'runs' from Lusaka to Luanda that I had to make very frequently in the early years were not much easier. By that time we had our own Learjet but we had to make a long detour through Namibia in order to avoid the UNITA missiles. Not that the Angolan government missiles were 'friendlier'. A plane carrying the President of Botswana was hit, but, thankfully, did not crash. And missiles were not the only danger. Entry and exit formalities had their own hazards. In August 1978 I arrived for a short visit and needed to get back by

Friday, because we would be moving house over the weekend from Lusaka to Chaminuka. The trouble with short visits was that they did not give enough time to get the exit permit stamp on my passport, without which I could not depart. Diamang did their best and at lunchtime on Friday they brought my exit permit. But not the exit permit for the Caterpillar representative, who would be taking a lift with me. He was anxious to get to Geneva and we decided to risk it. Escorted by Diamang personnel we managed the airport formalities without much hassle, but when the door of the plane closed and we were ready to taxi, a posse of military policemen armed with AK-47s arrived. We opened the door and they came on board. They wanted to check the passports again. Shivers went down my spine. Instead of helping Danae to move house, I had visions of myself in an Angolan jail for trying to smuggle an unauthorised American out of the country. But they were either not very clever or not very literate. The American who had been in Angola the year before, had an exit permit from his previous visit. They did not notice the difference in the dates and we got away with it.

We worked as contractors to Diamang, for the rehabilitation and main-tenance of the earth-moving equipment. Mining was carried out by a company called Mining and Technical Services (MATS), a publicly unacknowledged subsidiary of De Beers. Despite the distrust and dislike of each other the South African diamond mining colossus was running Angola's diamond industry under contract to Diamang, a company nationalised and owned 100% by the Marxist government of Angola. But in February 1984 the pot boiled over. Diamond production had dropped from some $250 million worth in 1980 to less than $50 million. The Angolans were convinced that the reason De Beers curtailed production was that the world price for diamonds had slumped. De Beers, on its part, complained of production problems caused by the war. In the end they parted company, the South Africans declaring that they could not subject their staff to the dangers of Angola any more. As we were on-site, willing and able, we were offered a contract to operate some diamond fields, as direct contractors to Diamang. This did not please De Beers, and Peter Leyden, a De Beers director from Johannesburg, whom I had known from the 1960s when he was working with the Anglo American Corporation (De Beers' sister company) in Zambia, tried to get in touch with me through our London office. I was not in London and he left a message that 'De Beers heard that we were seeking to start mining an area, which was under an agreement between the Angolan government and MATS and they considered this to be an unfriendly act'. He suggested that I meet Ted Dawes at the Diamond Trading Company headquarters in London. I went with my deputy. Mr Dawes had two others in his office, a Peter Gallegos and a John Mackenzie. The meeting took place on 24 July 1984 and the record was written by my deputy. It reads:

Dawes said that he understood that we had come at the behest of Peter Leyden. Sardanis said we had come because we understood they wanted to discuss Angola. Dawes said that rumour, and news stronger than rumour had it that Intraco [our Angolan company] was aiming to take over responsibility for the Cafunfo area despite the existence of a contract between Diamang and MATS running until 31 December 1984, and that Intraco had even been thinking about and were manoeuvring towards taking over the whole of MATS responsibilities for operating the Diamang mines. This could be considered not merely, in Peter Leyden's phrase an unfriendly act but a distinctly hostile one.

Sardanis said that ITM certainly had no intention of competing with De Beers as we had no capacity to do so, but felt an appropriate position for us to be that of taking the leftovers from De Beers. Our understanding was that they had abandoned Cafunfo and were no longer interested in it and Diamang has as a result asked us to become involved.

Dawes said that they had not abandoned Cafunfo. They did not return there after the February raid because the military situation was unsatisfactory and they were unwilling to risk British lives [quickly amended to British and Portuguese lives]. Other people may take a different attitude. However during his visit to Angola last week he had discussed the military situation both with the FAPLA [Forças Armadas Populares de Libertação de Angola – Popular Armed Liberation Forces of Angola] commander on the spot in Cafunfo and the general in Luanda responsible for the whole of Lunda Norte province and he was now satisfied that the security situation at least in a portion of Cuango division was good enough to resume operations. Thus MATS personnel would be returning to Cafunfo in the immediate future and taking up their normal tasks.

Sardanis said that Intraco had made a much earlier positive judgement on the military situation, so had had people in Cafunfo for a considerable time now carrying out repair work. No doubt, in view of this and perhaps because they were very concerned that MATS were not returning to Cafunfo and mining operations were not getting under way, the Diamang administration had asked Intraco to put up a proposal for full rehabilitation of Cafunfo as a mining operation. If Diamang now told us they no longer need such a proposal from Intraco we would bow out gracefully. If Diamang did so it would possibly be because they had achieved their objective of getting MATS back on the job ... There was discussion as to whether Intraco's original introduction to the Diamang project was as a result of De Beers' initiative. Dawes thought it was but Sardanis

31

emphasised that it was the result of Caterpillar's initiative, as an Intraco team visited Angola in August 1976, the year before the Diamang rehabilitation programme was first raised.

Dawes said there had been a good relationship between MATS and Intraco with Intraco in a subordinate role as a contractor to Diamang. He said that Intraco's manager was an excellent man who was very 'comme il faut' with the local situation. Sardanis agreed and said that we were proud of him. Dawes said that we must go back to a situation where Cafunfo was running normally again with Intraco repairing the earthmoving equipment. My deputy said that we were no longer just repairing the earthmoving equipment but now in Cafunfo repairing housing, the water pump systems, electrical reticulation, etc. and we were interested in doing more and more general repair and rehabilitation work. Mackenzie showed disagreement as to whether Intraco had indeed repaired the electricity generation plant in Cafunfo.

Dawes said he was glad to have had the opportunity to clear up the position but we should know that if Diamang in any way abrogated their existing contract MATS would not only withdraw from the contract and claim penalties but demand return of all monies advanced to Diamang. Also, we should know that he will always act to defend the De Beers interests and when necessary play very rough indeed, quite unlike his more civilised colleagues in Johannesburg with whom we were more familiar. Sardanis expressed jovial incredulity [here my deputy was being polite]; Dawes said he would stop at nothing defending the interest of De Beers and I shot back: 'Including eliminating us, Mr Dawes?'.

But the bully did not succeed in changing the mind of the Angolans. He probably knew that before the meeting. He had been in Angola the week before and he must have raised the threat relating to the De Beers contract supposedly running until the end of the year. Obviously, the Angolans ignored him, and the purpose of the meeting with us was to intimidate us to withdraw. If we had done so De Beers would have achieved its objective of curtailing production for a few more months and probably negotiating a more advantageous contract. But I do not get easily intimidated. As I was leaving I repeated that we were going to do what Diamang requested. We would bow out if it asked us to. But it did not. Our contract included production targets, which were set on the levels achieved by De Beers, and large bonuses if they were exceeded. Within a few months we were exceeding the targets three- and fourfold, which would indicate that the fears of the Angolan government that De Beers was suppressing production were justified – a point that worked in our favour as the bonuses became huge.

Except that payments were slow in coming. Diamang was succeeded by ENDIAMA (Empresa Nacional de Diamantes de Angola) after a reorganisation and payments became slower still. We would produce and deliver an average of over 100,000 carats every month, but ENDIAMA did not always pay within the stipulated period. It would sell the diamonds and collect the money, but it applied the proceeds according to the government's priorities, mainly to the military, instead of paying its contractors. Extracting payments for new equipment was an almost impossible task. ENDIAMA would confirm the order but not pay until the last possible moment. On our part we never delivered new equipment until payment was received – and in the nick of time it would arrive, though not without agonising anticipation. On one occasion we had a whole fleet of Caterpillar machines on board a chartered vessel in Baltimore, but the $9 million payment from ENDIAMA was still 'on the way'. As the vessel had to sail because the demurrage was mounting up, we gave instructions for it to sail to Abidjan. Luckily, the funds arrived before it reached there; otherwise we would have to send the machines to Europe instead of Luanda and look for buyers elsewhere, at tremendous extra cost and major loss.

As time went by the infrastructure of Angola collapsed completely. The roads became impassable and dangerous from lurking UNITA guerrillas. Truck convoys were escorted by the army and the journeys were long and hazardous. The only way to ensure timely supplies of parts, food and medicines was by air. Initially we worked in association with an Irish airfreight operator, but later we established Transafrik, an airfreight company in association with an Austrian entrepreneur. The planes, bought on the second-hand market, had to collect supplies from South Africa, a fact known to the government of Angola, which turned a blind eye. But planes cannot fly unless they file a flight plan and get landing permission, which could not be done from Angola in relation to South Africa. So we had to register the company in São Tomé, a minute island in the Atlantic about 1000 sq. km. in land area and with a population of 100,000. It had also achieved independence from the Portuguese at the same time as Angola.

The trouble with operating in buccaneering environments, as Angola and São Tomé were at that time, was that thousands of new problems cropped up daily and needed urgent solutions. And each problem presented a different opportunity. From the distance of London, New York or Lusaka, you knew that you did not want to get involved. But you found yourself involved anyway, because the local management acted before telling you, or with the permission of one of your senior colleagues who did not calculate the ramifications. In the end you found yourself doing things you never really intended to do and, worse, you realised that, without meaning to, you had created a number of baronies and associations that you could no longer control. They were all controlled by the local 'regent' – the term 'general manager' does not convey his importance and grandeur (the staff used to call our manager in Angola 'the Fuehrer' because of his arbitrary manner and German origin). He would have liked to declare independence but recognised the benefit of operating under our name. Such characters behave reverentially when face to face with you, but badmouth you and the organisation behind your back – a form of behaviour that I have since noticed amongst all employees who have something to hide. And when they get to that stage they can no longer be replaced, because in the countries they operate they have all the contacts and because they have done many favours to all the people that matter. One small mercy for us in the case of Angola: none of our senior executives was ever caught smuggling diamonds out of the country, a nightmare always at the back of my mind, which would have given us a bad name even though the smuggling would not have been with our knowledge and consent or for our benefit.

We did make good profits in Angola, and some members of our staff became very rich in the process. But we found ourselves running a hotel in São Tomé and passenger air services between São Tomé and Libreville; building apartments for rent, and villas and a fishing resort for some of our executives and those of our partners; and, to cap it all, spending money on an abortive oil exploration project for which we had neither the expertise nor the resources. Lots of group money was spent on rigs and drilling and sample analysis, the Fuehrer having been struck by an acute attack of 'black gold' fever. And in the end we found that the exploration licence and the contract were not held in our name but in his name. He assured us that the reason was 'local politics', but added that we should trust him as 'when oil is discovered the benefits would come to the group'. As oil was never discovered, this promise was never put to the test, but the abortive venture cost millions. The Transafrik planes would, at our expense, fly building materials from South Africa and furniture and carpets and everything that was needed to build and equip luxury villas in those highly unstable areas. But the Fuehrer would become unstoppable.

***

At some stage the Philippines appointed the Fuehrer as its consul in Angola, obviously because as our local manager he was in charge of all the Filipinos in that country. He took that appointment as recognition of his stature as an international statesman and an African expert and, using this newly acquired status, he decided to write to President Reagan asking him to change his policy on Angola. The letter was written on Philippines Foreign Service letterhead bearing the Philippines coat of arms and our Luanda address, which was also the address of the consulate. It was signed and sealed by the Fuehrer as consul, though he added an additional title under the consulate seal: 'President Mining and Project Management Division, ITM'. The letter, dated 3 February 1986, is a gem of megalomania and naiveté, but as it describes the situation on the ground at a very turbulent time and is amusing at the same time I thought it worth quoting from. It read:

> After much anguish and thinking I have decided to appeal to you personally in relation to developments taking place that will further destabilize the present situation in Angola...

After setting out his credentials – 19 years in Africa, eight years in Angola, Filipino consul and CEO of a Caterpillar dealership and a diamond mining operation that employs 350 expatriates, including Americans, Canadians, Filipinos, Portuguese and British – he continued:

> ...My appeal to you Mr President is specifically this: the further involvement or support by the United States Government to help the opposition forces of the MPLA namely UNITA will not only destabilise the political economic situation of Angola further but will at the same time endanger the lives and safety of Western foreign workers in this country. May I mention to you Mr President that in 1984, the Diamond Mine of Cafunfo was attacked and two of my employees (Filipino nationals) were killed and 33 of my employees, Portuguese, English and Filipino were kidnapped and taken into the south of Angola. On December 31, 1984 the same mine was attacked again after we had tried to rebuild the infrastructure and a further 17 Filipinos employed by this company were kidnapped.

After reminding Reagan that an American pilot had been killed and a Lockheed C-130 Hercules destroyed in the same raid, he continued:

> Mr President, I visited the site in Cafunfo Diamond Mines shortly after they had been attacked and I personally saw a mass grave of over 280 dead people who had been buried and had been massacred by UNITA forces. Some of these people testified to me [sic] that the remaining Angolan workers in the Cafunfo Diamond Mine had been killed and shot in their houses. A lot of them were women, children and older men. I mention this to you Mr President not for propaganda or other reasons but because I personally have seen this destruction

and my company and my staff have been involved in these attacks [sic]. Putting politics aside, whatever the involvement in the superpower game that is being done by the United States at present will adversely affect its reputation and its position in this country as well as in Africa. If your efforts to support UNITA have the result of producing more deaths and misery, surely they cannot be efforts that are correct. As a son of a Missionary and a poor Christian [sic] I appeal to your Christian values to consider the result that this type of action will produce and would have in causing perpetuation and increase of death and misery in this land. I do not think anything, even major political superpower manoeuvring justifies further deaths of innocent Angolan people as well as foreign workers and anything that contributes to this and causes further massacre cannot come from a country or a person with Christian upbringing and Christian beliefs. My appeal to you is humanitarian...

Then he warned Reagan:

With the many counsellors and advisers and political jockeys that must be around you I am sure it is difficult for you to come to a decision that will be right from a government and human standpoint. Let me say this, it is my opinion that a decision that affects the lives of people and their future is a difficult one to take and if the wrong one is taken the results are in the form of deep scars for many years to come...

The Fuehrer must have felt very proud of this effort of his because he sent me a copy. I do not know if he sent a copy to the Foreign Minister of the Philippines, but, as I did not hear that the Foreign Minister of the time had died of apoplexy, I assume he did not.

I am sure that Reagan's 'political jockeys' were thrilled to read the letter, which went on for six pages. More probably the Fuehrer's cronies in Angola read the letter, which must have enhanced his standing with the government. But America did not listen and the raids on Cafunfo carried on. After one particularly fierce battle UNITA guerrillas blew up millions of dollars worth of equipment, killed several workers and captured 77 of our Filipino employees and marched them to Savimbi's headquarters near the Caprivi Strip in Namibia, a journey of some 1000 kilometres, where they were released to the South African authorities. They arrived well and healthy despite their ordeal. We repatriated them, but many of them came back again.

Angola was not the first country that brought me into contact with diamond mining. In the early 1970s I had been on the board of Diminco, the newly nationalised Diamond Mining Company of Sierra Leone, which took control of Sierra Leone Selection Trust's operations.

4. THE STARS OF SIERRA LEONE

I felt like a sitting duck in Siaka Stevens' open-top car. But next to me the President of Sierra Leone looked calm and cheerful and did not seem to mind the five o'clock traffic in Freetown's narrow streets that slowed his car to a crawl. Sierra Leone had been a turbulent country and Stevens had been installed as President after a coup by non-commissioned officers. It occurred to me that if somebody decided to throw a bomb at him I would be one of the victims. Siaka Stevens had invited me to advise him on how to take over control of the diamond industry without interfering with its operations and upsetting production, because of my reputation as the architect of Zambia's economic reforms. We had just finished a meeting at his office and he offered me a lift to the Paramount Hotel, the only one in Freetown in those days, in his open-top Mercedes 600 – a huge car.

When the takeover was completed he asked me to join the board of the newly formed National Diamond Mining Company (Diminco), owned 51% by the government and 49% by its original owners, the Sierra Leone Selection Trust. I stayed on that board for about three years and during that period I watched the beginnings of the collapse of the country. The Sierra Leone diamonds were of jewellery quality and fetched high prices. But they were easy to mine, which invited many illegal diamond diggers. All they had to do was to dig a few feet into the ground until they reached the alluvial deposit – a few inches of sand set on the old river bed that had over the millennia silted and the river changed its course. They washed the sand and the diamonds remained at the bottom of the pan. Strictly speaking, the deposits were the property of the company and nobody else was allowed to mine them. But the diamond diggers, financed by Lebanese traders, would find all sorts of ways to evade the company. The most common was boys' initiation rites. A large area would be fenced and declared sacred ground out of bounds for the uninitiated. Inside the fence, though, instead of initiation ceremonies, the illegal miners were busy digging. I flew over such areas in the company helicopter and the spectacle was fascinating. The area within the fence looked like a sieve – all the pits, flooded and full of water after they had been mined and abandoned, looked like huge holes in a huge sieve. And the miners looked like ants busily digging new holes.

It was affecting the company's business because after an area has been 'raped' in this fashion it was no longer economic to follow up with proper mining. The board, at one of its meetings, appointed a committee to ask for the President's intervention. But Siaka Stevens was not very pleased with our initiative. He was a tall, big man with bloodshot eyes, not used to coming under pressure. He was annoyed and he showed it. He dismissed our argument that illegal digging was harmful to Sierra Leone's economy. 'Yes, the Lebanese finance the diggers,' he admitted. 'But the country does not suffer because the proceeds from the sales have to come back to finance more digging.' He was not prepared to see that the Lebanese were paying a pittance for the diamonds and were making huge profits outside the country. He did not see anything strange that Middle East Airlines, the Lebanese national carrier, had regular flights to Freetown, its only destination in sub-Saharan Africa. The flights were almost empty, but they were the only means of exporting the diamonds directly to Beirut without having to cross other borders and running the risk of being discovered by other authorities. Stevens was obviously benefiting from the illegal diamonds and did not take any action. His close ties with the Lebanese would become more open in later years, when a notorious Lebanese entrepreneur was regularly invited to attend Cabinet meetings.

I resigned from the board of Diminco over the sale of the Star of Sierra Leone – a 682-carat diamond. The company's consultants advised the board to sell the diamond by special auction. When the tenders were opened the highest price offered was £1,100,000. The consultants were confident that we could get at least £1,250,000 and advised us to try another auction three months later. There was deathly silence in the boardroom when at the next meeting I asked the general manager how much the Star of Sierra Leone fetched. After a lot of hesitation he reported that the diamond had been sold for £950,000 to a New York jeweller on the instruction of Siaka Stevens. By that time the corruption of the Stevens regime had become legendary and I decided that I no longer had a role to play on that board.

I went back to Sierra Leone, a few years later, after we had bought two international trading companies: Morison Sons & Jones, a nineteenth-century British trading house from the Guinness group, and Breckwoldt & Co., a 1930s Hamburg trading house, from the son of its founder. Both companies had subsidiaries in Sierra Leone, and I would visit three or four times a year. Business would take me to Sierra Leone for the next 20 or so years and I watched with great sadness that country's descent into chaos and civil war.

The reasons were not dissimilar to those of Liberia. While Monrovia became the citadel of freed American slaves, Freetown was the citadel of the 'recaptives' – the slaves freed from ships carrying them to the New World. Unlike the Americo-Liberians, who had a common language and religion, the recaptives had very little in common. They spoke different tongues and had different customs, yet over the years they kneaded together a community more enterprising and better educated than the indigenous people around them. They also developed Krio, their own patois, a mixture of local languages and English that has since spread to the whole of West Africa, with a variation for the French-speaking territories. By the middle of the twentieth century the recaptives had become the cream of Sierra Leone society, not just better educated but more affluent than the indigenous people. And they were at the top of the civil service too. When I visited for the first time I was very impressed with the quality of the top civil servants of Sierra Leone – almost all of them with British surnames, indicating their 'recaptive' ancestry. They were more sophisticated and better educated than most of their Zambian counterparts of that period – thanks to the Fourah Bay College, one of the oldest learning institutions in Africa, established in 1876.

Breckwoldt and Morison also had subsidiaries in The Gambia, Liberia, Ivory Coast, Ghana, Togo and Nigeria, which gave us extensive coverage of West Africa. Most of the businesses were vehicle franchises (Peugeot, Renault, Volkswagen), industrial chemicals, pharmaceuticals, toiletries and cosmetics and textiles. The textiles, mainly brightly coloured expensive brocades, were very popular amongst the elite in Ghana and Nigeria and to a lesser extent all over the rest of West Africa, where often husband and wife wear traditional dress made of the same material.

The Breckwoldt acquisition also increased the ethnic mixture of the group by adding a very large number of Germans. Contrary to the image I had of Germans being staid and imperturbable, I found the Breckwoldt staff highly emotional, almost childish in their dislike of change. The staff of the Hamburg head office predicted that we would lose all the franchises because German manufacturers would not want to deal with a British group (their perception of ITM). They were indignant at the claim in our promotional material that we operated on all six continents. After all, what they had learned at school was that there are only five continents on the globe – did the British create a sixth? I must confess that that is what I had learned at school too, but my deputy was a geographer with an Oxford degree, and who was I to contradict him? Their views of the British aside, they also seemed to have nothing but contempt for our choice of manager, a German we transferred from our Munich office. It struck me that the burghers of Hamburg considered their southern compatriots somewhat inferior.

***

Banjul felt like a run-down capital of a very remote province somewhere in colonial Africa. It is in fact the capital of The Gambia, the smallest country in mainland Africa and one of the many oddities of the continent. The Gambia is a sliver of land a few miles either side of the river Gambia, stretching from the coast for 295 miles upstream. Completely surrounded by Senegal, its total area is 11,300 sq. km., and its main resources are peanuts and tourism. The beautiful beaches around Banjul attract many visitors from Northern Europe, in search of light, sun and warmth during the European winter. After a few visits I ventured to ask why the Gambian immigration officers always made a last-minute inspection of the plane just before departure, particularly questioning Gambian youngsters on board. It was explained to me that some visitors at times smuggle their holiday lovers out of The Gambia, who end up destitute in some Northern European country or other after their hosts tire of them.

Unlike Banjul, Abidjan, the capital of Côte d'Ivoire, was a buzzing metropolis. But there was something un-African about it. First of all, I guess, were the many steel and glass buildings that dominated the town, and the state-of-the-art highway network that surrounded it. But what struck me in the early 1980s was the large number of French men and women performing jobs that in English-speaking Africa had long ceased to be done by expatriates. In Abidjan, there were French salesladies in shops, French barmen in hotels and even waiters in restaurants. And the ubiquitous baguettes sold on every street corner. The markets were, of course, very African and very colourful with men and women in their exotic costumes. Côte d'Ivoire and Guinea have been the leaders in African haute couture for decades.

***

There was an enormous difference in the post-independence behaviour of Britain and France towards their former colonies. After independence, Britain persuaded itself that the colonies had been a major economic burden and rushed towards cutting ties as fast as possible. It turned inwards, and its major preoccupation was to save the pound from devaluation. In the process it cut down many forms of assistance to its former colonies, including the topping up of salaries of British civil servants still working in Africa – an irrational act whose benefit I could never fathom, especially as these payments were made in sterling to the beneficiaries' accounts in Britain. The recipients lived on the emoluments they received from the host government. In the early 1970s, when the Prime Minister, Ted Heath, applied to join the European Economic Community, Britain also demolished the various commonwealth trade preferences – a measure that did not affect Africa as much as it affected the rest of the Commonwealth. And in the early 1980s Margaret Thatcher increased the tuition costs for foreign nationals wanting to study at British universities.

Somehow, Britain did not calculate the enormous benefits it derived from the colonial markets and the cultural influence associated with British higher education and Britons living and working in former colonies. As the British withdrew, their place was taken over by the Japanese, the Germans, the Italians and other Europeans, as well as Indians and Middle Easterners, particularly Lebanese, who brought new attitudes unburdened by a colonial past and new products of higher quality and lower prices. The vehicle market, for example, changed from being dominated by British-made cars and trucks to Japanese, Italian, German and Scandinavian in less than five years.

On the education front, the Soviet Union grabbed the opportunity to develop cultural ties with Africa by offering scholarships to its Lumumba University, to Leipzig and to many other institutions in the communist world. I did not think so at the beginning, but I now know that this worked to the benefit of the ex-colonies. The British withdrawal forced them into an un-expected cosmopolitan and economic emancipation they may not have been prepared for, like many had not been prepared for independence. Many economic disasters may have come about as a result of this forced self-reliance. But the English-speaking countries of Africa made those mistakes a few decades ago and are now much the wiser as a result.

By contrast, the French maintained close ties and control of their ex-colonies. For a start, the Bank of France guaranteed the free convertibility of the CFA (Communauté Financière d'Afrique) franc to the French franc at the rate of fifty to one, its original parity set at its inception in 1947. As a result the Bank of France had virtual control over all the central banks in French-speaking Africa, and in view of the free convertibility French business in the area thrived. In addition France secured preferential trade treaties with all its ex-colonies, in contrast to the British who dismantled them. So Frenchmen and French products and French businesses enjoyed preference over those of other countries. While Japanese vehicles and Japanese and American computers captured the English-speaking markets, Renault and Peugeot and Citroën vehicles and Bull computers were dominating the French-speaking ones. But this was not all. The French kept a grip on the choice of President of most French-speaking African countries and openly interfered in support of some long-serving strongmen or for the demise of others.

The different behaviour of the French and the British may have given the false impression that there was greater stability and prosperity in French-speaking Africa. This was not the case. With French patronage strongmen may remain in power for lengthy periods of time, but when they pass on they leave a vacuum that leads to instability and civil war. Côte d'Ivoire is a prime example. From a beacon of stability and prosperity in West Africa it has been ravaged by conflict and civil war since the death of Houphouet Boigny, its first and only President for over 30 years. Togo is following the same path after the death of Gnassingbe Éyadéma, another French protégé, a former sergeant who participated in the assassination of the first President of Togo in 1963 and took power in a coup in 1967. Upon his death Éyadéma's son was installed as President and has subsequently 'won' a controversial national election. But discontent is simmering below the surface.

We would expand further into French and British West Africa in later years, but in the early 1980s the ITM group turned eastwards to the Middle East, India, Sri Lanka, South-East Asia, Australia and the South Pacific.

5. AN UNPROFITABLE DIVERSION

'Like a mary-jane?' I had no idea what she was talking about, but then I realised that the Filipino girl was offering me a marijuana cigarette. I found her in my room – part of the hospitality of Usiphil, the Caterpillar dealers in Manila, when we went to visit them at the insistence of Caterpillar. Usiphil had protested vehemently that we were poaching its staff by recruiting in the Philippines for Angola, and Caterpillar felt so strongly about it that, in a letter demanding that we stop, a Mr Page, senior Caterpillar executive responsible for that region at the time, described our recruitment in the Philippines as an act of 'industrial piracy' and demanded that we stop. We were stunned. We thought we deserved praise for our initiative to resuscitate and keep the Angolan Caterpillar operations going, but we were being hit on the head instead. Despite the excellence of its products and its worldwide distribution operations Caterpillar remains essentially a Peoria, Illinois, company, with mentality to match. And when it gets on its high horse there is no point in raising the ethical principles of an issue, or the more down-to-earth argument that the Philippines is a huge country and its distributor there could not possibly be hurt by the recruitment of a few workers for Angola (not all our recruits were Caterpillar mechanics). So we went to the Philippines and our visit ended happily with an agreement to transfer our recruitment contract to Usiphil's recruitment affiliate, which must have been the reason for the fuss – hence the generous hospitality, not only to me but to every member of my team. Girls in your room seemed to be a common method of hospitality in the East as I would find later.

By then, Caterpillar was no longer the main focus of our attention. Apart from our own expansion, we now had to absorb Morison and Breckwoldt, which operated in West Africa as well as the Middle East, South and South-East Asia, Australia and the South Pacific. There was logic in the reasons why Guinness, a brewery group, wanted to get rid of an old trading house such as Morisons that operated in Africa and Asia, which we considered to be a good match with our other activities. We should have been more sceptical about Breckwoldt, which we bought from a consortium of German banks and other lenders. We were persuaded that the German group got into trouble because the founder, who was very old, had to retire and his son was not capable of running it. The son, downing a few cognacs with lunch during the negotiations, seemed to confirm that point of view. But, as we soon found out, European trading houses could no longer compete with the up-and-coming Malaysian, Chinese, Singaporean and Australian entrepreneurs in that region.

Nevertheless, these acquisitions gave us an international as distinct from just African flavour, and the opportunity to rationalise our operations and divide them into coherent subgroups. To emphasise our wide geographical spread, we chose Meridian (in what seemed to us its more elegant French spelling) as the brand for our international trade and finance operations, which traded largely as Meridien Trade and Meridien Credit Corporations.

A group brochure of the early 1980s describes them:

Meridien Trade promotes commerce among the developed and developing countries of the world through a global network of export marketing companies in the major commercial centres of the world. These are supplemented by branches, sales or liaison offices in many other countries so that Meridien has trading personnel ranging from big export houses of more than a hundred

Drilling for water in Makuno district in Eastern Uganda. An Ingersoll Rand drilling rig, one of the many products we distributed in many parts of Africa.

44

staff to small sales units of a couple of men in Angola, Australia, Belgium, Botswana, Canada, Egypt, Gambia, Germany, Hong Kong, India, Indonesia, Japan, Kuwait, Liberia, Malawi, Malaysia, Mozambique, New Caledonia, Nigeria, Papua New Guinea, Peru, Sierra Leone, Singapore, Solomon Islands, Sudan, Tanzania, Thailand, Togo, United Arab Emirates, United Kingdom, United States, Western Samoa, Zambia and Zimbabwe [a dizzying spread]. This extensive network enables it to offer exporters the widest market coverage wherever they may be and to bring the international market place to any importer's doorstep.

The Meridien International Credit companies finance the movement of goods from any country to any other country. The companies are strategically located in the major financial capitals of the world not only for the convenience of their clients on all six continents but also to tap the necessary funds for trade financing at the most competitive rates in the most suitable of a wide variety of currencies. Meridien's expertise in the sources, methods and techniques of trade related financing extends also to the procedures and programs of the various national agencies for export credit insurance and funding.

This was really the crux of the matter. As Africa sunk deeper and deeper into debt, we had to use the cover of the various export credit agencies of the major countries in order to finance supplies to Africa. These agencies guaranteed the convertibility of African countries' currencies into their own. So we needed cover from the Foreign Credit Insurance Association and Export-Import Bank of the United States, the Export Credit Guarantee Department of Britain, the Export Credit Insurance Corporation of Singapore, the Export Development Corporation of Canada, the Office National Ducroire of Belgium, Hermes of Germany, Coface of France and MITI of Japan to keep supplies flowing. When payments from Africa started drying up we discovered that the British were the most honourable payers under their policies and the Singaporeans the opposite.

The Caterpillar franchises in Africa were grouped under Intraco, head-quartered in New York. By that time we had operations in five countries (Angola, Liberia, Malawi, Mozambique and Zambia) and we expanded the range to complementary equipment, such as hydraulic cranes and shovels, off highway trucks, heavy-duty agricultural equipment, compactors, lift trucks, drilling rigs, etc. The building, civil, mechanical and structural engineering operations were grouped under the name Wade Adams Construction which operated in Zambia, Malawi, Botswana, and would later expand to Kenya, Tanzania, Uganda, Burundi, Sudan, Ghana and the United Arab Emirates. And we had a wide variety of other trading companies in Angola, Botswana, Egypt, The Gambia, Liberia, Malawi, Mozambique, Nigeria, Sierra Leone, Tanzania, Togo, Zambia and Zimbabwe.

Our sortie to the Far East and the Pacific did not last long. We soon found out that the troubles of Breckwoldt were not due to the perceived incompetence of the son. Times had changed and German products could not compete with those manufactured in the East, either in quality or price. To remain there we would have to reorient the Breckwoldt group to a different type of business. We considered embarking upon operations similar to the ones we had in Africa, but we decided that the field was unfamiliar and the area too far for us to give it proper attention, especially in its formative years. Places such as Papua New Guinea did feel a little like Africa but we found the business scene dominated by Chinese entrepreneurs and Australian conglomerates. Even though the country had been independent for many years, unlike Africa, the local people were content to leave business in foreign hands. So we gradually wound down those operations, selling the bigger ones, such as those in Papua New Guinea and Singapore, and closing others. But we did maintain offices in Bombay, Hong Kong and Sydney, because those centres handled exports to Africa and did business with some of our other operations.

India was the most relevant. Many Indian products were suitable for the African markets and their prices were low, even though the quality was not always consistent. And our frequent visits gave Danae and me the opportunity to become familiar with India and its people, as well as its history and monuments, and its art and other treasures that spread in abundance.

Hong Kong was the next important Far East post, sourcing goods from China and arranging finance from Hong Kong's financial institutions. It was a very attractive city, combining its Chinese origins and culture with Western architecture and business practices. The manager of our Hong Kong operation was one of the very few Germans who remained with us from the Breckwoldt group. He was very competent but remained very Germanic after almost a quarter of a century in a Chinese country. I don't think he had much love for the Chinese and he hated Chinese food so much that he would never have it even when he took us to a Chinese restaurant for dinner. He stuck to steak and beer, despite the waiter's protests, without the slightest embarrassment.

Australia has many of the characteristics of Africa. Perth looked like a Northern Rhodesian copperbelt town and, amazingly, I bumped into two ex-copperbelt characters during one of my stops there. One had been working for me as a mechanic in Chingola and the other owned the Chingola dry cleaners during the Northern Rhodesia days. Many white miners had emigrated from Northern Rhodesia to Perth after independence. The men in Sydney looked and behaved like whites in Southern Africa. The bars filled up immediately after work, with men downing beers at lightning speed before setting out on their way home. And their clothes, especially when wearing shorts, were two sizes too small for them, underlining their big beer bellies – exactly like those of the Rhodesians and the South African whites.

Singapore is not exactly out of Aldous Huxley's *Brave New World*, but it is the nearest the real world will ever produce. Its modern architecture almost obliterated all traces of previous cultures and its single-minded pursuit of higher economic goals has made this tiny city state and its inhabitants soulless and ruthless. We sold our operations in Singapore and withdrew, but we had to write off large sums in credit insurance claims that the Export Credit Insurance Corporation of Singapore refused to honour. And they produced a very good reason for it. Our manager, a Singaporean Chinese, received a bribe from one of our Indonesian customers. This led to the cancellation of all our policies and the repudiation of all our claims – not just those relating to Indonesia but also those from Africa and other parts of the world. The huge insurance premiums we paid over the years did not count. What hurts is that, with hindsight, I realised that the Singaporean insurers knew all along that they would never have to pay under their policies. Bribes are as much a way of life in that part of the world as they are in some parts of Africa and the insurance industry was running a good intelligence network. And, even though our entire staff, from the general manager down, was Singaporean and may well have followed tradition in their dealings with Indonesia and other surrounding countries, the business with Africa which originated from the group was entirely above-board. Corruption in Africa is often cited as the reason for the slow economic progress. But having been in South-East Asia, where corruption is equally rampant but the economies are thriving, I think that the reasons for Africa's ills have to be sought elsewhere.

In our accounts for 1986 we reported a write-off of $8 million arising from the closure of the Singapore and Malaysian operations. In Malaysia, most of our employees were Malaysian Chinese who had at one stage put us in touch with the Malaysia Chinese Co-operative, and we commenced negotiations for an amalgamation of their interests outside Malaysia. The Co-op had been buying businesses in the region and the idea was to combine them with our own operations not only in the region, but those in the Far East and Africa. We would become the managers of the resultant conglomerate. I have always been in favour of attracting Asian investment to Africa. As I said in *Africa: Another Side of the Coin*, Asian investors are less likely to be as sensitive to the African political climate as their Western counterparts. I thought that amalgamation with the Malaysian Chinese Co-operative would have been a good beginning. But after looking at the Co-op's portfolio we discovered that what they had bought was overpriced. And when a team from the Co-op board visited Africa it became apparent that they had no business experience and were unable to evaluate business opportunities. In the end the deal fell through. By that time the chief executive of the Malaysia Chinese Co-op was under investigation, and later he ended up in jail for the acquisitions he had made.

The Asian escapade was an interesting but unprofitable diversion. The real world for us was home in Africa.

6. JEWELS IN THE MAKING

I did not plan to spend my fiftieth birthday in Lagos. I never celebrated my birthdays anyway, always giving priority to my business schedule. I was scheduled to be in Lomé, the capital of Togo, that night and I thought that a quiet dinner with my team and our Togolese staff in some quiet French restaurant in town would be in order. There were plenty of those all over French-speaking Africa. But I was travelling in a British-registered Learjet and President Éyadéma was going through one of his Macbeth-like bouts of paranoia that mercenaries from Britain hired by the sons of Sylvanus Olympio (the first President of Togo, assassinated by him in 1963) would come by private plane to avenge the death of their father. We had arrived in Lomé from London for a number of meetings and intended to spend the night at the government-owned business hotel 'Deux Fevrier', named after the date Éyadéma survived a plane crash – proof that he had divine protection, according to his cronies. (A beach hotel in Lomé, also government-owned, was called Sarakawa and carried the name of the place where the crash took place – Éyadéma playing the survival card to the hilt.) We were allowed to have our meetings and stay the night but the plane was not given permission to overnight in Lomé. It had to go to Lagos, Nigeria (the next country on our itinerary for which a landing permit had been obtained), and come back the following day to pick us up. As the cost would have been exorbitant we decided to leave with the plane.

Travelling commercially between French- and English-speaking Africa in those days was only possible through London and Paris. Even travelling between two French-speaking or two English-speaking capitals, sometimes one had to go from Africa to Paris or London and back. So, for a quick and sensible trip, one had to use a private plane. But private planes had their own problems. For a start you needed clearances from each country you would fly over and landing permits from each country you planned to visit or stop in for refuelling. The Lear's endurance was only four to five hours, and as most civil aviation authorities never bothered to respond we used to apply to almost all the countries en route. But, even so, many times we had to get in the air without being sure where we would be allowed to refuel. Togo was the worst. On a different occasion we were refused permission to land in Lomé even though we had a telexed permit. Flying between Douala and Monrovia, as soon as we arrived in Togolese airspace we asked the control tower for the usual permission to start our descent in preparation for landing. 'You have no permission to land here,' was the terse response. We read our clearance number. 'The officer who keeps the permits is out and his office is locked': another unhelpful response. In desperation we said that we needed to land anyway because we were running out of fuel. 'You would be landing at your own risk,' was the chilling answer. To land in Togo at your own risk could mean a lot of things, but certainly arrest, long interrogation and detention. Deathly silence in the plane while we were trying to digest our predicament – and then a cheerful voice came over the speaker: 'You are only 15 minutes from Accra. Come down and we shall refuel you here.' The Ghanaians at their hospitable best saved the day.

We landed in Lagos the evening of my fiftieth birthday, without hotel reservations. The Federal Palace Hotel, where we had reservations from the following day, was fully booked, we were told. It turned out that the other couple of hotels of bearable standard available those days were also full. We faced the prospect of spending the night on the veranda of the Federal Palace, until late at night one enterprising colleague secured rooms at the additional cost of $30 per room – paid under the table, of course, and by then a greater cause for celebration than my birthday. We asked for champagne, but Nigeria was going through a bout of 'austerity' in order to prove its frugality to the world, which was pointing fingers at the waste of its oil income. No champagne, but, to our astonishment, the waiter

I celebrated my fiftieth birthday waiting for a room at the Federal Palace Hotel in Lagos, Nigeria.

produced two bottles of Château Haut-Brion for $25 each. A very respectable alternative, and at a giveaway price to be sure, except that red wine in that hot and humid climate needed some cooling. But we could not wait.

African countries have much in common, their ethnic differences adding spice and excitement. It was exhilarating to land in the chaos of Lagos airport after the relative orderliness and quiet of Zambia and the other East and Southern African countries. Nigeria is a vibrant country. Everything is done at high pitch. And everybody is a hustler improvising a living by hook or by crook: the guy who will try to pick up your briefcase (don't let him) and offer to get you through immigration and customs fast; the guy who wants to fill the forms for you; the guy who offers to get you a taxi; to get you a room at the hotel. You name it: for everything you need, real or imagined somebody is around offering service. And a visitor's needs were greater in the late 1970s and early 1980s when the price of oil was high and the Nigerian economy was booming, everybody rushing there to trade. The roads were congested and the hotels were always full. It would take two hours to get from the airport to downtown Lagos and more hours of waiting before you were given a room.

But the airport was only the first impression. Moving around Lagos you could not help but admire the entrepreneurial spirit of the Nigerians. Thousands of traders, shopkeepers, market women, jobbers, artisans, whoever, were running businesses big and small, from the sidewalks, from market stalls or from tiny shops. Their combined turnover must have been running into the tens of millions of dollars per day. And they did this, without much capital, never mind education. At the time – the mid-1970s and 1980s – this struck me as unique and I recognised it as the true foundation for African enterprise and the economic emancipation of the continent. It is wonderful to see that this phenomenon is now spreading all over Africa. In the so-called 'city centre' market of Lusaka, for example, one can buy all manner of things that are not available in the main shopping areas, or, if they are, cost many times more. What makes it amazing is that untrained, semi-literate people with very little capital can source after-market parts for vehicles, tractors and heavy machinery, computers, electronic equipment, pumps, compressors, builders' hardware and many other technical products.

The small shopkeepers and the marketeers were only the beginning of the evidence that set Nigeria apart. It also had the greatest number of universities in Africa and large numbers of sophisticated and highly trained people in the professions and big business, educated locally or abroad. It is for this reason that in the 1960s, when it went through the same processes of economic nationalism that most other African countries did, Nigeria did not have to resort to the nationalisations introduced elsewhere. The decree took the form of dictating Nigerian participation in businesses (60% in some and 40% in others), bringing about even greater participation of Nigerians in a business sector that was already substantially locally managed if not owned.

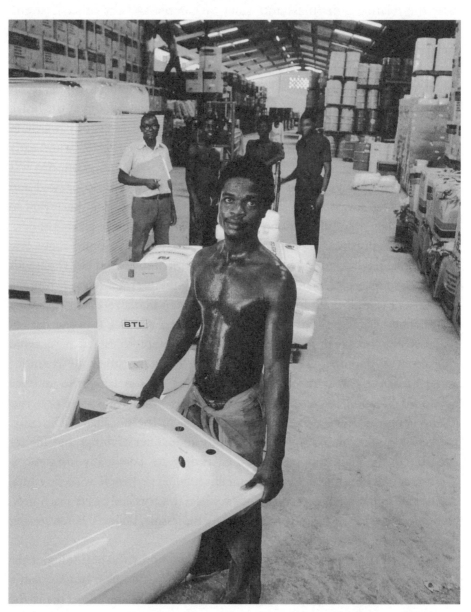

Inside the Lagos warehouse of Bisiolu Technical Ltd, our Nigerian affiliate that distributed building materials, engineering products and industrial chemicals throughout the country.

But the biggest economic paragon was still the government, with a major agenda for ports, roads and other public works and grand projects, such as vehicle assembly plants and steelworks – never completed despite the billions poured into them. And at government level the waste in Nigeria was legendary. The oil income made the government feel rich and it embarked upon public works in all directions. It did not seem to occur to the authorities that the country did not have the implementation capacity for all the projects at once. So the orders were placed (perhaps by people who were not interested in the project or its implementation but only in the commission that the order would bring) and shiploads of materials started arriving at the port of Lagos, which did not have the facilities to handle them. Congestion at the port was so bad that ships had to wait for up to six months before they could unload. And, by the time they got a berth, ships carrying cement unloaded concrete, the cement solidifying in the tropical heat and humidity.

Nigeria is a unique country. It is the most populous in Africa and it encompasses many tribes that can be roughly divided into three very strong ethnic groups with highly pronounced differences: the Hausa-Fulani in the north, with very strong Muslim fundamentalist leanings; and the Yoruba in the south-west and the Igbo in the south-east, both mainly Christian. There are constant antagonisms between these groups which frequently erupt into ethnic clashes. In 1967 the Igbo broke away from the rest and declared the Republic of Biafra, which resulted in a three-year civil war. In the end the Nigerian forces defeated Biafra and Nigeria was reunited in 1970. Since then there has been a succession of civil and military administrations, the latter mainly led by some strongman from the north. But, in spite of all these stresses and strains caused by ethnic and religious differences, Nigeria remains united as a federal republic. Its people share many common characteristics, the most pronounced being self-confidence in abundance, self-reliance and enterprise. And they seem to have determined that the best way forward is to remain united as one country constantly reviewing their constitution and creating new states in order to solve local rivalries as they go along.

Expatriates everywhere tend to live in their own cocoons and have very little understanding of local realities. We discovered that the Germans of Breckwoldt knew less than most. But as Africa was home ground it was easy to replace them – with Nigerians, of course, who were more capable, better connected and cost a fraction of what the Germans did. The Breckwoldt sales of expensive textiles to rich Yoruba for their traditional dress was doing well but our biggest business was a builders' hardware trading operation we set up with a Yoruba accountant who had fled Nigeria during the Biafra war and had worked for the

Industrial Development Corporation of Zambia when I was its chief executive. Many educated Nigerians, mainly Igbo, spent the civil war years in Zambia in positions such as university lecturers, doctors and accountants, and it was pleasant to meet them again on their home ground in equally high positions. Their hospitality was boundless but one had to be careful of Nigerian food. I remember once filling my plate with chicken that was swimming in a sauce, the colour of which was a beautiful shade of red. It turned out that the sauce was chilli, not tomato as I had thought, and I almost choked on the first mouthful – the hottest chilli sauce I ever tasted.

Nigeria is moving forward. After the experience of a series of military dictators culminating with General Abacha, who plundered unashamedly (more than $2 billion have been identified in his various accounts since his death, at least half of which had been remitted through British banks), the country has been shaken to its senses and realised that a cleaner and more conventional form of government is the only way forward. Olusegun Obasanjo, the general who handed power to a civilian administration in 1978, has been elected President and in 2006 was serving his second and final term. The economy, boosted by high oil prices, is doing well again. And, despite the constant bickering between regions and clashes in the oil-producing areas, where the local people are in constant conflict with the international oil companies and are constantly agitating for a greater share of the oil wealth, Nigeria can look forward to a more stable future. In 2005 the Minister of Finance (a lady) achieved a businesslike settlement of Nigeria's external debt without having to resort to the various 'carrot and stick' conditions devised by the IMF. The negotiations took place on an equal-to-equal basis, a very gratifying novelty for Africa.

***

Ghana has many of the characteristics of Nigeria without as many problems of ethnic diversity. The high prices of cocoa before independence created a prosperous middle class that could afford to educate their children in British and American universities, as long ago as the 1950s. As a result, Ghana probably has the highest proportion of university graduates in Africa and a large, well-to-do diaspora around the world, particularly in Britain and the United States. Yet this highly sophisticated and, unlike Nigeria, reasonably homogeneous country had an equally dismal record since independence, with a series of coups, counter-coups and short-lived civilian administrations.

Ghana was the first African county to be granted independence in 1957 when Kwame Nkrumah was Prime Minister – he had to be released from prison in 1951 to become leader of the government, and Prime Minister the following year after his party won a majority in the general election. Ghana became a republic with Nkrumah as its President in 1960, and in 1964 a one-party state with him as Life President. Those who have been involved in African independence movements have a soft spot for Kwame Nkrumah. He may have had many faults, but he was a committed pan-Africanist, generous in his support of the liberation movements of the other African countries, and his vision of a United Africa still inspires. Sadly, the younger generations of Ghanaians think that Nkrumah's pan-Africanism and the money spent in assisting the liberation movements of other countries was a generosity that their country could not afford, much as the younger generations of Zambians resent Kaunda's dedication to the liberation struggles of Southern Africa and the economic burden that Zambia has had to carry as a result.

Nkrumah had the courage of his convictions and he never wavered from speaking out. He was outraged, as all Africans were, at the break-up of the Congo, the secession of Katanga and the overthrow and assassination of Patrice Lumumba, the only Congolese leader before or since who had a chance to unite the vast, amorphous Belgian colony that the greed of Leopold II created at the end of the nineteenth century. In a broadcast in Ghana he accused the United Nations of connivance in the Belgian-led and Western-supported conspiracy to dismember the Congo and kill its Prime Minister. And he had a tempestuous relationship with John F. Kennedy despite America's financing of the Volta Hydroelectric scheme because of his conviction that the CIA was involved in the death of Lumumba and the installation of Mobutu as the Congo strongman, an act that America would come to regret decades later. But the CIA may have had the last laugh on Nkrumah. The belief in Africa is that it was the CIA that organised the coup against him while he was in Beijing en route to Hanoi at the invitation of Ho Chi Minh, during the Vietnam War. The Americans tried to prevent that mission because it would have implied recognition of North Vietnam, and as Nkrumah did not listen, their only way of aborting his mission was the coup.

The received wisdom in the Western world is that Nkrumah brought about his own downfall through political and economic mismanagement, which led to stagnation and food shortages. But, as one learns from Geoffrey Bing's (Ghana's first Attorney-General) biography under the title *Reap the Whirlwind*, the economic problems of Ghana were not dissimilar to the problems that would engulf the whole of Africa a few years later after the collapse of commodity prices brought about by the rise in the price of oil. For some reason the price of cocoa, Ghana's mainstay, had dropped by 70% from £467 per ton in 1954 to £139 in 1965. And the price of gold, Ghana's other major resource, was held firm at $80 per troy ounce under the Bretton Woods agreements. Such a huge drop in the price of cocoa without a compensating increase in the price of gold inevitably caused the economic stagnation and hardships that were given as the cause of the coup. But Ghana's economic problems were not solved by the coup, or the succession of unstable governments that followed.

Ghana's stagnation lasted until the early 1990s. I remember the neglect and decline in Accra that struck me on my first visit. Everything at the airport was falling apart. The taxi that took us to the hotel was ancient and dilapidated, the roads potholed, and the only international hotel was badly in need of a coat of paint and complete refurbishment. The bed sheets were torn and the bath towels were unusable. One look at the dining room was enough to put us off dining there. We did have a good dinner at a Lebanese restaurant nearby but when the bill came we had the shock of our lives: $525 for a dinner for four at the official rate of exchange for the cedi, the local currency. I called the owner and protested. His response was: 'What money do you carry?' He accepted $100 and was so pleased that he offered cognacs on the house. In other words, the real value of the cedi was just 20% of its official value at the time.

The problems of Ghana engendered a succession of military coups and counter-coups, with a sprinkling of civilian administrations in between, yet none of the administrations that followed Nkrumah was able to improve the economy. Eventually Flight Lieutenant Jerry Rawlings came on the scene in 1979 with a coup that led to the installation of a civilian administration, which he overthrew in a second coup on 31 December 1981, after which he became President. By that time Ghanaian society was craving for stability, which allowed Rawlings to impose painful economic programmes, inspired by the International Monetary Fund (IMF) and the World Bank, which caused a lot of suffering for many years. But the resurgence in the price of gold and cocoa, the development of tourism, and the return of many Ghanaians after the liberalisation of the economy that started with Rawlings and was consolidated by his successor, brought about an economic transformation that is enviable in Africa.

But transformations were also taking place nearer home, in Southern Africa.

7. RHODESIANS NEVER LEARN

'We must remain loyal to those who helped us during our difficult times of sanctions.' I nearly fell off my chair hearing this statement from the marketing manager of one of Zimbabwe's biggest industries. I was enquiring if they could supply cast-iron bathtubs to our Hong Kong branch. (Cast-iron bathtubs were no longer produced in most countries, but they were very popular with the Chinese because they keep the water hot longer.) That the sanctions were imposed against Rhodesia in order to force the change to Zimbabwe, the country where he now lived, did not seem to matter to the Rhodesian manager, who intended to show his gratitude to his sanction-busting agent in Hong Kong, ignoring the fact that the agent's actions had been inimical to the interest of the new nation. The Rhodesians (I shall be using this term to distinguish the whites from the black inhabitants of Zimbabwe) may have lost the war but this did not dent their confidence in their superiority or their belief that they would be able to always have it their way. And, amazingly, they did during the first couple of decades after Zimbabwe's independence. But their attitude would inevitably lead to the backlash at the beginning of the twenty-first century.

The struggle for majority rule in Zimbabwe had been long and bloody with many twists and turns. Some take the view that the declaration by Harold Wilson, the then Prime Minister, that Britain would not take arms against its kith and kin in Rhodesia gave Ian Smith the signal for the Unilateral Declaration of Independence (UDI) in 1965. I do not subscribe to this view. The Rhodesians would have done it anyway. They always lived in a fantasy world and really believed that the blacks in Rhodesia were the happiest in Africa – as their Prime Minister, Ian Smith, often repeated. They had a warped view of what was happening in the rest of Africa and they discounted land and freedom as factors in the independence struggle. After all, they looked after their blacks very well, they continually declared. They ascribed the demand for independence to a few agitators who were influenced from outside the country. They calculated that UDI would give them the ability to deal with the agitators the way they deserved, and everything would be peaceful thereafter. And, after UDI, they did put the black political leaders behind bars.

But this did not stop the liberation war. After some years of preparation outside the country Zimbabwe guerrillas started infiltrating through the north-eastern provinces in the early 1970s, coming in through the FRELIMO-liberated areas of Mozambique. They were successful in enlisting the support of the local population, and after Mozambique's independence in 1975 their infiltration intensified. The guerrillas could have won earlier, but too many obstacles were cast in their way because too many meddlers and too many manipulators saw opportunities for their own plans: John Vorster, the South African Prime Minister who had a dream of South African domination of moderate African States, took the opportunity to start a dialogue with Kenneth Kaunda of Zambia, hoping to use him as a stepping stone to the front-line states; Kenneth Kaunda who pursued a multitude of contradictory plans as he tried to bring the war to an early end, either in order to stop the drain on Zambia's economy, or to lend a helping hand to Joshua Nkomo, whom he would prefer to be the leader of an independent Zimbabwe; Bishop Muzorewa, Ndabaningi Sithole, Joshua Nkomo and many other black politicians, all hoping to become President one day; Henry Kissinger, US Secretary of State, siding with the whites and threatening to lift sanctions in order to pre-empt Soviet influence in the region because, along with most Southern African whites, he believed the freedom fighters were communists; and Ian Smith, who had a talent for misleading the Western countries, lent him a hand. In September 1976 he announced that he would agree to the principle of black majority rule within two years if the sanctions were lifted. Incredibly he was taken seriously, and Kissinger thought that he had pulled off a Rhodesian settlement. All these interventions gave Ian Smith the opportunity to hang on, misleading himself and the whites, who supported him to a man that the war was going well or that another compromise nearer to their liking was around the corner.

The Rhodesians never saw the root causes of the war. It never entered their minds that the Africans were aggrieved over the seizure of their land and their expulsion into remote and crowded reserves. Nor did they ever consider redressing the land grab legalised by the Land Apportionment Act of 1930, when the Rhodesian Parliament allocated 50% of the total area of the country to the settlers, whose numbers were minute at the time. Even after the many amendments of the Act, the settlers, who made up less than 5% of the population in 1961 still owned more than 45% of the land.

Zimbabwe's total area is 390,759 sq. km. or 96,558,503 acres. In their book *The Struggle for Zimbabwe*, David Martin and Phyllis Johnson provide the following table of land apportionment between white settlers and blacks:

	1931	1962
	Acres	Acres
European areas	49,149,000	35,384,000
Native reserves	21,600,000	21,020,000
Native purchase areas	7,465,000	4,216,000
Special native areas	–	19,150,000
Unassigned or unreserved	17,793,000	5,416,000
Wankie game area	–	3,324,000
Forest area	591,000	6,650,000
Undetermined	88,000	
Total	96,886,000	95,160,000

Not only did the settlers allocate to themselves 50% of the land. They got the best land (some say that they owned 80% of the agricultural land) and pushed the blacks into remote areas, with poor soils and low rainfall and far away from the market place. Overcrowding in the reserves would inevitably lead to overgrazing and soil erosion. When this came to pass, instead of allocating more land to ease the congestion, the Rhodesian government in 1951 introduced the Native Land Husbandry Act, limiting land ownership for blacks to eight acres and five head of cattle per family. The Africans, who had to sell their cattle in a hurry under pressure from the local district commissioner, had to sell at any price. The alternative of solving the land erosion problem by allocating more land for the native reserves was never considered, yet statistics at the time showed that the best land was in the hands of only 6400 white farm owners and 1400 white tenant farmers and only 3.5% of it was under cultivation (*The Struggle for Zimbabwe*).

In the mid-1980s I was offered one of those huge farms. It belonged to the Brook Bond Company, which had been taken over by Unilever. They wanted to sell it because it did not fit into the rest of their operations in Zimbabwe. It measured some 900,000 acres in south-west Zimbabwe, and apart from cattle ranching it had an antiquated abattoir and meat processing plant. Unilever were very wise to try and sell it, but they wanted £4 million, an unrealistic price. The

Downtown Harare, in the early years of independence. ITM businesses in Zimbabwe included construction, builders' hardware, the manufacture of paint, concrete pipes and structural steel products and the extraction of black granite in the Mtoko region for export to Italy.

response of Unilever's Rhodesian managers to my argument that the land was so huge that surely the government would expropriate it one day was to say that the government would not know what to do with it, which epitomises the post-independence attitude of the Rhodesians.

In the early years of independence the government of Zimbabwe, amazingly, did not make any attempt to change the status quo in either business or agriculture, so the Rhodesians came to the conclusion that they were indispensable. Like the white settlers of Zambia in the 1960s they did not recognise the aspirations of the new nation and made no attempt to change their ways. And in the 1985 election, the last that allowed them to vote for their own representatives in parliament, they voted for Ian Smith and his party as if nothing had changed in the country. It was still Rhodesia and it was business as usual, as far as they were concerned. Farms were bought and sold and prices remained buoyant. Sure, in order to complete the transaction they needed a certificate from the government certifying that it did not require the specific farm. They ignored the caveat 'in the foreseeable future' that the certificate carried, persuading themselves that the blacks would never be able to run farms properly and therefore would not want them anyway.

The deluge finally occurred in 2001, when President Mugabe, worried over his political fortunes, decided to use the land issue in order to attract support and nationalised the farms in a hurry. There has been a lot of justifiable criticism at the way Mugabe carried out the farm nationalisations, most of it missing the point. Like all the other African countries did in the 1960s, led by Tanzania and Zambia in 1967 and 1968, four years after their independence, Mugabe should have started taking measures at a similarly early stage to show that he meant to change the Rhodesian status quo. Had he done so then, the change would have been gradual and without the catastrophic effects on the economy that occurred in the early years of the new century. To be fair to him, he did make an attempt at land reform in 1990 when he announced his intention to redistribute 13 million acres to peasant farmers (*The Fate of Africa* by Martin Meredith). But he backed down after a storm of protest by the white farmers, supported by Britain, the United States, the World Bank and the IMF. A second similar attempt in 1998 suffered the same fate (*The Fate of Africa*). Mugabe introduced land reform too late and then, under pressure for his own political survival, compressed it into a very short timescale, with disastrous effects on the economy of Zimbabwe. At that stage, instead of looking realistically at the land problem and trying to solve it, he played to his own party's gallery and took brutal action for maximum political advantage.

There were many nationalist solutions that he could have introduced. He could have decreed that all landowners should distribute a certain acreage of their land to their workers, either gratis or at a price per acre agreed by negotiation between the government and the farmers union. Or that a farm worker after a specific number of years of continuous service should be allocated a piece of land by his employer on similar terms. Or that a tenant after so many years of residence on a property should acquire rights over a piece of land of a certain size. And the Rhodesian farmers could have been compensated through a combination of formulas including government grants and/or instalment/rental payments by the new tenants over a period of years. Such policies would have redistributed the land to trained black farmers, because it would have

Zimbabwean workers fabricating steel in the workshop of Wade Adams Engineering in Harare.

favoured farm workers – and farm workers are farmers too. And, in this way, the owners would have retained part of their land, and they would have been paid for what they sold to their workers over a period of time. But Mugabe's policies were not aiming at solving the land problem. Their real aim was to get maximum political leverage, and they destroyed Zimbabwe's economy in the process.

The West, which praised Mugabe for his responsible handling of the economy in the 1980s (read: not rocking the white boat), is now up in arms. But the West must understand that Mugabe's measures, not unlike Idi Amin's expulsion of the Indians out of Uganda, are popular not only in Zimbabwe but the whole of Southern Africa. I remember the applause Mugabe received at the second inauguration of President Thabo Mbeki of South Africa. It was deafening and second only to Mandela's in enthusiasm. And the West must also accept that events were caused as much by the attitude of the Rhodesians, a combination of the foolhardy and the bloody-minded, as by Mugabe's political opportunism; and it must understand that the make-up of the Movement for Democratic Change (MDC), a conglomeration of black trade unions, white businessmen, professionals and farmers, make the people of Zimbabwe and the neighbouring countries suspect that it is a front for the Rhodesians who finance it, a suspicion that is continuously reinforced by the vitriolic campaign against Mugabe by Britain and other Western countries and the shrill demands for Thabo Mbeki to intervene in Zimbabwe. The most ludicrous in this genre was an article in Johannesburg's *Business Day* of 13 August 2003 by a Mr R.W. Johnson. He admonished Mbeki:

> …Thus Mbeki, instead of spending time on Charles Taylor would do better to get rid of the torturer and murderer next door: for state collapse and civil war are now not far away in Zimbabwe. Moreover with Zimbabwean president Robert Mugabe openly threatening to use British and US citizens as hostages, the prospect of western military intervention there now inevitably exists. Should this occur, the Mugabe regime would not last one afternoon but Mbeki will not escape the fall out from these fresh Zimbabwe ruins.

This kind of thinking seemed to be very prevalent amongst the Southern African whites in 2003. I used to receive many e-mails on Mugabe and his policies over the land and other issues. I found the ones from a Gordon Cormack particularly silly and distasteful, so I sent him an e-mail asking him to take me off his mailing list. I received the following reply:

> …I will take you off my mailing list today. I suppose it is a bit embarrassing when one finds one's favourite 'Sons of the Soil' have very muddy, clay feet! Good luck, old chap, and I hope the rivers keep running for all in Zambia, as

Zimbabwe completely collapses and South Africa becomes overwhelmed with violent crime. Yes, I am pessimistic re: SADC region's future. There is no order and there is more AIDS than Aid. *[I am sure such thinking makes perfect sense to Cormack and his friends, but its logic escapes me]*

Old and new technologies working side by side. Wade Adams' workers building a new canal in Zimbabwe.

By the end of 2006, three years later, none of Johnson's and Cormack's wish lists were fulfilled and the rivers of the region, bar the drought, kept running. On the other hand, the Movement for Democratic Change was in disarray.

The economy of Zimbabwe was in ruins at the end of 2006 due to Mugabe's action. But adversity in Africa, particularly in the rural areas, is commonplace and as a result the peasants' patience is inexhaustible. The peasants, who are still the majority, have for ever put up with adversity and seen their land and their rights taken away in the twentieth century with little change in their fortunes since independence. The difficulties of Zimbabwe are not as distressing to them as economic statistics suggest. Drought-induced famine aside, peasants in Zimbabwe were not better off in the remote reserves that they lived in for the best part of the twentieth century, or the overcrowded 'protected villages' they were forced to live in by the Smith regime during the liberation war in the 1970s in order to prevent them from giving food and shelter to the freedom fighters.

The above notwithstanding, Mugabe cannot be absolved of blame for Zimbabwe's predicament. His method of land reform is one of the many blunders he has committed. He is culpable for many others, including atrocities committed against minority tribes and political opponents. His operation 'drive out trash', in 2005, which destroyed the homes and livelihoods of some 700,000 people in the major cities, is a disgrace to Africa and unbecoming of a liberation hero. I do not think that he calculates, as the Western press has speculated, that by forcing his urban political opponents to return to the rural areas he was going to neutralise them. He knows enough about his people to realise that angry urban sophisticates are more likely to influence their rural relatives against him than vice versa. The operation 'drive out trash' was, more likely, the result of demands from the urban middle classes to achieve 'urban beautification' – i.e. tidy streets around their properties so that they do not lose value. The whites want the same thing, and I can imagine the Rhodesians praising him for the 'drive out trash' campaign in the pre-land reform era.

But the worst aspect of the initiative is that it is undermining the emancipation of the people. Mugabe should have been proud of the urban poor for their enterprise in trying to make ends meet and he should have tried to help them, not destroy their livelihoods and their homes. Prim, clean towns with tidy streets, though desirable, may be an unaffordable luxury at the moment. Zimbabwe, like almost every other country on the continent, first needs to develop the earning capacity of its people before it can look to such luxuries, which matter more to the middle classes than to the poor who are used to the wretchedness and overcrowding because they cannot afford any better. And he should have removed from the statute book the legislation he used to carry out this exercise. It was promulgated by Ian Smith with the specific aim of cleaning the cities of 'subversives' – i.e. the freedom fighters. A Zimbabwean government should not have made use of that law, 25 years after independence, against its own people, who, as in many other parts of Africa, have shown commendable initiative and ingenuity in order to earn a living. Perhaps Mugabe should send some of the proponents of the 'drive out trash' campaign to Lagos and the other big cities of Nigeria to teach them the facts of urban life.

We set up our first company in Zimbabwe in association with a Zimbabwean friend I had worked with in Chingola in the 1950s. But as time went by we expanded into the whole range of our operations, engineering, pharmaceuticals and cosmetics, construction, etc. One of the more interesting businesses we had was mining granite and exporting it to Italy. Most of our other operations were also partly owned and managed by locals, but as Zimbabwe business in the 1980s and early 1990s was still under Rhodesian domination we never made as much progress as we had originally expected.

8. A PAN AFRICAN BANK IS BORN

The 1980s was the most difficult post-independence decade for Africa. Oil prices ballooned and commodity prices collapsed. Hard currency became scarce and most African currencies went into free fall time and again. In my chairman's statement of 1984 I described the situation:

> Turnover is below last year's but this apparent reduction was the result of currency translation rather than a decline in the group's real growth rate... Continuing economic difficulties in most developing nations have imposed changes in traditional patterns of trade. While new projects are mainly aid-assisted, the emphasis has shifted towards imports of only the most essential inputs for agriculture and local industry, transport equipment, plant spare parts and technical supplies. Consumer goods are either given low priority or have been largely eliminated from a country's imports. Exports are being vigorously encouraged with various incentives the most significant being allocation to the exporter of part of the foreign exchange earned.

There was no change in 1986, when I again said:

> Our traditional business remains good and profitable despite difficulties experienced in most African countries. The massive devaluations of many currencies brought about by the realisation by many countries of the need to restructure their economies in order to face up to what has turned out to be a permanent economic contraction, has in fact improved trading conditions. I have no doubt that with the measures taken, most countries will achieve substantial exports in non traditional products and we have geared our international operations to assist and profit from this development.

And then I indulged in some wishful thinking:

> The devaluations have had a severe effect on our balance sheet... Even though in accounting terms the value of our assets had to be adjusted downwards, I do not

believe that their true worth has been in any way affected as is evident from our results.

Despite all this our business remained good and profitable. In 1987 I said:

> The year 1987 proved a record year in all respects. Turnover rose to $624 million and net income to $11.9 million. But the group's balance sheet does not show the full benefit of this profitability as our reserves again suffered some diminution due to the downward movement of some currencies, though to a much smaller extent than the previous year.

The reality, which I was reluctant to believe and acknowledge, was that de-valuations eroded our equity – a problem that still haunts businesses in Africa. We tried to mitigate the problem by acquiring businesses in more stable economic environments in order to balance our portfolio. Thus we bought a tractor and a pharmaceutical business in Britain and started a construction company in London specialising in property rehabilitation, but we soon discovered that we were not able to generate sufficient volume to make the UK business worthwhile and withdrew.

Payment patterns from Africa remained erratic right through the 1980s and most countries built up huge foreign currency arrears. They rationed their meagre hard currency earnings according to the government's perception of priorities. But the government priorities very rarely had any relevance to the real economic needs of the country. First they had to keep the multilateral institutions sweet, in order to get good marks for the innumerable rounds of debt rescheduling by the Paris Club (the creditor countries). That meant making some payments against maturing debt, so that the Paris Club would allocate more to pay the balance. (In 1996 Oxfam, the UK charity, would accuse the International Monetary Fund and the World Bank of creating a 'financial circus', in which more and more aid was being recycled in the form of debt repayment while the debt stock was increasing. Oxfam calculated that repayments for the debt had increased from $1 billion or 20% of total debt servicing in 1980 to $3.3 billion or 50% in 1994.)

Other priority hard currency allocations included government and political requirements, which very seldom coincided with real needs. In Zambia, ZCCM, the government-controlled mining company, had to surrender all its hard currency earnings to the government and then put out the begging bowl in order to get allocations for its requirements. And all it got most of the time was enough to purchase essential supplies in order to keep the plants running.

Regular scheduled maintenance, rehabilitation and equipment replacement were never a priority.

This is what inspired the creation of Meridien Bank. As our customers became unable to finance their purchases we had to provide medium-term credit for them. As Caterpillar dealers we had, until then, been reasonably successful, because the Caterpillar equipment received priority coverage from the Export-Import Bank of the United States and our Meridien Credit Corporation in New York was able to raise the finance. But, as the 1980s wore on and the country arrears built up, EXIM Bank, suspended coverage for one country after another. And, as the group range of products spread, we needed greater access to the financial markets in order to carry on business. Out of this need the Meridien Bank was born in 1982.

It was registered in the Bahamas but operated from a representative office in New York for easy access to the financial markets. And it did produce some innovative financing. Where EXIM Bank would not give cover, AIG, or Lloyds of London would. The premiums were higher, but as the customer did not have many options and was prepared to pay it did not matter. By 1984 Meridien was able to boast that it provided $40 million financing for Zambia, $90 million for Angola and $30 million for a forestry project in Congo-Brazzaville.

The Congo project involved the supply of equipment as well as technical assistance and product support for a period of three years, to be provided by our Angolan operations. Some of the equipment was from Caterpillar, which upset the Caterpillar dealer in the Congo. Even though we did pay him the encroachment fee according to the Caterpillar code, he wanted to take over the maintenance and technical support contract. He tried to enlist the support of Caterpillar in Geneva and began keeping a diary of the visits of our technical staff. He reported them to Caterpillar, who in turn relayed them to us. I became progressively annoyed with this unacceptable monitoring of people's movements and my patience snapped when I received a telex from the Caterpillar office in Geneva saying that Chris, our manager in Angola, 'was again seen in Brazzaville yesterday'. I sent a sardonic telex back that 'I shall tell Chris to grow a beard next time'. They got the message and the telexes stopped. But in the end the Congo authorities defaulted and our claim on AIG that gave us insurance cover for the project ended up in the courts.

There were some dinosaurs, of both American and Swiss origin in the Geneva office of Caterpillar who seemed to resent newcomers and have distaste for all progressive ideas and initiatives. Ideally, for them, Africa should have remained the sleepy, peaceful continent that it was under colonial rule – that made their job easy. I remember the dirty looks I received in the Caterpillar office in Geneva in April 1980. The Rhodesian elections had just finished but, instead of hanging around for the results to be announced, Mugabe embarked upon a whirlwind visit to Dar es Salaam and Maputo to see the Presidents of Tanzania and Mozambique. The Rhodesians' wishful interpretation of Mugabe's departure was that he had fled the country having realised that he lost the election. One of the dinosaurs asked my view. 'He knows that he won the election,' I said, 'and he has gone to thank Nyerere and Machel for their support and consult them about the future of the struggle in Southern Africa. While the votes are being counted he has plenty of time on his hands – from next week he is going to be a very busy man.' The frigid silence that followed embarrassed the Zambian team that accompanied me. They tried to cover up, telling me that I had been out of the region for too long and was getting out of touch, which pleased my interlocutor. But within a couple of days I was to be proved right.

Meridien grew from strength to strength. In 1986 it reported:

> As the African marketplace becomes increasingly difficult economically and some banks and financial institutions are disengaging from it, it is encouraging that Meridien continues to find both sound new business and the appropriate financing packages to make it bankable.

In 1987 Meridien boasted the successful completion of 'very complicated and time consuming' aircraft lease financing packages for Zambia and Angola. The Zambian package involved two ATR-42 turboprop passenger aircrafts for Zambia Airways. The Angolan deal was much more interesting. It involved the lease financing of a Lockheed C-130 Hercules for Endiama, the government-owned diamond company of Angola. It was not just the difficulty of organising the finance for the Angolan plane during the civil war, there was the added difficulty of obtaining an American export permit for it that had to come from the White House, which at the time was the Reagan White House. We were very pleasantly surprised when we did get the permit because such planes could be used for troop transportation and Endiama was 100% owned by the government of Angola, which was anathema to the Reagan administration.

As is obvious from the inimitable letter sent to President Reagan by the Philippines consul (and Fuehrer of our Angolan operations, quoted in Chapter 3), America at the time was a strong supporter of Savimbi, the Maoist guerrilla leader who was fighting the Angolan government led by Dos Santos, a Soviet-educated politician with close ties to Cuba. I do not think that the American government was supporting a Maoist against a Soviet communist as the lesser evil. Savimbi had very powerful lobbyists in Washington, paid from the proceeds of his diamond smuggling operations. They created an image of a dedicated, Western-oriented leader, fighting for democracy and justice in his country, which could not have been further from the truth. America stopped supporting Savimbi after the collapse of the Soviet Union and the change in the administration. As far as we were concerned we were very pleased that commercial sense prevailed over 'evil empire' ideology and the export permit was granted, which enabled us to conclude a very profitable deal.

And, despite the recession, opportunities in Africa seemed endless.

9. MARCHING ON

Roan Selection Trust (RST) had started life as Rhodesian Selection Trust in 1928. It was formed by the British company Selection Trust Limited, and in partnership with the American Metal Company started the development of the Roan Antelope Copper Mines (RCM) Ltd. Roan got its name from a roan bull that was shot by a prospector in 1902. It fell on a malachite-stained rock and the ore body was discovered. Over the years RCM developed the Luanshya, Mufulira, Chibuluma, Chambishi and Kalengwa mines. It also expanded into other operations in both Northern and Southern Rhodesia, until in 1969, under the Matero economic reforms announced by President Kaunda, it sold 51% of its mining interests to the government of Zambia but retained the contract to manage the mines. I conducted the negotiations on behalf of the government of Zambia, and describe them fully in *Africa: Another Side of the Coin*. After 1974, when the government consolidated the mining industry under ZCCM (Zambian Consolidated Copper Mines Ltd), AMAX (American Metal Climax, as the American Metal Company was renamed) owned RST, whose main interests were an insignificant 7% shareholding in ZCCM, a large farm in Mazabuka and a number of other insignificant companies in Zambia and Zimbabwe.

Under government control ZCCM seldom, if ever, paid dividends, but when, in 1984, AMAX wanted to get out of copper and Africa and approached us to buy RST I jumped at the opportunity. By that time we had decided to open a commodity trading business and our Meridien Bank was looking at raising finance for ZCCM. I thought that having a small shareholding and a seat on the board would be very useful for the group. I approached Kenneth Kaunda for his reaction with some trepidation. At the time everybody thought that he was aiming at 100% control of ZCCM, and RST would have given him the opportunity to increase the government share from 66% to 73%. But he had been under pressure from the IMF and the World Bank to stop expanding the parastatal sector and he must have seen my approach as a good opportunity: a

Zambian group led by me as a shareholder of ZCCM would be preferable to an American.

That was the first and last time I shared any of my business plans with Kaunda. The same year Meridien International Bank received a licence for the establishment of Meridien Bank Zambia. That application was handled by the local branch of the international accounting firm Deloittes, Haskins and Sells, and went through the normal channels of the Bank of Zambia despite the fact that ten years later, after the debacle, the governor who had granted the licence would claim that he was instructed by State House otherwise he would never have issued it. No such instruction was ever sought and none was given.

In my chairman's statement in 1984, after announcing the establishment of Meridien Bank Zambia I went on to explain our thinking:

Meridien Equity Bank's spacious premises and colourful customers in Lagos, Nigeria.

This first move into local commercial banking is a very useful expansion of the activities of Meridien International Bank (MIBL), which has hitherto concentrated on arranging short term finance and short and medium term credits for African countries from offshore. Through the new Zambian Bank, and other local Banks and financial institutions to be established in some of our other major markets in the future, MIBL will increase its client base and improve its ability to package project finance including the local component. It will also seek export opportunities for its clients and provide the necessary export finance.

And in preparation for the latter we established in New York, at the same time, a commodity trading house under the name of RST Resources Inc. It became very successful, trading in both metals and soft commodities, specifically cocoa and coffee, sourced mainly from Africa and South America. One of its early successes was the purchase of copper concentrates from a mine in Katanga, in the Democratic Republic of Congo, near the Zambian border, which it toll-processed in Mufulira, Zambia, into copper cathodes.

The next Meridien Bank was established in 1986 in Liberia, and the following year it took over the Chase Manhattan Bank's Liberian assets, thus becoming the biggest private bank in that country. By 1988 we had acquired Chase Bank Cameroon and took minority participation in two new banks in Burundi (25%) and Nigeria (40%).

**

Our partners in Burundi were all Tutsi, who constituted only 15% of the population of that country but had been running it since its independence from Belgium in 1962. Our staff were mainly Hutu. Prominent amongst them was our credit manager, Melchior Ndadaye, a very bright and pleasant man in his late thirties. He was very good at his job but he was also a prominent member of FRODEBU, the Hutu political party. Our Tutsi chairman hated him for that and tried repeatedly to get him out. Ndadaye sensibly avoided the baiting and stuck it out until 1993, when he resigned and ran for President under a negotiated new constitution that inevitably ushered in a Hutu government.

I met him at the presidential palace in Bujumbura after his election. He was as modest as he had always been, and with the characteristic sparkle in his eyes he expounded some of his plans to reconcile the two communities. Unfortunately, he was assassinated in a Tutsi-led army coup four months later. The coup was followed by massacres and an exodus of refugees to the Congo, starting a new bout of strife between the two communities that carried on until a new 'reconciliation' was achieved with help from South Africa in 2005. Hopefully it will last this time. Regrettably, I have the uneasy feeling that one of the Tutsi members of our board, an ex-army officer, was one of the prime movers of the coup against Melchior Ndadaye.

***

The Meridien Equity Bank of Nigeria (MEBN), 60% owned locally, mainly by northerners, turned out to be a very difficult bank to manage. The shareholders interfered constantly in the management of the bank. We could not get a manager to last. The only one who did was a South Asian, himself a Muslim, who knew how to flatter them and facilitate 'perks' for one thing or another. When matters became really difficult I would attend a board meeting to lay down the law and bring some semblance of short-lasting order. The board meetings always started with a prayer. It was usually led by some member of the board in one of the Nigerian languages. I was taken aback one day when the chairman called on me to say prayers. Praying is not on my agenda and I do not have a ready repertory, nor do I know what people say in such circumstances. I did not want to refuse in case I caused offence, but in my panic inspiration struck. I remembered a passage from Pericles' funeral oration, which stuck in my mind from my schooldays, and I recited it in Greek:

' Φιλοκαλοῦμέν τε γὰρ μετ' εὐτελείας καὶ φιλοσοφοῦμεν ἄνευ μαλακίας· πλούτῳ τε ἔργου μᾶλλον καιρῷ ἢ λόγου κόμπῳ χρώμεθα, καὶ τὸ πένεσθαι οὐχ ὁμολογεῖν τινι αἰσχρόν, ἀλλὰ μὴ διαφεύγειν ἔργῳ αἴσχιον.

For we are lovers of beauty, yet with no extravagance and lovers of wisdom yet without weakness. Wealth we employ rather as an opportunity for action than as a subject for boasting; and with us it is not a shame for a man to acknowledge poverty but the greater shame is for him not to do his best to avoid it.

(Translation from the Loeb Classical Library Edition of Thucidides, *History of the Peloponnesian War* Book II.)

High-minded morality on which the Greek civilisation was founded! Maybe I should have translated it into English and given them a lecture on the subject, instead of holding a board meeting.

Hard-working, meticulous and concentrating. Zambian mechanics assembling a Skania truck in Mazembe's Kitwe premises.

Towards the end of the 1980s conditions in Africa started improving. After reporting a record turnover of $950 million and net income of $18 million for the year 1989 I went on to say:

> Our performance was helped by the economic conditions in Africa, which, as anticipated, remained stable as a result of the genuine effort made by governments to come to grips with their various problems. A quiet revolution has in fact been taking place on the economic front with most governments taking drastic and very difficult measures, which would have been unthinkable a few years ago. Massive devaluations, substantial reductions of government subsidies, elimination of price controls, reasonably realistic interest rates and tight liquidity conditions are now the order of the day in most countries. As a result many are now on the path to economic recovery, self sufficient in food and generating exportable surpluses, and regional trade is on the increase. The international community has responded cautiously so far with a mixture of measures such as debt forgiveness and increased aid, both of which have contributed to the improvement of the business climate.
>
> However a more permanent improvement requires innovative and massive investment in new ventures as well as in the rehabilitation of existing plants and the infrastructure which has been neglected over the years because of the lack of hard currency. The investment for infrastructure will come from multi-lateral organisations and unilateral aid. The initiative for some of the investment in business ventures will come from overseas but most of it needs to be primed from within Africa, not by governments as in the past but by the many local entrepreneurs who have emerged in recent years. ITM is part and parcel of this group inasmuch as it has its origins on the Continent and in most of the 19 African countries where it operates is in some form of association with local entrepreneurs...

Wonderful plans, full of good intentions and hope! But the storm clouds were gathering. In ITM's 1990 chairman's statement, after proudly reporting that sales exceeded $1 billion with net profit of $21 million, I went on to announce that we had had to close down our Liberian operations because of the civil war. At a stroke we lost $19,677,000 – the book value of our investment in that country. What hurt more was that during the year our investment in Liberia had jumped by almost $3 million, from $16,801,000 the previous year. We owed this 'favour' to a Mr Vuillamoz, one of Caterpillar's Geneva bullies, who early in 1990 had put pressure on our Liberian management to increase the parts inventory, threatening to withdraw the dealership otherwise. Naively, our local management consented, and, ignorantly, our London office agreed to make the funds available, despite the fact that the Taylor invasion of Liberia had started the previous Christmas and by that time anybody who had eyes to see would have realised that the days of President Doe were numbered. The following year we had to write off an additional $5.4 million: the unpaid parts account owed by Libtraco, Monrovia, to Intraco, London. A memo from Libtraco reports that an inventory audit had revealed that the loss of inventory resulting from the looting of its premises amounted to $1.9 million, and added:

> It will be very difficult for Libtraco to pay up its total indebtedness to Intraco, especially following two years of destruction and inactivity and the problems anticipated in the collection of $3.3 million in receivables short term. We should therefore request a partial capitalization of the liability, which is $5.4 million as at February 28, 1992.

Another $5.4 million down the Liberian drain.

As if the losses of the Liberian collapse were not enough we came under increasing pressure from the Caterpillar dinosaurs to slow down our localisation programme. Naturally localisation meant release of expatriates, a measure that Geneva viewed with distate believing that with fewer whites the efficiency of our operations would suffer. This infuriated me sufficiently to ask for a meeting with the chairman of Caterpillar during his next visit to Geneva. I took with me the senior management of all the dealerships (the managing directors of Zambia, Liberia and Malawi were local) and each one made a presentation of his individual operations. I closed the presentations thus:

> In the eighties we embarked upon an earnest and serious localization program with great success. Our dealerships are now, not only managed by indigenous people but where local conditions permit they are majority owned locally. Our localization program brought about greater market penetration and improved profitability as it is apparent from the presentations made to you... I would like Caterpillar to understand that we are an African organization. As you see, our executives in the market place are all local. We see Africa and its future in a different light from foreigners. Our efficiency is African and it may be short on reports and social graces but it is very effective because it comes with our intuitive knowledge of the market place, a knowledge that comes from total immersion in the environment where everything concerning the market is in our nostrils, on our skin and in our gut...

The chairman seemed rather pleased with all that, but the hard-liners of Geneva began sharpening their knives. They would have the last laugh.

And the damage in Liberia was done, and the additional $3 million in 1991 and the $5.4 million in 1992 could not be recovered. In addition, a large part of an $18 million Meridien loan that financed the earth station of the Liberian Telecommunications Corporation (LIBTELCO), in 1987, was still outstanding. In the ITM report I said:

> An unforeseen event was the civil war in Liberia, which ravaged the country for most of 1990 culminating in the suspension of business activities in July. We decided, in consultation with our auditors not to consolidate our Liberian companies nor to take into account the 1990 profits and to make substantial provisions against loans, which became non-performing because of the cessation of business activities. These provisions affected mainly the results of Meridien International Bank.

But Meridien Bank reported, optimistically, that it was hopeful that in 1991 civil strife would end and Meridien Bank Liberia would resume normal activity. It also reported that the premises of the bank were largely intact and its personnel ready to resume business. We would open fitfully during the next couple of years until the civil war encompassed the entire country and our senior management had to be evacuated, some to Sierra Leone and others to the United States. The civil war would last for another decade, bringing about almost total devastation in the country. But my optimism about the future in Africa persisted:

> Elsewhere, even though African economies have been again affected by the high oil prices resulting from the threat of war in the Gulf, new political and economic factors give reason for optimism. Orthodox economic policies are now pursued as a matter of conviction and not as unpalatable impositions by the IMF and the creditor countries. More significantly, though, they have led to a radical change in political thinking. Constitutional changes have taken place or are in the process of doing so in most countries. These acknowledge opposition parties and afford the electorate a choice from a wider body of people and views.

With all this in mind ITM was poised for further expansion in the 1990s. In 1990 we reported that we had taken a majority share in the Goldenrae alluvial gold prospect in Kwabeng in Ghana, financed through loans from DEG of Germany and FMO of the Netherlands. The project was expected to produce 20,000 ounces of gold per year and had an anticipated life of seven years. We also reported that we had acquired another gold prospect, San Martin, near Kisumu in Kenya. Both projects were alluvial, and we relied on the expertise we had gained in Angola mining alluvial diamonds to run them. Both would come to grief a couple of years later.

But Meridien was also ready for a huge leap forward. On 27 August 1990 we signed a memorandum of understanding with the Central Bank of West Africa 'for the establishment of a new holding company to acquire participations in banks of the BIAO network and to assist in the restructuring of that network'. We commissioned S.G. Warburg, the British merchant bank, to advise us with regard to capital restructuring and raising capital and Price Waterhouse to make comprehensive financial investigations of all the BIAO banks, and we sent various teams from our banks to review the operations of each bank and the organisation and methods of BIAO.

Part 2

Stepping Into the Abyss

10. A HORNET'S NEST

Rereading the final project report that was prepared for BCEAO (Banque Centrale des États de l'Afrique de l'Ouest – Central Bank of West Africa) in respect of the BIAO network, I now wonder why we went ahead with the deal. The total net worth of the network was negative $209.17 million, though after deducting the deficits of the banks in Côte d'Ivoire and Senegal, which in the end were not included, this reduced to $91.83 million. The banks that made up this deficit were in Burkina Faso, Central African Republic, Congo-Brazzaville, Gabon, Guinea, Mali, Niger and Togo, as well as the branches in London and Hamburg (the last being the only one with a positive net worth, of $7.26 million). Eventually Congo-Brazzaville and Guinea, where BIAO had 21% and 34% shareholdings were not included in the deal. Our own Banks to be included in the deal at the time (Cameroon, Liberia, Nigeria, and Sierra Leone) had a combined book value of $16.28 million.

On the other hand, we found – as we said in the report – that 'notwithstanding the months or years of difficulties and operating losses and the consequential outflow of deposits, customers and business, BIAO has retained much of its historical image in the market place and been able to keep a reasonable share of the market up to now which demonstrates strong customer loyalty at grass root level'. We did not say in the report that it had become obvious from our investigations that it was not the local banks that caused the problems but the recklessness of the hydrocephalic Paris headquarters that constituted a drain on their resources, and, in addition, charged blindly into South America – together with all the big banks of the world – at the same time.

BIAO was a relic of the French colonial administration. It had been the central bank of French West Africa and it used to issue the currency for the whole region, a matter of great pride for its officials, who would show off the old banknotes printed with the BIAO name. Its palatial headquarters in Paris were located in Avenue de Messine, in the 8th arrondissement, close to those of the other major French banks. The main entrance was guarded by two large Alsatian dogs, which 'had been trained to bark only at African clients', officials would proudly boast. The lifestyle in Avenue de Messine was reminiscent of colonial splendour, with long, sumptuous lunches and excellent wines. Who paid for this extravagance? The African affiliates, of course. They were being charged exorbitant fees for 'assistance' that was in no way related to the services they received, or the size and the results of each bank. With steady income from Africa the Paris headquarters launched into sovereign lending outside Africa, mainly into Latin America. The whole edifice collapsed when the Latin America debt crisis hit the markets. BIAO was both unprepared and lacking in the resources to provide for the losses. The only way out was to make Africa pay and to seek the help of both the French Treasury ('le Trésor') and BNP, a major French bank and BIAO's biggest shareholder.

BNP jumped at the opportunity to monopolise the banking business in francophone Africa and prepared a rescue plan that provided for the absorption of the BIAO network into its own. Most BIAO Paris staff acquiesced with the Trésor/BNP plan, hoping to keep their jobs with BNP, but the managing director at the time, Jacques Bayle, resigned, joined l'Européenne de Banque, a subsidiary of the Crédit Commercial de France (CCF), and embarked upon his own rescue operation. Jacques Bayle had an exaggerated idea of his importance and his powers. A graduate of the French elite civil administration college, ENA, he had served in the French Ministry of Finance, ending up as director-general of the Budget, the main tax official in the Ministry, before being 'farmed out', in typical French fashion, to become director-general of the BIAO, a move that could be interpreted either way: promotion or demotion.

The Trésor/BNP plan did not go down well in West Africa. The then governor of BCEAO, Alassane Ouattara, a former senior official of the IMF who would later become its deputy managing director, was concerned at the consolidation that would take place within the banking system of West Africa, with BNP potentially controlling up to 50% of the deposit base. He gathered the support of key ministers in the various member countries and commissioned Bayle and S.G. Warburg of London to see whether an 'African solution' to the rescue of the BIAO network could be found. He assembled a BCEAO task force, headed by a Mr Adji, a former Finance Minister of Niger, to work with his new-found advisers. As was to be expected, the reaction of BNP and the Trésor was undisguised fury at what they considered the spoilers, especially as Warburgs was a non-French bank. Bayle had little support among the Paris-based former BIAO staff and his only acolytes in his venture were two senior executives – Georges Atlan and Jacques Chanard. (Bayle's cynical comment on this was: 'Typical of my compatriots; only a Jew and a Corsican are willing to stand up and be counted.')

At the same time, the general managers of the various branches in Africa also worked to protect their own individual positions: they hoped to pull their banks out of the old network, negotiate their own correspondent banking arrangements in Europe, and build up their own local fiefs. Bayle tried to keep them in line, and promised that he would defend their interests. (He did not really mean it. He had little loyalty to anybody, one of his aphorisms being that 'a promise commits only the person who hears it'.) Major US and European banks were pulling out of Africa at the time (we had bought Chase branches in Cameroon and Liberia) and new investors into banking in Africa were scarce. Standard Bank of South Africa was approached but was interested only if, by 'saving' the BIAO network, it could acquire the Avenue de Messine bank and, consequently, a banking licence in Europe. Predictably enough, the Trésor was opposed to such an approach – it was before South Africa's majority rule. With all these goings-on and the French authorities – whether in the shape of BNP or the Trésor – in opposition, Ouattara and his advisers had an uphill struggle on their hands.

Finally the quest for a new partner ended with only two candidates: Ecobank based in Togo and managed by a group of ex-Citibank officials, and us. As I understand it, in the eyes of the BCEAO team Ecobank was considered to have the management experience and skills, even though it was small and lacked capital. We were more of an unknown quantity: we had a successful banking network in East/Southern Africa, but Meridien was part of ITM, an industrial group, which had its pluses and minuses. And in the final analysis we were 'culturally' different. The francophone Africans saw themselves closer to France than to anglophone Africa and the cultural divide was large. I would later discover that a major issue that irked them was the thought that they were being taken over and managed by 'Zambians'. But in the end, to our misfortune, BCEAO selected us.

When we decided to go ahead with the deal our understanding was that our participation would be only 51% and that the African Development Bank (ADB) would take the lead to raise the balance from various institutional and private interests. In the end, only the African Development Bank and the West African Development Bank came forward, subscribing 24% between them. The International Finance Corporation (IFC) of the World Bank made a long-delayed decision against participating, which was communicated to me when I was already in Abidjan to sign the ADB participation. The behaviour of the IFC had indeed been curious. It initially signalled strong support for the Meridien–BIAO merger and promised equity participation, quite publicly. Then, step by step, it tried to wriggle out of this commitment. It was never clear what drove this process, though I became convinced that the French authorities were putting pressure on the IFC to pull out, and, naturally they succeeded. With so many bureaucracies involved and with one delay following another we found ourselves sliding into this investment to a point of no return and ended up holding 76% of an insufficiently capitalised banking network, the Meridien BIAO Group.

The only international commercial bank that indicated interest was the NMB Bank of the Netherlands. They indicated that they would initially take a 5% share, raising it to 10% later. They asked for a seat on the board until they made up their mind, and we gave them observer status. They attended all our board meetings and received all board papers, and they seconded one member of their staff to Sofimer, our Paris service company, for about a year, but they did not proceed. NMB's official reason for not proceeding was their merger with the ING insurance group (NMB has since taken the name ING Bank), which did not want expansion in Africa, but I learned later that the Bank of France put pressure on them too, through the Dutch central bank.

But undercapitalisation was not the only problem. The liquidity of many banks was very tight, because their main assets represented non-performing government and parastatal obligations, and much of each bank's capital was locked into real estate. As we were to discover, each bank owned huge luxury headquarters, way above its needs. Some architects had gone wild and some contractors must have made huge profits, and maybe some managers got big kickbacks out of those premises. (Grand premises of public enterprises seemed to be a tradition in French-speaking West Africa. Huge, ornate buildings tower over modest, drab and dusty towns in poor Sahelian countries, the most impressive being the headquarters of BCEAO in each country, all of which are several storeys high.) The investment in banking premises was unrelated to the realities of the market place and was way above what the various BIAO banks' balance sheets could support. Making accounting adjustments for this extravagance, the deficit I mentioned earlier would have been much worse. We would also discover later that additional adjustments should have been made for the obligations by governments and public bodies, which we took at face value even though none was current, and they later turned out to be non-performing and not collectable.

The idea behind the Meridien–BIAO merger was to create an African-based banking network with a better understanding of Africa's needs, catering for the indigenous people of Africa, and assisting in the development of African private enterprise. In addition to governor Ouattara's worries about BNP controlling 50% of the deposit market he, together with the president of ADB and me, felt that the major international banks operating in Africa were geared towards multinational and settler-owned companies and they were not prepared to take risks on local enterprise – a phenomenon that obtains to this day. We were determined that Meridien BIAO would fill the gap. While we were pursuing these lofty goals we unwittingly made enemies in France.

Most of the Paris managers of BIAO supported the Trésor/BNP plan in the hope that they would find positions in Paris, while the two who attached themselves to the Bayle plan were hoping that we would not know how to operate in French-speaking Africa and we would depend on them to run it. They even prepared the business plan requested by BCEAO, but we had one look at it and scrapped it. It was a plan for another colonial-style operation, with an expensive operation in Paris and all senior positions in Africa reserved for French expatriates, who would average around 13 for each bank. This was contrary to the philosophy of the ITM group, which gave priority to local people and employed expatriates (African, Asian and European) only where local skills were not available. The plan was worthless and we had to rewrite it from beginning to end.

The first attack on us came in a French publication in April 1991. It said (in free translation):

> The group chaired by Andrew Sardanis is no longer unanimously supported by those who supported him in his seduction act. Some senior personnel of the bank, including Jacques Chanard, former director in charge of the international network of BIAO, openly say they were cheated by the Cypriot-born businessman. In side conversations, his enemies cannot find harsh enough terms to describe him and denounce the way his empire was built. 'For him the world is split between the people that bring the money and the boys.' Over the last few months the bank became his 'thing' and its future depends only on him. 'Such an attitude is very different from the consensual way of operating, which had always prevailed within BIAO,' say some whilst remembering bitterly the meeting of 8th December, 1990, in Abidjan which showed the true personality of Meridien's strongman.

I had called that meeting of chief executives of the BIAO and Meridien banks in West Africa in order to meet the BIAO managers and gauge their thinking on how they expected the network to operate under Meridien. I had 24 people around the table, including the general managers of BIAO banks in Guinea, Gabon, Hamburg, Côte d'Ivoire, Senegal, Mali, Niger, Burkina Faso and the Congo, the manager designate of our proposed office in Abidjan, the managers of the Meridien banks of Liberia and Cameroon, representatives from the Ministries of Finance of Gabon and Guinea, a couple of Meridien group executives and two representatives of S.G. Warburg. The minutes were taken by Warburg. Even though the article went on to say that they were up in arms, the record of the minutes says the following:

> Kossi Paass of Togo as spokesman for the group of managing directors declared that apart from Bayle, Meridien could get rid of all the other Paris based BIAO staff. According to the minutes, Bayle was judged essential given his past relations with the managing directors, local political authorities and political heavyweights in Paris.

Perhaps we should have kept Bayle, but I came to the conclusion that the importance of his Paris political contacts was exaggerated, particularly after he had been seen as leading the anti-BNP/Trésor solution. And he was not a 'banker' but a bureaucrat, and his goal would have been to maintain his status in the French establishment, which was irrelevant to us and would turn out to be very expensive. With hindsight we are all wiser, but one of our failures was not to find a credible French banker to take over the day-to-day management of the French-speaking banks. He might have been able to recruit better-quality staff than we did; we resorted to reappointing some of the Frenchmen who had served in Africa before, and most of them turned out to be worse that any expatriate in English-speaking Africa I ever came across.

But the insults were coming thick and fast. In its February 1991 issue *Africa International*, trying to divine my background, came to the conclusion that I was a total unknown – which was true enough as far as French-speaking Africa was concerned. But it proceeded to insinuate that I had drug connections, as follows (in free translation):

> People are astonished that many ex-employees of the Arabo-Pakistani Bank BCCI that was implicated in drug-money laundering can be found with Sardanis.

No direct accusation, no libel, but in a cunning way it connected me to drugs and it stuck. Some months later *Jeune Afrique*, the French magazine most widely read in Africa, asked me for an interview. It was long and wide-ranging. By that time the contrived connection between me, the BCCI employees and BCCI drug money had been replaced in the French press by a certitude that irrevocably associated me with drugs and drug money laundering. *Jeune Afrique* asked (in free translation):

> Some people say that there are links between your bank and the network of drug laundering.
>
> I responded: 'I heard about that. Some of your colleagues have tried to establish that type of connection. What can I do against such rumours? I lived in Africa for 41 years, most of my colleagues are African and I assure you that our business is clean. Many people will be able to tell you so in Africa. Nothing stops you from checking it out. What is true is that we have recently recruited people formerly employed by a Bank, BCCI, which laundered narco-dollars. What does it prove? I employed six former BCCI employees: one from Nairobi, one from New York, one from London and three others from Harare. How would they have been mixed up with the BCCI scandal? You have to be serious. We are in the banking business; we get many applications and choose the most capable people for the African network. This was the case for these employees.

Jeune Afrique also wanted to know what my relationship with the French government was, and I replied that we never met anybody from the government of France. That was not strictly true. I did have a meeting with Mr Philippe Lagayette, the deputy governor of the Bank of France, in the company of Micha Spierenburg, Warburg's Paris manager, but as I walked into his office he told me that he was seeing me as a courtesy to Warburg and if I said to anybody that we had ever met he would say that I was a liar. Writing about this now I realise that I do not remember what we discussed – not surprisingly, my mind must have gone blank after such a 'cordial' reception.

In the meantime we bravely embarked upon integrating the network. That is when we found that there was no network but a series of autonomous fiefdoms. Either the senior Frenchman conspired with the senior local to declare their independence or the senior local aligned himself with a local politician to ward off any interference. What all this meant was that we had to tread very carefully in order not to antagonise them.

11. HEAT AND DUST AND CAMELS AND BIKES

The harmattan was raging when we landed in Niamey, Niger's capital. The dust cloud was so thick that, through it, the sun shone like a silvery moon. By the time we reached the hotel I could hardly breathe and coughed uncontrollably. But as the afternoon wore on the harmattan cleared – or so we thought. We sat on the veranda for a drink as darkness fell over the river and the desert beyond, a beautiful, peaceful evening, the mirror-calm river reflecting the fading light, and the fishing canoes barely moving with the river's leisurely flow. Niger cools down in the early evening, which means that the temperature drops from the mid-forties to the high thirties (from 115° F to 100° F); but the difference makes it feel cool. I must have ingested a lot more dust during that time. I ended up with a terrible attack of asthma and had to spend the night on a chair.

Niamey is a nondescript town covered by a blanket of dust. Dust is everywhere: in your mouth, in your nostrils, on your hair and your skin, on the roofs of the buildings, on the walls, on the few trees that survive in that harsh climate. It makes everything look dirty and miserable and there is no way to get rid of it. Buildings, shops and government offices look old and neglected, but I am sure that is the effect of the dust. The BIAO bank building stood out in its magnificence, all four storeys of it. The two lower floors were occupied by the bank. The other two were empty, but the bank had to keep them air-conditioned, at great expense, because cooling the lower floors and leaving the top ones hot would cause the building to crack. The city residents looked like sleepwalkers, slowly moving amongst camels that were making their way nonchalantly to the markets and other delivery destinations loaded with firewood, vegetables and other merchandise. Surely, Niger must have the biggest population of camels in the Sahel, I thought.

It struck me that the problem with Niamey was that it had no personality to project. It seemed stranded, marooned from the rest of the world. And it was wallowing in its isolation while the rest of the world passed it by. The country is drought-ridden and undeveloped, and apart from a short economic boom in the 1970s when the price of uranium was high it remains the poorest country in Africa, and the only one where slavery still exists, even though the government

Camels, carrying supplies to the markets, pass by the magnificent building of BIAO Niger, in Niamey.

denies it. I cannot remember which military strongman was in charge in the early 1990s but Niger, until then, had only known one-party dictatorships or military strongmen since independence, no doubt the cause for the apathy that seemed to dominate.

Rush hour in Ouagadougou, the capital of Burkina Faso.

The strongman of BIAO Niger seemed to mirror his national leaders: he lay down the rules and expected everybody to follow. Even though we owned 84% of it, he did not want any interference from us in the affairs of 'his' bank. The problem was that he ran the bank single-handedly not allowing any initiative to his senior staff. The branches were heavily laden with bad debts that he was not inclined to pursue. But he was a good politician and he cultivated the local shareholders. And to support his case he embarked upon a campaign to protect their interests. I would meet those shareholders later. They were honest-to-goodness local businessmen, mostly Fulani, who had been conned by BIAO Paris to subscribe capital at an exorbitant premium in 1985 and had never received a dividend. I sympathised with their predicament, but their problem was hardly ours. However, as a gesture of goodwill I agreed to pay a 10% dividend to them that year.

**

'Land of Incorruptible People' may sound like a joke but it is the name of a country, believe it or not: that is what Burkina Faso means. Captain Thomas Sankara who with the assistance of his close friend Captain Blaise Compaoré, took over power from the previous military strongman in a bloodless coup in 1983, renamed Upper Volta to Burkina in 1984. He was an austere man and he did embark on some remarkable projects, aiming to eliminate corruption, improve the status of women, curb the powers of the chiefs, eliminate waste in government (he replaced the Benz with a Renault 5 as the ministerial car). He also launched a campaign to plant 10 million trees. Some if his many slogans 'Fatherland or death – we shall overcome!'; 'Burkina Faso is not for sale'; 'Shame on imperialism'; 'Work is freedom' (the infamous inscription of Auschwitz 'Arbeit macht Frei', or just a coincidence?); 'Plant trees'.

But trying to enforce austerity in government did not endear him to his lieutenants and in 1987 he was assasinated together with 12 aides in a coup d'etat organised by his close friend Blaise Compaoré. Compaoré, who many believe was at the airport at the time of Sankara's assassination ready to board a plane if the coup did not succeed, like Brutus, did love his friend and legend has it that he spent three days locked in his house in mourning. He was persuaded to emerge and take over the reins by two accomplices (they would be executed a few years later) and promptly declared that Sankara's death was an accident. Compaoré has since turned from military strongman to an elected leader – elected unopposed twice so far. He was a handsome man oozing innocence and sincerity – a true Dorian Gray I thought when I met him.

Burkina is as poor as Niger and equally colourless. Instead of camels it has motorbikes, but, even though wheels are faster than camels, the pace of the country did not seem any faster than Niger's. But it did have more trees, and it was not as dusty and hot. There was no BIAO in Burkina; there was Banque Internationale du Burkina (BIB), with 60% local shareholding (53% owned by the government and the balance by some individuals). BIAO had a 40% share and we were aiming at managing BIB. We were received courteously enough by the general manager. At dinner at his house we met the Prime Minister and we learned a little of the history of BIB. The Prime Minister had been its previous chief executive and, as the evening progressed, it became clear that the current 'general manager' was his locum. We also discovered that, instead of the usual purpose-built grand premises of the other BIAO banks, BIB had bought a downtown hotel from a Lebanese and converted it. We were assured that the price paid for the hotel was extremely good, but we took that information with a pinch of salt. The next day, when we were escorted into the bank building by gun-toting soldiers, we would discover that it is not easy to convert a hotel to banking premises without a tremendous waste of space and complex work flow. And it was not easy to run a bank with a $53.2 million deficit. But that was the controlling shareholder's problem, i.e. the Prime Minister's, we thought hopefully.

***

Mali is the most colourful country of the Sahel. Its history goes back to the pre-Christian era and its geographic position as the centre of trade between the Arab north and the African south of the Sahara created a succession of rich and powerful empires over the centuries. They left behind a mixed population of various African tribes (dominant amongst them being the Bambara) and Berbers, whose sub-group, the Tuareg, still lead a nomadic life in the north of the country and are in constant friction with the authorities. (I attempted a few times to visit Timbuktu, a city built in the eleventh century, famous for its Islamic tradition and Arab architecture, but every time I was refused permission to land because of troubles between the Tuareg and government troops.) Mali's colourful past produced a mixed culture rich in music and sculpture with many distinctly different carving traditions in different parts of the country. Mali is poor and drought-stricken like the other Sahelian countries, but its people are self-motivated and entrepreneurial and if they cannot make ends meet at home they are ready to emigrate to other countries in the region, or elsewhere in Africa, the Middle East, Europe and America. Immigrant remittances constitute a substantial portion of the country's foreign income. Bamako does not give the decaying feeling of its sister capitals. Though equally hot and dusty, with some parts of it equally poor, it does not seem to be overwhelmed by poverty and dust.

Malian politics after independence followed a different path from the other countries of French West Africa. Mali initially distanced itself from France and issued its own currency, but returned to the CFA franc fold in 1967. It remained substantially non-aligned, though, and avoided the repeated coups of its neighbours. The bank building in Bamako was reasonably modest and its manager was young. BIAO had only a 54% shareholding in the Malian bank and the balance was held by 150 individuals, including employees. As the bank had a deficit of $9.2 million, it needed an injection of $15 million to cover the deficit and provide minimum fresh capital. We thought that this might be difficult for some of the local shareholders and offered to give them a year to raise their subscription. But the manager was very sanguine about that. He was sure that if he made a trip to Paris and met members of the Malian diaspora in France he would raise the necessary funds and more. The manager appointed himself as their spokesman in advance and tried to negotiate his independence. He did not succeed, but I had to put up with bouts of proposals and counter-proposals in the hotel the first day of my arrival. In later visits I would discover that many members of the staff disliked him

The manager of BIAO Mali, standing in front of the Bank's premises in Bamako in his magnificent Malian traditional costume.

intensely and were afraid of him. Nobody dared question his decisions which were often capricious. There was an outcry that he did not take action against the perpetrators of a fraud that cost the bank F CFA 522 million ($1 million) over a three-year period on the excuse that the fraud was covered by the bank's insurance policy. As his English was good, we decided to move him to the Meridien BIAO Africa Headquarters in Lusaka – an action that may raise eyebrows in management terms, but in terms of political appeasement in those early days I considered necessary

***

Conakry, the capital of Guinea, was a pitiful sight. Its streets were a museum of jalopies, most of them 30 years and older. That they were still running was a testimony to the ingenuity of African poverty. The tarmac had long gone from the surface of the streets, which were now rutted and lined by pools of stagnant water, as the sewers were obviously blocked. The newest buildings in the town were ugly apartment blocks of the type I later saw in East Berlin and Saint Petersburg, obviously donated by the Soviet Union, Guinea's patron for many years. The hotel was of the standard I had encountered in Accra in the mid-1970s and which I described in an earlier chapter.

Guinea, the only country to reject participation in the French Community and break away from France in 1958, had had a rough time since independence. In Africa there are many tales of the revenge of the French, who on departure are reputed to have vindictively vandalised as much of the infrastructure as they could. However, Sékou Touré's rule which lasted for 26 years until his death in 1984, and his love affair with the Soviet Union must be held responsible for the devastation of the country. Guinea is not without resources. It has rich bauxite and iron ore deposits as well as diamonds and some gold. Before independence it was a major coffee producer and its climate is similar to the rest of the West African coastal countries such as Ghana and Côte d'Ivoire, both large producers of cocoa and palm oil. Even though there have been attempts to open up the country to Western investment after Sékou Touré's death, narrow-minded nationalism and suspicion of the West had become so deeply ingrained that negotiating sensible business deals was impossible.

The governor of the Central Bank of the Republic of Guinea had those characteristics in abundance. The government had a 51% shareholding in the Banque Internationale pour l'Afrique en Guinée (BIAG), BIAO had 34% and Sifida, an African investment fund based in Switzerland, 15%. The Minister of Finance indicated that he wanted to buy the Sifida share first and then sell back to us the 51% controlling share. A convoluted way of going about it, perhaps, but it made sense to the mind of the Guinean government. The governor was conducting the negotiations and he kept changing his mind. After many months of fruitless discussions, I gave up. There was only so much effort one could sensibly put into taking control of a bankrupt bank with a negative net worth of $4.3 million in a country devastated by neglect that did not want to change its ways.

**

Togo, by the sea, was a breath of fresh air after the desert countries and Guinea: luxury hotels, beautiful beaches, paved streets, French restaurants and an amiable if not very effective manager of BIAO. He liked his drink, and had had one too many during the sumptuous dinner he gave us on the veranda of his villa. And for musical background he chose Beethoven and Mozart, as he had heard of my musical tastes. He was one of many mixed-race Togolese with German surnames. We discovered that they and many others hold the view that the worst thing that happened to Togo was the end of German rule in 1918. Their view was that 'they were replaced by the French, with the resulting chaos' ('pagaille' was the word used), as opposed to Teutonic order. And after so many years there are still unmistakable signs of nostalgia for the Germans, like a Munich-style beerhouse in Lomé and pilgrimages to Germany in search of ancestors.

We paid a courtesy call on President Éyadéma, the dean of francophone Africa's strongmen at the time. He did not look as evil as Mobutu but he was not exactly a compassionate leader. He railed against debtors who did not meet their obligations and said that they were thieves and that they should all be put in jail until they had paid off their debts. I guess I was expected to admire such 'progressive – investment-friendly' thinking but I could not let it pass. I pointed out that, from jail, the debtors might have some difficulty paying up.

Our tour ended in Abidjan for consultations with Alassane Ouattara, who had initiated the project when he was governor of BCEAO but was now Prime Minister of Côte d'Ivoire.

But political developments in Zambia were taking an interesting turn.

12. NEW BROOMS AND HIGH-HANDED ACTIONS

'How can a President lose the election?' That was one of the directors of BIAO Gabon and cousin of President Bongo, questioning me on the results of the Zambian presidential election that had just taken place at the end of 1991. 'Bernard will never lose an election in Gabon,' he said. Albert-Bernard were the Christian names of Omar Bongo, the President of Gabon, before he converted to Islam in 1973, and obviously the members of his family still called him Bernard. Fourteen years after that conversation, at the end of 2005, 'Bernard' aka Omar Bongo was again re-elected as President of Gabon for another seven-year term, so his cousin knew what he was talking about.

It had been a crushing defeat for Kenneth Kaunda. As the election campaign progressed, we all came to realise that he was going to lose, but no one was expecting a margin of three to one. He did not have to hold the election in 1991. His term was not due to end until 1993, but, to his credit, as soon as he realised that the country wanted to move away from the one-party system he proceeded speedily in 1990 to prepare a new multi-party constitution. He had the ability to pass it through Parliament, which his party controlled 100%, in a shape favourable to him, but he proceeded to negotiate it with his opponents. He did not have to do that, and maybe he should not have done it, because the final version was a bastardised, Westminster colonial-type constitution with presidential powers as draconian as those of the colonial governor for whom it was designed. Such constitutions had already proved unsuitable for Africa and have been discarded in most countries. But I suspect that the British High Commission, which was heavily supporting the MMD (Movement for Multiparty Democracy), had an input, as well as some of the white members of the party and some blacks who had worked for the government of Northern Rhodesia and were still nostalgic for the past.

It was inevitable that Kaunda would lose the election after the paralysis and stagnation of the 1980s, about which I wrote extensively in *Africa: Another Side of the Coin*, and the excesses of the one-party system. And it was inevitable that the MMD would get enthusiastic support because it was preaching the right gospel. It promised to do away with the one-party system, with its corruption and incompetence, to reintroduce democracy and free enterprise, to cut down the size of government and liberate the economy from excessive government control, etc., etc. (It did nothing of the sort and as far as corruption is concerned it elevated it to levels never before experienced in Zambia.) But I knew most members of the leadership of MMD and I knew that some of them did not give a hoot for those lofty goals. There were crooks and drug dealers amongst them whose aim was to get into government in order to have a free hand to pursue their nefarious activities. I had never met Frederick Chiluba, their leader, but his sermons on democracy did not ring true. He had been the chairman of the Zambian Congress of Trade Unions for many years and he was known as a cunning manipulator (hence his longevity in that post), not as a democrat.

Another aspect of the MMD that I found objectionable was that it unashamedly solicited and accepted support from the De Klerk government of South Africa. De Klerk was anticipating constitutional negotiations in South Africa at the time and he must have thought (naively) that an MMD government in Zambia would be preferable to Kaunda's, which had given so much support to the African National Congress (ANC) over the years. By contrast, the ANC gave Kaunda moral support (it did not have any money, I guess). I gave a lift on the company plane to Nelson Mandela and Oliver Tambo to visit KK, who was campaigning in the Northern Province and Mandela spoke warmly on camera about KK and urged the Zambian people to vote for him. This angered the MMD and after the election its publicity secretary made an arrogant statement asking Mandela to apologise to the Zambian people for trying to mislead them. But the MMD leader would get a direct response from the South African people, in 1994. As part of the celebrations for the advent of democracy and majority rule a football match had been arranged in Johannesburg between the Zambian and the South African teams. Naturally both Kaunda and Chiluba were invited. Chiluba's entrance to the stadium was greeted with deafening silence, Kaunda's with deafening applause.

The Western countries took the view that Kaunda must go and they openly supported the MMD, ignoring diplomatic conventions. And they had the ability to influence the World Bank, which suspended food aid to Zambia in August 1991, three months before the elections. I went to see the American ambassador and gave him a rundown of some of the undesirable elements in the MMD. He did not want to listen. Chiluba, Kaunda's opponent, was a great guy, he had embraced liberal economics, and that was what Zambia needed, he told me. It was small comfort that, when I saw the same ambassador again just before he left, he was wondering what kind of a man Chiluba was. And Kenneth Kaunda told me years later that the ambassador, who went on to work for the Carter Center apologised to him for misreading the situation at the time. But, unfortunately, foreign diplomats do have the ability to influence events when they are around. They get transferred a couple of years later, leaving behind sometimes serious long-term problems they helped create.

The election campaign was vicious, and even though I was not directly involved I became a target because some people liked to believe that I was a front for Kenneth Kaunda and that the ITM and Meridien groups belonged to him – not an unusual situation in Africa, where public opinion is singularly uninformed, particularly on financial and business issues, and feeds on rumours cleverly put about by interested parties. I was chairing a meeting one morning when a crowd of screaming youngsters surrounded the office carrying placards and shouting insults against me. The dominant theme was 'Imperialist Sardanis get out'. I was dismayed to learn later that a personal friend who harboured a deep hate against Kaunda and was angry that I was supporting him had had a hand in organising that demonstration. The screaming youngsters were collected at his farm and were transported by truck to our office. They were dropped outside the gate and they rushed in unfolding placards on the way. There was a guard, but as the gate was always open during the day and they were so many of them there was nothing he could do to stop them. The office was some 250 yards from the gate and I heard the screaming before I saw the placards. It was hard to remain composed and carry on with the meeting as if nothing was happening. And the participants were dying to have a look. I adjourned the meeting and everybody rushed to the windows. But the demonstrators must have had instructions not to linger. Abruptly they made an about-turn and walked out.

Chiluba would prove a master in misleading the West and making them happy at the same time. He started from day one. His Cabinet was as large as Kaunda's, even though a small Cabinet was one of the cornerstones of his election campaign. But he was fierce against Kaunda's lieutenants. The *African Analysis* magazine was jubilant. Under the title 'Kaunda's cronies ousted' it wrote:

...Nonetheless there is widespread relief in Zambia that the iron grip of Francis Kaunda, chairman of ZCCM [the government-controlled mining company] has been broken. Although he was not related to ex-President Kenneth Kaunda he was one of his closest confidants ... The well publicised ousting of Francis Kaunda [armed police raided the ZCCM offices and bundled him out of the building the day following Chiluba's election] from his Lusaka office and his replacement by Edward Shamutete, general manager of Nchanga (ZCCM's most profitable mine), has been paralleled by events in Zimco House its City of London headquarters. The managing director there, Joseph Banda, was ordered to leave instantly by a new temporary incumbent, Derrick Mhango who displayed a suitable sense of theatre by arriving in a chauffer driven Rolls Royce ... Banda was accompanied into the street outside Zimco House by his two white secretaries. His senior secretary was told by Mhango to leave her company BMW behind ... Another top level industry executive suspended in London was Lawrence Mutakasha, head of Memaco, which handled ZCCM's mineral sales world-wide ...

The new government is known to have no intention of taking any hostile action against the Zambian interests of Andrew Sardanis, despite his close association over many years with both Kenneth Kaunda and Francis Kaunda. From modest origins in retailing on the Copperbelt in the early 1960s, Sardanis now has Africa-wide interests in banking (Meridien), trading (ITM) and construction (Wade Adams) ... His associates say that he is profoundly depressed by the shattering defeat of Unip, the former ruling party with which he has links going back for 25 years. One previously powerful figure in State House, never likely to be seen there again is the wealthy Mahadeva Ranganathan, an Indian ex-teacher of arithmetic who had acquired an almost hypnotic hold over Kenneth Kaunda ...

So Chiluba reneges on day one on a very important governance issue, but everybody is happy because he was fierce against Kaunda's cronies. As *African Analysis* said, I was spared from direct action, but I was a friend of Kenneth Kaunda, so in the eyes of some in the new establishment, especially those who felt out of place and insecure, a legitimate target. The first to throw a stone was a Dr Guy Scott, the new Agriculture, Food and Fisheries Minister. A couple of weeks after his appointment he made a statement ostensibly on the expected arrival of maize ordered by the Kaunda administration to alleviate shortages resulting from the previous season's drought. He told the press that, though the maize was worth $25 million, the loan procured from Meridien Bank was $31.25 million, and added: 'The $6.25 million is apparently tied to other various transactions to which the Chibote group of companies is an interested party. There is no other explanation to this.'

If he had bothered to check the agreement that had been signed with the Canadian governor of the Bank of Zambia (BOZ), an IMF appointee, he would have found that it contained a 'cash collateral' clause providing that '20% [$6.25 million] of the gross outstanding amount throughout the life of the loan to be invested with Meridien at LIBOR plus 2% p.a.'. In other words, part of the loan remained on deposit with Meridien and it was interest-neutral, earning the BOZ interest at the same rate as it was paying for the loan. It is a necessary banking condition (especially when there is a worry that the borrower may not be able to meet instalments on due date) and its purpose is to ensure payment on time. (Meridien had syndicated the loan and had to pay the other lenders promptly as instalments fell due whether the funds were received from Zambia or not.) I would not have minded the comment if it had come from anybody else in government, but the honourable minister had a first class degree in economics from Cambridge and had been a businessman for many years.

Dr Scott's ministerial career was very short. Sometime in April 1992 he appointed Fairtrade, a one-woman company operating from her house in Johannesburg, to supervise the transit of Zambian-bound maize through South Africa. For her pains he agreed to pay her in Switzerland, at the rate $3.50 per ton-in-transit plus expenses. And as a measure of goodwill he made an advance payment to her company's Swiss bank account amounting to $200,000. But governments do not normally launder money through Swiss bank accounts, and the Zambian government could not very well do so for a South African company owned by a South African resident in order to relieve her of paying income tax for the work she performed in South Africa, or help her to evade her country's exchange control regulations. Dr Scott did it without going through the correct government channels in Zambia. Not unnaturally, the contract caused a furore amongst political circles, which ended up with an investigation by the then Attorney-General. The above description of the deal was taken from the 'summary of events' as they appear in his legal opinion dated 3 July 1992. And one amusing comment from the Attorney-General's report: 'Fairtrade did not obtain Central Bank authority in South Africa to receive hard currency payment of $200,000 as deposit.' Dr Scott was dropped from the Cabinet in April 1993, without explanation. Three other ministers – the cream of Chiluba's Cabinet – were dropped at the same time.

But back to Gabon.

13. PRESIDENTIAL PALACES AND PORNO FILMS

We had arrived in Libreville in November 1991, for meetings with the governor of BEAC, the Central Bank of the Central African States (Cameroon, Gabon, Equatorial Guinea, Chad, Central African Republic and Congo-Brazzaville), and the Minister of Finance on the many problems of BIPG (Banque Internationale pour le Gabon). The government had never paid its capital subscription of F CFA 300 million, yet it was behaving as if it owned the bank and appointed various functionaries, including the managing director, who may have been politically important but had no banking expertise. We complained to the governor. That was not his concern, he said. As far as he was concerned he wanted to see urgent recapitalisation of the bank and he was sending his inspectors to determine how much was needed, etc. The fact that at that time, strictly speaking, Meridien BIAO had not as yet come into being, because neither the African Development Bank nor the West African Development Bank had paid their subscriptions (it would take another year to do so), did not concern him either. We received no sympathy from the governor. The Minister of Finance sounded more sympathetic, but was equally unhelpful.

Amazingly, Gabon, a country with a per capita income of $2500 per annum, one of the highest in Africa at the time, had fallen into arrears on its international obligations and had to resort to constant rescheduling. The government owed $21 million to BIPG and we were anxious to know if we were ever going to get that money back, and when – preferably as soon as possible. And as we were under pressure from the central bank to inject liquidity into the BIPG we needed to collect at least the interest arrears immediately. The game of sending you from pillar to post is very common in Africa, especially if you are a foreign visitor and they know that you have a tight timetable and you are anxious to leave as soon as possible. To gain time the minister arranged that we meet President Bongo.

I have been to many presidential palaces in Africa and I always expect some delay in my meetings with Presidents, but the delays with Bongo and, I would discover later, Mobutu were the worst. Presidential security was in the hands of fierce-looking Moroccan soldiers, who made a thorough job of it, treating everybody as a potential assassin before we were ushered into the waiting room. It was full of people and we had to wait for hours for our turn.

Bongo's office was a large, square room, with the desk in the far corner. The sitting area was near the entrance, with a sofa and a couple of chairs for the visitors and a tall throne-like chair facing them for the President. The 'throne' was elevated and had a step to it that looked like a footrest. The purpose of this arrangement was to bring Bongo to the level of his visitors, who were sitting on the sofa. He was less than five feet tall and so conscious of it that there is a story that he blacked out the word 'pygmée' from all the dictionaries sold in Gabon (I did not check it). By the presidential desk, diagonally across the sitting area, two television sets were switched on and were visible sideways from where we sat. The discussion took place through an interpreter and during the translation my eyes wandered towards the TVs. One was showing CNN news and the other was showing a film. As I looked, it dawned on me that the kiss being shown was taking rather a long time, and then I realised that I was looking at a porno film. The president of the Meridien BIAO group who had accompanied me, a very prim Englishman, could not wait until we got out of the palace before he asked: 'Did you see what was showing on the TV?' Needless to say, we got no joy from the President for our requests. He did not involve himself with financial issues, he said. That was the responsibility of the Minister of Finance, who was there with us, having arranged the meeting.

Bongo would get headlines in the United States in November 2005, when a Washington lobbyist was indicted on federal fraud charges. It transpired that, amongst other activities, the lobbyist in question had been negotiating in 2003 to arrange a visit for Bongo to meet President Bush, for a fee of $9 million. Bongo did in fact visit Bush ten months later, on 26 May 2004, but the White House explained that the visit had nothing to do with the lobbyist: 'It was part of the president's outreach to the continent of Africa,' the spokesman explained. During the hearings it also transpired that the same lobbyist had been acting for Mobutu, who also had a penchant for porno films, as I would discover a year or so later when cruising on *Kamanyola*, Mobutu's luxury river yacht.

***

I was attending a meeting of the African Business Roundtable in Kinshasa, and President Mobutu decided to entertain us. He invited us for lunchtime drinks at N'Sele Palace outside Kinshasa, which had been designed and built by Taiwan, in exchange for diplomatic recognition. The sudden sight of a Chinese palace with pagoda-style roofs of shiny tiles on the banks of the river Congo in the middle of Africa, as we turned the corner, was disorienting. The garden was Chinese, too, with a large gazebo in the same style, and there we were served pink champagne (Mobutu's favourite drink, and that of the nouveau riche society of the Congo) and canapés. But that was not the end of Mobutu's generosity. When I decided that the lunchtime drinks had taken too long and that the canapés were meant to be our lunch, a fleet of limousines arrived and whisked us all down a broad boulevard, unfinished, but lined with palm trees all the way to the river Congo, where the *Kamanyola* was anchored. We sailed upstream and downstream for two or three hours; more pink champagne on the middle deck, where, in the lounge, a TV set was showing porno films; and, later, lunch on the top deck – a four-course meal served by white-gloved waiters with a different wine for every course. What floored me was the fruit served on silver platters at the end. Plums, apricots, kiwi fruit, apples, grapes, blood oranges and tangerines probably flown from Fauchon's in Paris. No tropical fruit, no mango, no pineapple, no papaya. It might have been an enjoyable day if one did not cry for Africa at the end.

The Meridien BIAO Bank in Zaire (now the Democratic Republic of Congo) was not exactly a bank. It was more of a glorified bureau de change. With inflation rates of 2000% it simply was not possible to run a bank. So the management concentrated on buying dollars and converting them into zaires (the local currency) or vice versa. The dollars were generated by the many diamond dealers, and the zaires by various traders, including many Greeks. It was a very basic but profitable bureau de change operation, but Meridien BIAO had a full banking licence. This must have been the reason that prompted the invitation I received from Mobutu, the President of Zaire, to visit him in Gbadolite, where he lived most of the time after the riots in Kinshasa in 1991. I set up the visit as a transit stop on my way from Lusaka to Abidjan. Danae and my son Harry, who had been on a visit to Zambia from the Abidjan office of Meridien BIAO, where he was working at the time, and his wife, Wendy were with me. We flew to Kinshasa, picked up one of Mobutu's 'consultants', a Belgian lawyer, through whom the invitation came, and flew to Gbadolite,

Mobutu's home village, where he had built a retreat. On the plane the Belgian sang the praises of the great man, who, he informed us, was now his father – his natural father had died and he decided to 'adopt' Mobutu as a father instead (a rather 'downside-up' process, I thought).

Gbadolite, not very far from the Ubangi River which forms the border between the Congo and the Central African Republic, had the unmistakable signs of stillbirth. Abandoned buildings standing next to half-finished ones, bearing names of state corporations, insurance companies and banks, lay on either side of an unfinished boulevard, all decaying in the tropical heat and humidity. We had arrived mid-morning and were met at the airport by a protocol officer, who took us to one of the luxury guest houses for a rest until the great man was ready to see me – he was chairing a Cabinet meeting, we were informed. The protocol officer arranged a tour of the town, and the hydro-electric scheme on the Ubangi, which supplied power to the palace and the town. At the presidential garage, where we went for refuelling, we saw parked in huge sheds row after row of black Cadillacs. There were 35 and they were all bulletproof, the driver proudly informed us, and they were kept for visiting heads of state and major international events. It was for the same reason that the large airport where we had landed earlier that morning was built to handle Boeing 747 aeroplanes (Mobutu's personal plane was a 747, of course). The drive to the 'barrage' some distance out of town gave us the opportunity to see village life in that part of Africa. The soils are fertile, the vegetation lush and the villages looked prosperous, with cassava fields and yams and goats, and pigs and chicken and well-nourished children. The hydroelectric scheme turned out to be only a half scheme. Mobutu had built the dam wall on his side of the river, but the Central African Republic had not done the same. The wall on the Congo side, though, raised the water level sufficiently to run a small power station to satisfy the needs of Gbadolite.

I made some rough calculations and came to the conclusion that the annual cost of running the extravagance of Gbadolite, which by that time had shrunk to the palace and its compounds, should be in excess of $20 million a year. Supplies needed to come either by barge on the Congo and then the Ubangi, but the Ubangi was navigable for only three or four months a year. There was no road to Gbadolite from Kinshasa so, for the rest of the year, supplies needed to come by air – i.e. the Congolese Air Force. Back at the guest house, the steward brought pink champagne, but there was no sign of lunch – we were informed that lunch would come from the palace, and it came rather late. No word about when the great man would deign to see me. I was fuming. After lunch I sent a message that I would be taking off at 4 p.m., and I was called to the palace immediately.

It was built at the top of a hill. Midway up the hill we had to pass a big gate, like those of medieval castles with high walls on either side. (I do not know if the wall went around the hill.) Outside the palace some 20 or so Mercedes were waiting to drive the ministers back to their guest houses or to the airport for the flight to Kinshasa. I was taken through the gardens to a veranda, where the Belgian lawyer was waiting. Mobutu took some time to come and when he joined us he was accompanied by his Minister of Mines. He explained that he needed to resuscitate the economy of the country and he asked if Meridien could raise a loan of $150 million for the rehabilitation and development of the copper mines in Lubumbashi and Likasi. The Congo was bankrupt and no loan was possible, but in order to avoid embarrassment I asked for the usual information, project report and statistics and promised to see what I could to. The Minister of Mines undertook to send the information to London.

We chatted a little more, and this gave me more time to admire the view that held me spellbound from the moment I sat on that veranda. It was breathtaking. Dark blue rainforest covered with a faint mist spread for miles and miles below us. And on the right-hand side of the vista the forest ended abruptly in a perfectly straight line and the adjacent savannah looked like a field of green and yellow grass – as if some extraterrestrial surveyor had demarcated the two fields for different crops. While we were talking it started to rain, and the rain darkened the veil over the forest and increased the mystery that enveloped that majestic view.

I was mesmerised, and I wondered if Mobutu ever saw that great beauty I was looking at.

The architect must have done, though, because he had designed wide verandas and ceiling-to-floor glass windows so that nothing got in the way of the view. But either the architect or Mobutu had gone mad in the size and the finishing of that edifice on that beautiful hill. As it was raining I could not return to the car through the garden and was escorted through the palace. From the veranda we entered a huge room, with a very high ceiling at the lower level of the hill, reducing as we were climbing up. It covered six lounges, in open plan on three different levels, three on each side of the inclining passage that separated the room into two. I was walking through and did not have much time to study it, but my mind was absorbing rapidly what my eyes were taking in. The walls and the floors were covered in shiny pink and lime-coloured marble that did not seem very happy in that humid and hot environment

– patches of mildew were spreading all over it. The furniture seemed to have come from different countries, with Chinese carpets and Chinese and Japanese consoles in prominent display, full of porcelain and other artefacts of Far Eastern and European origin. Groups of people were lounging around, and at the top a few men were standing around a bar chatting. A large door led to the foyer, where a huge, ornate Belgian marble-top table was standing in the centre, and a huge *belle époque* gilded mirror placed at an angle covered the back wall.

The Congo is an inexhaustible source of African art for collectors. But not a single piece could be seen in Mobutu's equatorial Versailles. Chinese porcelain and Belgian tapestry, yes, but not a single piece of Chokwe, Lulua, Luba, Kuba, Pende, Songye or, nearer his home area, Mangbetu art.

14. THE NEW DEMOCRATS

'Come on, Mr Sardanis; it was Marxism, pure and simple.' That was the response of Frederick Chiluba, the new President of Zambia, to my analysis of the thinking behind the Zambian economic reforms of the 1960s. During the election campaign Chiluba and the MMD, prompted by settlers and foreign embassies, had made a very big issue of the economic reforms of the 1960s and the parastatal sector; they classified them as Marxist and gloated at their failings. They promised to abolish the parastatal sector and open the Zambian market in order to attract foreign investment. I thought the new President needed some briefing on the evolution of business in Zambia, the economic nationalism that prompted the Mulungushi reforms, and an assessment of the foreign direct investment possibilities and their consequences that he seemed to be banking on. I asked B. Y. Mwila, who had worked for me in the Industrial Development Corporation of Zambia and who was Chiluba's cousin and Minister of Defence, to introduce me to the new President. Early in January 1992 our Zambian chairman and I received an invitation to lunch at the government guest house where Chiluba was staying until the renovations of the presidential villa were completed.

I gave him a rundown of the economic reforms around Africa in the 1960s and explained to him that, regardless of their individual flavour, they all had a common motive, and that was economic nationalism. I tried to make him understand that, if the governments of the 1960s had not taken the measures they had, business evolution in Africa would have remained in foreign hands and training would have been non-existent. I pointed out that in Zambia government participation in business had achieved its purpose: it had brought about substantial Zambianisation of the business sector, and more importantly, the development of Zambian business executives and managers. In view of this the parastatal sector could be privatised provided measures were taken to ensure maximum Zambian participation. Chiluba's implementation would turn out to be haphazard in relation to some businesses he did not care about and highly selective in relation to others – a subject that I shall cover later.

On foreign direct investment I cautioned him to lower his expectations, because investment in Africa was not one of the priorities of foreign capital. I explained that foreign direct investment would certainly be attracted to petroleum and the mining of other primary commodities, as well as large agricultural, hydroelectric and telecommunications projects, but it would bargain hard and demand extremely generous concessions that would override the country's business norms and tax legislation for years to come. And, in an attempt to instil some African backbone in him, I gave him a present of Basil Davidson's book *The Black Man's Burden*. But he held on to his electoral campaign momentum and the lunch conversation was dominated by his electoral slogans: free enterprise, democracy, the evils of state enterprise, corruption, Kaunda's Marxism, etc. For a man whose three sons are called Castro, Tito and Mikoyan, the metamorphosis was remarkable.

A couple of months later Chiluba attended his first OAU heads of state meeting in Senegal, where he stunned everybody with his sermon. It was brimming with evangelical fervour (he is a 'born again') warning his fellow

Some of Chiluba's spare shoes: 50 pairs of them in psychedelic colours on two-inch heels. They were kept in a warehouse in 21 trunks and 11 suitcases, together with 150 suits and 300 shirts. Nobody knows how many he kept in his house for everyday use. (Picture courtesy of the *Post*, Zambia's independent daily).

heads of state that the day of judgement was nigh and that they had to repent and change their ways. They should stop building monuments to themselves and start building silos instead. (Ironically, after Chiluba's demise his own half-finished 'monument' intended to house his grandly called 'Institute for Democracy and Labour Relations' went under the hammer, because the new government refused to complete it.) In the meantime, in Zambia, Chiluba set about persecuting his predecessor. The verdict of his then Minister of Justice was that a presidential pension becomes operative only when an ex-President retires from politics. On the grounds that Kaunda was still head of his party, Chiluba vetoed Kaunda's terminal benefits, which would have included a house to be provided by the state. Kaunda did not have a private home in Lusaka to move to and after a few weeks in the ZCCM guest house he was forced to leave, and moved into a house owned by a friend. He would later move to a rented house, but even though the government promised to pay the rent the owner had a long struggle to get paid. The government did not even provide vehicles for Kaunda's removal and we had to help out with one of our trucks.

The next twist was a police complaint that Kaunda had stolen State House property (his books which he kept on the bookshelves of his study at State House). Front-page pictures of KK standing amid packages and books strewn all over a warehouse floor, with policemen around searching for government property, may have gratified Chiluba, but they highlighted his meanness and revolted many Zambians. (Chiluba would get his just deserts in 2004, when, facing charges of plunder, his property received the same photo opportunity in another warehouse. Chiluba's 'loot' was not books, though: according to his claim, the government confiscated 21 trunks and 11 suitcases containing 150 suits, 300 shirts and 50 pairs of multicoloured shoes on elevated platforms – Imelda Marcos would have been proud of him. Chiluba was indignant at the pictures of his apparel spread all over the front pages – it was after all, his own – but the state's contention was that it was procured from a Swiss outfitter at the cost of many hundreds of thousands of dollars and paid for through a government account.)

And then the real witch-hunt started against Kaunda, his senior lieutenants and his friends, which included me. As a first act, I was removed from the board of ZCCM, courtesy of the Anglo American Corporation, which had taken upon itself the right to nominate the directors on behalf of the minority shareholders and was hell-bent to please the new government. What rankled was the front-page report in the *Weekly Post* of 20 March 1992 under a banner headline: 'ZCCM board shows ITM boss the door: Sardanis Booted Out'.

As fresh evidence of gross mismanagement in ZCCM surfaced this week, ITM boss Andrew Sardanis was expelled from the company's board for undisclosed reasons. Anglo American Corporation (Central Africa), the second major shareholder in ZCCM, championed Sardanis's expulsion from the company's board on Tuesday. Anglo's Managing Director, Anderson Mazoka, confirmed Sardanis's expulsion but declined to elaborate. ITM who are the minority shareholders in ZCCM have been heavily involved in Zambia's copper transactions and have had a lot of business with the mining conglomerate. Business analysts believe that its loss of representation on the ZCCM board may have serious financial consequences for the ITM group. The group, which made its fortune from Zambia, may be forced to find a new base. Sardanis had been a close friend of former president Kenneth Kaunda and played a major role in the setting up of Zambia's parastatal companies...

The author, Jowie Mwiinga, was a bright but inexperienced young journalist, and in line with the trend he could not resist a little uninformed speculation in order to make his story sensational – a common problem in African journalism. And in order to connect me with the 'gross mismanagement' he had started his report with, he proceeded:

And as the board made heated consultations on Wednesday, investigations into malpractices by the former ZCCM management extended to Tanzania where deputy commissioner led a team of police and SITET officers to Dar to probe reports of irregular copper transactions...

But, as it turned out, they did me a favour. Even though my initial reaction was to fight, more mature thoughts prevailed and we sold the ZCCM shares instead, thus bringing into the group much-needed liquidity to relieve some of the cash drain caused by the BIAO acquisition.

But that only gave us a short respite. I should have walked out of the BIAO deal, which was taking for ever to conclude, and it was straining our cash and human resources. With the approval of BCEAO (the Central Bank of West Africa) we signed the deal with the liquidator and bought Afritrust International, the French holding company that held the BIAO banks' shares in Africa, on 19 April 1991; but it was not until 11 March 1992 that we were officially informed that the African Development Bank had taken a decision to subscribe $7.5 million (10% – we had been expecting 20%) in the capital of Meridien BIAO SA (MBIAO), and it was not until 10 April 1992 that the legal department of ADB came into the act, scrutinising articles of association, statutory records, etc. It was only at that stage that BOAD, the West African Development Bank, started having a serious look at the project, and it was not until the second half of 1992 that the ADB paid for its shareholding and the end of the year that BOAD did so too.

In the meantime we had to carry the burden for almost two years, from the time we had made the original agreement with BCEAO to the time the new shareholders subscribed, and then for only half the anticipated contribution.

15. CAMEROON AND OTHER DISASTERS

The interim existence was surreal. We had the meeting in Abidjan with the general managers of the various banks on 9 December 1990, at which we made some nuts and bolts interim operational decisions. Afterwards we made visits to the various countries described earlier, and realised that almost everywhere a rearguard action was going on behind our backs to subvert us and the network. And depending on the inclinations and connections of the local manager or the senior Frenchman there were many authorities and bodies that could be called upon to throw spanners in the works. For example, on 14 August 1991 we received a letter from the Central Bank of Togo informing us that we had no authority to change the name of BIAO, Togo, or change the logo, or appoint directors on its board. It was difficult to determine who had authority for what, anywhere. We had understood that BCEAO was the central bank for UMOA (West African Monetary Union), to which all these countries belonged, and BCEAO had branches in each country. Yet, depending on the whim of the man in charge (who in Anglo-Saxon terms would have been described as the branch manager), this man could choose to behave as the governor of an independent central bank and there was nothing we could do about it. But we soldiered on. The determination to create a pan-African banking network was so strong that at every obstacle we drew a deep breath and tried to overcome it.

So, in my ITM chairman's statement for the year 1991, I proudly reported that 'Meridien BIAO SA comprises 18 banks with 100 branches, making it the most extensive banking network in Africa'. My chairman's statement did not seem to take too seriously the drop of pre-tax profit from $35 million to $27 million. I attributed it to the Gulf War, the instability caused by the transition to multi-party democracy in Africa and the expenses of the BIAO acquisition, but the reality was that BIAO absorbed too much of our energy and resources and the core businesses suffered. And I went on to appeal to the Western world for more help to Africa:

Democracy, to flourish requires a fairly significant economic base to mitigate the effects of restructuring, which in the third world context implies difficult decisions: reduction of the public sector work force, removal of all controls, trade liberalisation, consequent increased competition for local enterprises, etc. In other words countries are attempting to introduce democracy and restructure their economies at the same time regardless of attendant political risks. Possible food riots, nationwide strikes, attempted coups d'etat and general political discontent can frustrate the process. It is therefore important that both multilateral and bilateral donors understand Africa's dilemma and remain alert to its problems some of which require urgent solutions…

In the same statement I announced that 'we negotiated with the government of Cameroon for the merger of Meridien Bank Cameroon and BIAO Cameroon, which occurred on 1 June 1991, and we are at the final stage of the negotiations to acquire the last remaining BIAO bank in Africa, BIAO Equatorial Guinea'.

***

We were sweet-talked into the merger of Meridien Bank with BIAO in Cameroon. On the other hand, it was foolish on our part to agree to merge a perfectly profitable small bank with a bankrupt Goliath in the hope that we would make a profitable unit out of the two. But by that time we could not see the wood for the trees: the BIAO deal and its successful conclusion had become an end in itself.

Like the governments of Côte d'Ivoire and Senegal, the government of Cameroon had taken over directly from the liquidator the local BIAO, which was bankrupt, and it appointed a provisional administrator to run it. BIAO Cameroon should have gone into liquidation, but those were turbulent political times and the government was afraid of the public outcry that would follow. The cry for democratisation (Cameroon was still a one-party state at the time) that started with the beginning of the 1990s was as strong in Cameroon as in most countries in Africa. There were demonstrations and violence in the major towns, especially in anglophone Cameroon. And there was another very potent weapon there: 'les villes mortes', the ghost cities. People paralysed the towns by not getting out of their homes to go to work, or shop, or carry out any of their daily activities. So the government could not close BIAO, but needed some credible solution.

Meridien Bank Cameroon, having started life as Chase Bank Cameroon, which we had taken over in 1988 was a very successful bank, so much so that in 1990 we decided to increase its capital by F CFA 1 billion (a couple of million dollars) to enable it to expand its portfolio. Our application for the capital increase went to the Minister of Finance, who also gave approval to the sale of shares to 'public and private interests' – a god-sent solution for the government to offload its BIAO problem on Meridien.

The agreement with the government was signed on 17 April 1991. It provided that the takeover would be based on the two banks' management accounts as at 28 February. The government promised a 10% (F CFA 635 million) participation in the capital of the merged bank and securitisation of the bad debts (due mainly by government and parastatal bodies), which constituted most of the portfolio of BIAO and regular servicing of its own obligations. Naively, instead of insisting on cleaning BIAO's portfolio in advance, we agreed to do so at the end of a six-month period. We understood the process to be pretty much automatic, but we would discover that it turned into a battle royal, the government reneging on the agreement time and again.

Problems arose as early as June 1991, two months after signature. The government had to pay its capital subscription, but it never did. It was not until December that we got a hearing from the Minister of Finance to discuss the problem. A memo from the manager of our Paris office, who flew down for the purpose, reports that a Mr Astier, described as 'French technical advisor/ Banking sector', did all the talking, and bluntly said: 'The government is short of liquidity so payment would be difficult.' He said that 'he might support a partial payment of around F CFA 250 million with the balance to be paid "as waiver of certain taxes"' – this would later be forbidden by a presidential decree. The government's capital subscription was never received and no bad debts were accepted.

I have in my files a document dated 6 January 1995, titled 'negotiations de la dette de L'État – chronologie des événements', cataloguing all the abortive negotiations with the representatives of the Ministry of Finance led by Astier and, later, a Mr Astruc. An entry dated January 1994 records that the total government debt to Meridien BIAO Bank Cameroon was reconciled at F CFA 53,835,359,231, and an entry dated December 1994 records the debt of three major parastatals, Société Nationale d'Investissement, Société de Développement du Coton and Cameroon Development Corporation, at F CFA 27,284,992,950, which brought the total government indebtedness to some F CFA 81 billion against the bank's total assets of F CFA 120 billion. In other words, two-thirds of the bank's portfolio represented non-performing government obligations. The penultimate entry in the 'chronologie' records that 'a letter from the

Ministry of Finance dated 25 October 1994 nominates Maitre (attorney) Gilbert Manceau in consultation with the Ministry of Finance to arbitrate the interpretation of the agreement signed on April 17, 1991' – back to square one,

The façade of the Meridien BIAO Bank grand headquarters in Douala, Cameroon. With 26 branches it was the biggest bank in the network.

four years later. The government's intransigence may have been driven all along by the fact that it was bankrupt and did not have the ability to meet its obligations, but I could not help suspecting that it was also partly due to the various French functionaries who were in charge of the negotiations. They never wanted the merger of Meridien and BIAO and they took the opportunity to dig the knife deep.

Cameroon turned out to be the most difficult country we operated in. It had been a one-party state since its inception in 1961, when the small British section joined the French Cameroon in a federation. Ahmadou Ahidjo was President from the beginning until 1982, when he resigned for health reasons. The story in Africa was that the French gave him the push. After he was diagnosed with cancer he was persuaded that he only had a few months to live and was made to appoint his Prime Minister, Paul Biya, as his successor. He kept for himself the position of party president, hoping that he would control Biya from the back seat. But he found out, like many others before and since, that it is the person who holds the post that has the power and not his erstwhile patron. Ahidjo in fact lived for another couple of years and the story goes that he wanted to make a comeback but was prevented. Biya became President in 1982 and even though, after a public outcry, he had to introduce a multi-party constitution, he has 'won' all the elections since. Under the constitution his latest seven-year term, which ends in 2011, is meant to be his last, and even though he will be 83 years old by then, a campaign started in 2005 to change the constitution to allow him a further term. And he does not seem to care about either the government or the country. He spends most of his time in France, and when in Cameroon he prefers to live in his home town instead of the capital, Yaoundé. The country seemed pretty much headless in the early 1990s and I understand the situation today is the same.

***

My first encounter with Equatorial Guinea occurred in New York in the mid-1980s. We were approached by a group that had entered into a contract (or so they claimed) with the government of Equatorial Guinea to set up dumps for New York refuse on one of the islands. We were asked to raise finance for the barges that would transport the trash across the Atlantic and the vehicles and equipment that would transport it on the island and bury it. I rejected the project with horror. Apart from my own personal objections to such a project, the last thing I wanted Meridien to be associated with was dumping First World trash on African soil.

Tropical Gangsters was the title of a book published in 1992 by Robert Klitgaard, a World Bank officer, after a tour of service in Equatorial Guinea. The gangsters he refers to were the President and the government of the country.

Equatorial Guinea was a comical anomaly in sub-Saharan Africa in the early 1990s. A Spanish colony that was granted independence in 1968, it retained all the pomposity and pretentiousness of the Spanish society of yesteryear and the features of a country of shanty towns. Shanty towns usually emerge on the outskirts of major cities in Africa, but in Equatorial Guinea the capital, Malabo, was itself the shanty town. All the ministers were 'Don' and were addressed as 'Excelentissimo' and our discussions took place in flowery language that had to be translated from Spanish to French to English. My high school Latin came in handy, because it allowed me to follow the convoluted Spanish phraseology, which I found very amusing at the time.

The President, Teodoro Obiang, took power in 1979 having deposed his uncle, Macias Nguema, the first President of the country who had made himself President-for-life in 1972. Obiang was notorious as a ruthless despot and his regime ranked as the most kleptocratic in Africa – hence the Klitgaard book title. Equatorial Guinea now, after the discovery of oil, is a much richer country and Obiang is still the President, and much richer too, despite the efforts of some latter-day Cecil Rhodes and Leander Jamesons from Britain to engineer his removal. (Amongst them: Sir Mark Thatcher, son of Britain's former Prime Minister and other upmarket Britons. They recruited mercenaries in South Africa and Zimbabwe in preparation for a coup but the plane that was due to carry them to Malabo was intercepted at Harare airport, so the coup never got off the ground.) Nevertheless, we were received very courteously and we did open the bank, but it was not really worthwhile. Its total balance sheet amounted to only $15 million in 1995.

Our 1992 report gave some ominous hints of the looming disasters we would have to grapple with the following year. First there was UNITA's total occupation of the diamond mining area we operated in Angola. Then there was another cessation of all activities in Liberia, the last one, I think, after just a few months of resumed operations. But the most worrying one was this:

> ...Many of our operations in Africa were adversely affected by recession and the severe drought, which impacted East and Southern Africa. The Caterpillar dealerships in Zambia, Malawi and Angola had a disappointing year...

Despite the above comment I concluded that we did not expect business conditions to worsen during 1993. What I did not foresee was the mindless economic policies of Chiluba's government in Zambia, which would maso-chistically set about destroying the economic base of the country in 1993 through overzealous and prolonged implementation of the IMF 'structural adjustment programme'. The average base lending rate in Zambia rose from 60.6% at the beginning of the year to 214.4% at the end of March, 241.7% at the end of June, before it started falling to 239.9% at the end of September and 132.5% at the end of December.[1] Even the World Bank was up in arms with the Zambian self-flagellation, and on a visit to Washington some officers asked me if I could do something about it.

I decided to go and visit Chiluba. I had not seen the man since our first encounter at the beginning of 1992.

16. GREEN CROCODILE LEATHER SHOES AND STORM CLOUDS

Chiluba was sitting behind the desk in the presidential study at State House in Lusaka, where over many years in the past I had countless meetings with Kenneth Kaunda – familiar ground for me. The desk and the furniture were the same, arranged in the same order as they always had been: the desk opposite the entrance, with a large sofa to its right and an easy chair facing it, at right angles to the sofa. But there was a difference. Whereas Kaunda used to work mostly in a golf shirt, Chiluba was in suit and tie. He stood up to greet me and he did not go back to the desk. He showed me to the easy chair and he sat on the sofa. I explained to him the reason for my visit and my worries over the effect of prolonged high interest rates on the economy. He immediately went into a sermon on the structural adjustment gospel. 'Mr. Sardanis, I sleep structural adjustment, I dream structural adjustment, I breathe structural adjustment… We have to kill inflation.' He carried on with a chant on the effects of inflation on people's incomes, etc.

I do not mind arguing with Presidents, but when reasoning gives way to slogans I switch off. I sat back observing his performance, my mind not even taking in what he was saying. He is an extremely small man, with unusually small eyes, set deep into his skull, and at that time he seemed 'possessed' by his sermon. But what struck me most was his attire. Light grey suit with darker pin stripes, grey shirt and a very colourful tie, with splashes of blue and yellow and green, over grey background, a similar handkerchief hanging down from his breast pocket. When his shoes came into focus (crocodile leather, coloured green, sitting on two-inch cork platforms), I decided I was wasting my time. The vanity displayed by his attire seemed to underline his empty head: his inability to think and put what he heard to logical test and make a judgement. I concluded the meeting and left, and never set eyes on the man again until six years later.

And the interest rates remained high for almost the whole of 1993, killing whatever industry remained intact after the foolish free-market policies that had also been decreed by the IMF, and Chiluba religiously followed ostensibly in the interest of better prices for the consumers. (Since then, I have developed a theory about the readiness of some African leaders to comply with the flood of advice they get from multilateral institutions and donor countries. Most of those who accept it wholeheartedly and preach it enthusiastically do so because they have figured that it wins them the approbation of the donors, who in turn do not scrutinise too closely the rest of their actions, and in this way they can get away with everything else they want to do, particularly in the personal enrichment game.) And some consumers of Zambia did indeed get better prices but only in 'salaula'. (Zambian vernacular slang for second-hand clothing, developed on the copperbelt. Roughly translated, it means 'carry on choosing', and it is a typical example of self mocking folk humour. Another such example: the name of the street in Chingola that leads to the cemetery is called 'Mudzabwera', which translates into 'you will come'.) And the clothing industry of Zambia, one of the few industrial successes, which had already achieved an export breakthrough, with expanding sales to Europe, folded, leaving thousands of workers jobless. By the time Chiluba's term ended, no more than a dozen clothing factories were still operating.

The problem of second-hand clothing needs to be looked into, especially by international charities, which I believe are the main recipients of such donations in the Western countries. I once had a visit from two very nice Danish ladies, asking me for a donation to a 'street kids' programme they were running. They explained that their funds had run out, but their problem was temporary. They had large consignments of second-hand clothes on the way and as soon as those arrived and got sold off, their funds would be OK again. I explained to them that I did not approve of the way they were funding their programme. I tried to make them understand that maybe some of those street kids would have a working father or mother (that was in the early 1990s, before AIDS became a devastating pandemic and the mother of all street kids) if second-hand clothing had not destroyed their parents' jobs. I could understand donated second-hand clothing for free distribution to the needy, but not as a revenue-earning industry destroying jobs in developing countries, especially when received by charities that are exempt from duty. I do not think that my argument registered, but it does merit consideration.

But it was not only the interest rates and 'salaula' that caused the stagnation of the early 1990s. The haphazard privatisation policies and the indecent haste in dismantling existing institutions had disastrous consequences. A prime example was the abolition of the National Agricultural Marketing Board

(NAMBOARD). I do not know when it was established, but I assume that it must have been during the war years, when the government of Northern Rhodesia needed to have control of the distribution of grain in the country. It was certainly operating when I arrived in Zambia in 1950, because I used to deliver to it all the groundnuts and other produce I bought in the North Western Province. During the federal days it came under the control of the Federal Ministry of European Agriculture, and it was used as the tool to subsidise the European farmers, paying higher prices to them and lower prices to the Africans. After independence the board had a chequered history with the Kaunda administration, vacillating about which way to handle the farmers. Eventually, in the 1980s, Kaunda seemed to have found the right formula, which resulted in increased food production in the rural areas. I recall the Northern Province producing 2.5 million bags in 1985, a record for that part of the country.

But the IMF ordered the abolition of NAMBOARD without giving much thought to what would replace it. It probably expected the millers to fill the vacuum, but it did not bother to investigate if they had the financial capacity to do so. So Chiluba decided that the party faithful should come to the rescue and make some money in the process. He gave out generous loans to all his cronies who were willing to buy produce in the rural areas, while at the same time he pushed the interest rates to over 200% per annum. It did not need a financial genius to calculate that one would be better off buying treasury bills than buying produce. So the produce was left to rot and the following season the farmers did not have any money to buy seed and other agricultural inputs. And most of those loans to party faithful have not been repaid. As late as the beginning of 2005 the Food Reserve Agency (FRA), which inevitably had to be created in order succeeded MAMBOARD, was pursuing repayment.

***

The combination of the drought and the destruction of the agricultural marketing infrastructure in Zambia, the civil wars in Angola and Liberia, together with business problems that some would say were of our own making would make 1993 a nightmare year. In my chairman's statement I said:

> The year was the most difficult in the history of the group with many adverse circumstances combining to produce a loss for the first time since ITM was formed 20 years ago. The conflict in Angola was still raging as was that in Liberia for part of the year. The economies of several southern African countries

The ill-fated floating washing plant of the Goldenrae mine in Ghana that came into production in 1990 and never managed to achieve its anticipated capacity.

important to the group did not show reasonable recoveries despite their satisfactory harvests. Political problems in Malawi brought that economy to a standstill. In Zambia, low copper prices and erratic implementation of the structural adjustment programme produced stagnation, factory closures and massive unemployment. In West Africa the lack of confidence in the CFA franc combined with political uncertainty and huge budget deficits in some countries led to economic stagnation. The effects of these factors on the group was a loss before tax of $4 million and a loss after tax and minority interests of $11.5 million...

The dismal general picture described above omits the many specific problems that hit us during the year. First, there was a construction scandal in Botswana. I was never directly involved with the construction part of the group, but I had heard many stories of contracts going awry and losing their owners a packet. The particular contract that went wrong in 1992 for Wade Adams, our construction group, was with the Botswana Housing Corporation. From what I was told there was a design fault relating to the prefabricated material used for low-cost housing, which had to be replaced and consequently cost the corporation large sums of money. Our local construction company was accused of overpricing with the connivance of a senior local politician, who was to share the loot with our local manager and a Zambian engineering consultant. A commission of inquiry was set up and in its report it quantified the overpricing at Botswana pula 8.5 million, or some $3 million. It accused the Zambian engineering consultant who was involved in the project of conspiring with our Cypriot manager to launder the money through a series of shell companies controlled by the latter, and in the process sharing the money with two senior Botswana politicians.

The Zambian consultant fled to Zambia and our manager fled to Cyprus, and they left us holding the baby. I have never met the Zambian consultant and never seen our Cypriot manager since he fled so I do not know if the conclusions of the commission were justified. But the Botswanan authorities were determined to extract blood, and they did – from us. As most countries do in Africa and elsewhere, they unleashed the income tax department on our construction company and they extracted huge payments – not by any justifiable assessment but by arbitrary demands. The senior inspector assessed a tax of Botswana pula 6 million and a penalty of 200%, making a total of P18 million on a take-it-or-leave-it basis. He then threatened to cancel the contract, in which case he declared that he would collect P13 million in unpaid certificates and retentions and the corporation would cash our contract bond of P20 million and complete the contract. Bloody-minded apparatchiks can be very dangerous in Africa. But foreign ones, as the one in question was, wanting to show face to their employers can be deadly. We paid P13 million, but the overall profits of Wade Adams for 1993, according to the accounts, declined by only $1.7 million to $5.2 million.

The real killers were the mining division, which made a loss of $5.3 million, and the African manufacturing and product distribution operations, which lost $17 million.

There was always a worry at the back of our minds that one day the diamond mining operation in Angola, one of the very profitable divisions of the group, could come to an abrupt end. We tried to mitigate this looming disaster and at the same time build on the expertise we had developed over a decade of mining alluvial diamonds by looking into expanding elsewhere. We first looked into the possibility of searching for diamonds in Zambia, but a report by an engineer who had worked for De Beers during their investigations in Zambia did not look very promising. He identified four possible areas: one in the Kafue National Park, in an area called Kafue Hook; one in South Luangwa on the river Kapamba, a tributary to the Luangwa; one in Mpika on the Muchinga Hills, on a tributary of the Lwitikila river and one in Isoka, near the Tanzanian border where the geological data were difficult. They were kimberlitic deposits, which would have meant deep mining, of which we had no expertise. A year later an opportunity arose in Kenya with the offer of St Martin's, an alluvial gold project near Kisumu. We commissioned a mining consultant, a retired mining executive with Zambian and Chilean experience, to look at the prospect, and he was very enthusiastic in his assessment. His report read:

Ray, Andy and I are all enthusiastic about this project. The potential for gold production is enormous – 100,000 ounces a year is a realistic target – compared with the price of $4 million for 85% of the company. ITM is unlikely to find a comparable opportunity in mining anywhere. This should be seized in spite of two negative factors specific to Kenya…

The other was the Goldenrae Mining Company in Ghana, another alluvial gold project. The opinions over Goldenrae were mixed. The manager of our diamond mining operations in Angola was worried that the deposits were underwater, but our consultant did not share his scepticism. Yet in the end it was the floating plant that he ordered for underwater mining that was found to be unsuitable. Our fears about Angola materialised in October 1992, when Jonas Savimbi and

126

his UNITA guerrillas captured the mine at Cafunfo. Our staff had to flee, leaving everything behind, including 22,000 carats of diamonds in the safe. In 1993 losses from the Kenya and Ghana projects and write-offs of the Cafunfo operation in Angola caused the mining division to report a loss of $5.3 million against a profit of $6.3 million the previous year – a negative turnaround of $11.6 million.

But the biggest disaster came from the African operating companies, which produced a combined loss of $16.5 million, against a profit of $2 million the previous year. Our annual report attributed this to

> …reduced activity in key sectors such as mining and agriculture; reduced donor funding for capital projects, plus high inflation and wildly fluctuating currencies with high interest rates in many countries also made business difficult especially for the companies distributing and supporting heavy equipment.

It also goes on to report that, of the two main Liberian companies, the Caterpillar dealership was unable to operate because of its location, while the Toyota dealership remained open – but not for very long. In 1994 we would have to close down completely in Liberia, and a $20 million investment there would be lost irretrievably.

But the nightmare of 1993 seemed set to continue. An insert in our 1993 annual report read:

> After completion of this annual report but before its publication, the CFA franc was on January 12, 1994 devalued by 50%. As is apparent from the Chairman's statement we warmly welcome this move. The effect it would have had on our balance sheet if it had occurred on 30 September, 1993 is shown in note 21 to the accounts. One effect is a very substantial improvement in the capital adequacy ratio of the Banking division of the group. In the short term the devaluation necessarily means that values in the accounts in US $ terms of buildings and other fixed assets owned by our subsidiaries in the CFA zone halved overnight but we do not regard this as realistic because a devaluation of this scale will inevitably lead to enhanced values in local currency. If to take the extreme position fixed assets and properties held for disposal maintained their US $ values despite the devaluation the estimated figure for shareholders' funds mentioned in note 21 would be higher by approximately US $ 16 million.

But note 21 does not mince its words. It read:

> … The Directors estimate that in broad terms had the devaluation occurred on 30, September 1993, the effect on the balance sheet shown in these financial statements taking account of hedging arrangements then in place would have

been to reduce total assets from US $1,911,281,000 to $1,405,000,000 and shareholders funds from US $76,207,000 to US $74,000,000.

All that over and above the fact that, in 1993, we suffered the first loss in the 20 years of our existence ($11.5 million), but worse still we lost $20 million from our reserves writing off civil war-impaired assets and devaluation losses.

We were truly punch-drunk, but *Euromoney* magazine decided to give us another blow on the head.

17. HATE AND VENOM

'The High-wire act of Andrew Sardanis' was the title of an article in the *Euromoney* issue of December 1993, written by a stringer, Stephanie Cooke. By way of introduction it said in bold letters: 'Two years ago, Greek-Cypriot-born Zambian Andrew Sardanis bought himself control of Africa's most extended banking network and a legacy of banking woes. By skilful juggling of resources he has kept the Meridien BIAO group afloat, but few western bankers or regulators are impressed. Sardanis, defying scarcity of capital and the cancelling of credit lines, isn't quitting – in fact he is expanding.'

The article was four pages long and very detailed, with many tantalising tit-bits provided by executives who, as the article said, had resigned over the past year 'complaining about the way the group was run'. Obviously in view of its sources, some disgruntled and all of them vengeful, the article was sensational and caused maximum damage. The opening paragraph was lethal:

> A Luxembourg-registered holding company and its Bahamian-registered bank. A network of faltering Third World Banks riddled with bad debt. Complex inter-group transactions. An autocratic entrepreneur, executive jets and champagne lifestyle. Sounds familiar? The bank in question is not technically a bank at all but a banking network known as Meridien BIAO. Thus it has no banking license, nor home supervisor nor central bank of last resort. Like its ultimate parent company, ITM International, Meridien BIAO is registered in Luxembourg but does not operate there. The creation of African entrepreneur Andrew Sardanis, it is a holding company with equity stakes in 30 subsidiaries including 20 banks in Africa, service companies in New York, London and Paris and a subsidiary in Hamburg. But Meridien BIAO is severely short of capital...

After giving a reasonably accurate account of the merger with BIAO it quoted a former executive of the banking group as saying:

The complexity of the job of running it is huge because of the diversity of the entities, the two different cultures, the shortage of foreign exchange and trained personnel and personal safety. I mean, staff get killed [an utterly malicious comment against us and against Africa – nobody ever got killed or had been in immediate danger]. But Africans hope the Sardanis gambit will give them a chance to succeed where colonial power failed. Sardanis is viewed as an African's African…

And it continued:

Against a background of severe recession and political turbulence and precious little hard currency, Sardanis, however well intentioned, took on perhaps more than he could handle and may be expanding too rapidly. He is playing a high-wire act say former executives to keep the banking network together. While he and his senior executives live a champagne lifestyle flying in chartered aircraft, first class or Concorde and staying in top hotels wherever they go – the group has just bought a $9 million second hand Gulfstream jet which Sardanis insists is needed to overcome the difficulties of travel in Africa – the meagre profit suggest the group has little money to throw around. Yet the fundamental problem is less of extravagance and more that the group's capital resources are being severely stretched…

It went on to describe me as 'charming, affable and hard-working', and concluded:

…He also lives well. He keeps apartments in both London and New York, [bought in 1971 and 1975 long before Meridien was even thought of] as well as a large, modern open plan house [a parody of Chaminuka – it was designed after an African village; the land was bought in 1973 and the 'village' was completed in 1978] surrounded by its own private game park [the first in Zambia, licensed in 1979 – long before we had anything to do with banking]…But Sardanis is first and foremost a businessman with a Mediterranean instinct for trading and autocratic management style, according to former colleagues. He respects ruthlessness in business having applied it himself on more than one occasion…

By the time the article was written we had been in existence for more than 20 years. It would have been unnatural if the original team had remained intact. People leave for greener pastures, others to set up on their own, yet others are asked to leave or are dismissed having reached their level of incompetence. This is life and this is a normal business process, and I never claimed that ITM was a welfare organisation. The article, I learned later, was prompted by an executive who had left MIBL a few months earlier. He fancied himself as a great deal-maker and sneered at all other banking work, but as time went by his deals became more fancy and convoluted, and so few and far between that I decided that he could not chew gum and walk at the same time and was costing too much money. But the article managed to present my parting with senior staff as a failure unique to myself and the group.

If the truth be known the opposite was in fact the case. I did not recognise early enough that some of the original partners were not capable of rising to the demands of running a much larger and complex group. And that the prejudices and personal goals of others were at variance with the thinking and strategies of the group. A minor catharsis took place in the late 1980s when we parted company with some of the original partners. I should have taken that as a signal for more radical reform. I should have closed or radically reduced the London office then.

But, instead, I took the departures as an inevitable process. We had started the group when we were all very young; we were a kind of rainbow coalition with very diverse backgrounds but a common goal: to create an African enterprise; not a foreign conglomerate operating in Africa, but an enterprise that placed the development of Africa and its people at the top of the agenda. But personal goals change with the years as families grow up and different social needs and influences take over. Ethnic backgrounds also play a role in people's outlooks, especially in mid-life years, when most people tend to get closer to the collective thinking of the society they originate from. In some Gujarat families, success is more likely to be measured by the size of one's personal wealth or one's own business and not by any other achievement or the prestige of an executive position. So I was not surprised to see colleagues from East Africa opting out in order to start on their own. I helped by buying their shares in ITM or by selling to them group companies that no longer fitted into the group's game plan, and gave them an opportunity to start. We always tried to be generous, and most ITM executives who left us to go on their own prospered, building on the nucleus they had obtained from us. They remained friends and most of them were grateful for both the ITM experience and the new start we provided. Except for two Gujarati brothers from Tanzania, who left in 1987; they sold their shares to us and they bought from us some companies and other assets in the UK and Tanzania. But three years later, in 1990, after they had read our 1989 results, they wanted more. In a letter dated 13 February 1990 the older brother wrote to me:

> It would be hypocritical of me not to admit that my family and I are not quite bitter and sensitive [sic] about the way we were treated by nearly all of our

previous partners whom we considered as more than our closest friends. We feel we have been taken advantage of especially at our weakest point by totally insensitive and inequitable actions taken individually and collectively. However it does not help to go over history in too much detail. We think that now that the group has had a good two years and can see a bright future some amends can be made by both parties to at least balm the wounds.

He went on to calculate that, on the basis of the 1989 accounts, the net asset value of the group had risen to $292 per share and the profit to $70 per share, and he wanted more for the shares he had sold three years earlier. But, as the saying goes, 'you cannot eat your cake and have it too'. He had had his cake in 1987, I told him, and he could not have it again in 1990.

Another partner had to leave because I did not trust him any more. The saying 'he arrives late, he leaves early and in between you do not know where he is' fitted him perfectly. And in his case it could be expanded to 'or who he works for: the group or himself'.

A major contributor to Stephanie Cooke's article was David Campbell a former senior executive of RST Resources, our New York commodity trading company. He had left us in July 1993 to set up his own group 'Global Mineral and Metals'. He was an extremely astute trader and I did not want to lose him, but in December 1992, he got it in his head that we should participate, together with Sumitomo in a copper squeeze on the London Metal Exchange (LME) and make lots of money. RST stood to make $40 million, he said and he needed the bonus that would come with it, in order to build his dream house in the Hamptons, on New York's Long Island. He had asked us for a $2 million loan for this purpose, but, after a quick consultation with some of my senior colleagues, I refused. (My number two who would later become the chairman of Global Minerals and Metals (GMMC) had suggested that I should buy him a copy of Tom Wolfe's *The Bonfire of the Vanities*, instead.)

The tactic proposed had been suggested by 'Mr Copper himself', who promised to provide the finance and underwrite possible losses. 'Mr Copper' was the nickname of a Mr Hamanaka, the Japanese trader in charge of Sumitomo's copper division. He was also referred to as 'Mr 5%', because he was reputed to be handling 5% of the world's traded copper. The proposed tactic had come up before and I asked for legal advice. Our lawyers were unequivocal that the operation would be illegal in the United States. And worse than that, as far as I was concerned, it would have been frowned upon in Zambia. I refused to sanction RST's participation, whereupon Campbell embarked upon a well-coordinated plan to break away from the Group. Together with other RST executives they set up a Delaware company in April 1993, while they were still working with us, and over the next several months they all left. At one stage they indicated that they wanted to buy RST and we commenced negotiations, but they wanted it for nothing, which they effectively achieved by poaching its staff.

Hamanaka in association with various metal trading companies including Global, did indeed carry out some spectacular market squeezes on the LME over the next couple of years, but inevitably the scandal broke out in mid-1996. Sumitomo had lost some $3 billion on copper trades, and Hamanaka ended up in jail for forgery and fraud. The New York trio, reduced to a twosome by then, did face a number of class action suits, and together with Sumitomo had to pay large sums of money in out of court settlements. And the US Commodities Futures Trading Commission (CFTC) also opened a case against them, but after five years of investigations the Division of Enforcement filed a motion asking the Commission to dismiss the case.

The order of dismissal of the CFTC complaint against Global Minerals and Metals Corporation, its principal, R. David Campbell, and its chief copper trader, Carl Alm, stated:

> The Division asserts that the case has consumed an unexpectedly large amount of time and resources and it will require a disproportionate share of resources for the foreseeable future. The misconduct alleged occurred nine years ago, the complaint was issued five years ago, yet no hearing on the merits has taken place and none is imminent. Other actors in the manipulation scheme at issue here have settled with the commission and paid significant civil monetary penalties. In these circumstances and as further discussed below the Division states that its limited resources could be used more effectively on other matters.

In giving the background of the case the order of dismissal added:

> The Complaint also charged Merrill Lynch & Co., Inc. and two of its subsidiaries with aiding and abetting Global and Sumitomo. The subsidiaries settled the charges, agreeing to pay $15 million civil monetary penalty, and the Complaint was dismissed against the corporate parent. ...A separate enforcement action against Sumitomo resulted in a settlement pursuant to which it paid $150 million in civil monetary penalties and restitution...

After discussing its reasons in great detail the Division of Enforcement concluded:

> The Commission's interest in discovering and deterring manipulation generally and the copper scheme in particular was vindicated substantially through its successful prosecutions of Sumitomo and Merrill Lynch. At this juncture, the Commission cannot prudently continue to spend limitless sums on a case in

which major goals have been achieved, but which cannot be concluded without litigating ancillary issues that have no likely prospect of being resolved expeditiously. The Commission's overall policies will not be irreparably damaged if the case against these respondents cannot go forward...

So, my ex-employees survived. But a lot of evidence was collected by CFTC, and my lawyer in New York obtained copies of thousands of pages in preparation for a lawsuit I commenced against them. Some faxes exchanged between Hamanaka and Campbell in their own handwriting, for confidentiality purposes, no doubt, make interesting reading. The elaborate mating dance, circumspectly phrased in case the note fell into the wrong hands, the anxiety expressed by Hamanaka about 'their joint operation' being found out, and the need 'to find perfect excuse to protect me [Hamanaka] to continue our relation including joint operation' and the rallying cry ' I will try my best and I am confident with my ability... to manage everything for big success on someday in the near future; let us think and work hard for our dream' sound a bit pathetic now, but no doubt they pumped the adrenalin then.

Campbell's responses reserved large doses of venom for RST and the ITM Group. Phrases such as 'GMMC [Campbell's company] has the ability to make very large, and serious trouble for RST/ITM in Zambia, thereby eliminating ITM/RST as competitors', 'We must first kill ITM/RST and then establish the business [GMMC].' 'To succeed we must kill ITM and RST', constantly repeated in Campbell's faxes, are chilling even now, 13 years after the event. And the gradual recruitment of RST's staff over a period of time, gave him the added advantage of making him privy to RST's business plans and strategies, which manifested itself throughout that weird correspondence.

The previous chapters show that our liquidity took a turn for the worse when we took over BIAO, first, because it took almost two years before we received the ADB and BOAD capital subscriptions, and because we were not able to get additional subscribers and had to absorb 74% of the combined group instead of the 51% we had originally anticipated. But the liquidity problems had been exaggerated by the renegade team spreading rumours on the New York market, initially to make me sell RST cheap and later in order to knock RST out as a competitor. ING Bank, one of our main bankers, was unequivocal about it: 'We are firmly of the view that a great deal of information about RST and ITM, not all positive, was put into the market by the former management of RST itself.' We did lose some bank lines but, by the time the *Euromoney* article was written, I had been able to replace most of them.

But *Euromoney* provided a new opportunity to spread the rumour to an even wider audience and left them with the impression that we were squandering depositor's funds. Apartments in London and New York and a 'modern open plan house surrounded by its own private game park' (a philistine's view of Chaminuka, which was modelled after an African village) reeked of extravagance and made people think that depositors' money had been misused, but all those were acquired in the 1970s, long before we got involved in banking. And how do you explain to Stephanie Cook and the public at large that, in the eyes of the family, Chaminuka was a labour of love and not an extravagance, and that all the money that had been invested in it belonged to the family, long before Meridien was even conceived, and that we were planning to retire there because we had made Zambia our home wholeheartedly and irrevocably, and our decision was non-negotiable. The alternative, I guess, should have been to follow the expatriate standards and invest for our retirement abroad.

All those, and private jets, do go with luxury hotels, champagne and high living, and are sure to offend the sense of probity of the average person and raise question marks in the minds of the average banker about extravagance and waste. But we had planes before we bought BIAO, as the reader will have gathered from previous chapters and the various planes we operated over the

In the company plane with Henry Shikopa, my friend and partner since 1958. There were always papers to read and discuss between destinations.

135

years were always stationed in Lusaka and used as African workhorses (they never left the continent unless they needed service), where distances are huge and means of communication are scarce. As I say in Chapter 1 of this book, we used private aeroplanes to travel from day one – otherwise we could not have grown the way we did.

Sure, you could fly from Niamey to Bamako on Air Afrique, if you had a few days to waste. Sometimes you might have to go to Paris or Abidjan to get there. And if you wanted to go from Lusaka to Lagos you could do so via London, or if you wanted to chance it you could use the Bulgarian Airways weekly flight from Sofia via Harare, which we did do from time to time. But the Bulgarian airline might fly in to Harare or it might not, and if you set up appointments in advance you might not be able to honour them. The 'Caviar Vodka and Hope' (our translation of Bulgarian's flight identification letters: CVH) airline was not exactly reliable, but it did serve Russian caviar and vodka on board. And if after Lagos you wanted to return to Lusaka you could do so in CVH via Sofia, or more likely via London; or, if you needed to go to Abidjan, you could again use Air Afrique, if it happened to be flying, or fly to London and then Paris.

As regards luxury hotels, I am sure there must be plenty to choose from in Bangui, Ndjamena, Niamey, Ouagadougou, Bamako, Dakar, Banjul, Conakry, Freetown, Monrovia (before and during the civil war), Accra, Lomé, Abidjan,[1] Lagos, Douala, Yaoundé, Libreville, Luanda, Gaborone, Francistown, Harare, Maputo, Dar es Salaam, Kampala, etc. Except that, unfortunately, I did not come across any. Personally, I was grateful to find running water in a hotel (I hated having to use water out of buckets in the room, when the town water was cut off). Even though the town water was fine to use for a shower one never brushed one's teeth with it. And I never accepted ice cubes in my drink in most of those towns. After an experience in Ndjamena, when my entire party except me got sick, I came to the conclusion that ice must be the preferred carrier of salmonella. And high living? I guess you can find it in Africa, but I did not.

But the aversion to planes was not confined to *Euromoney*. My number two made the following comments in writing when he signed the resolution for the purchase of the plane Stephanie Cooke talked about in her article:

At the risk of boring all concerned beyond measure I would like to place on record that in signing this document I am bowing to majority opinion. I have not been convinced of the wisdom of the transaction and I personally do not support it. However, henceforth I shall shut up about it.

But his objection was not against using planes to travel within Africa. He thought that chartering planes was preferable. It might have been, if the only source of planes was not South Africa and if the white pilots from South Africa did not feel so out of place in remote Africa in those days, and if they knew how to handle the flight controllers when they were filing flight plans or paying landing fees, and if we did not have to pay for the dead leg Johannesburg–Lusaka–Johannesburg.

But a bigger avalanche than the *Euromoney* would hit us within a few months.

18. THE ELUSIVE SUPERVISION

I was quite sanguine about the 50% devaluation of the CFA franc, which had been overdue by almost a decade, because the various participating countries could not agree at what level it should be devalued. In fact, the CFA franc is a contrived kind of currency, made exchangeable at par between countries whose economies are at such variance that they might as well be on different planets. There are two zones, the West African and the Central African. In West Africa at that time the biggest economy was Côte d'Ivoire's and in Central Africa it was Cameroon's. But there were countries in each zone that were amongst the poorest in the world, such as Niger, Burkina and Mali in West Africa and Central African Republic and Chad in Central Africa. The logic behind maintaining the same parity for Cameroon and Chad or Côte d'Ivoire and Niger, for example, escaped me. That the devaluation was going to happen early in 1994 had been common knowledge from the middle of the previous year. Final consultations between the various countries and France had been going on quite openly. But we could not have hedged against the impending devaluation loss because there was no market for the CFA franc.

The only way to hedge against the possible devaluation losses was by keeping the network banks' spare cash out of the two zones, but the central banks became very strict about it. While it was easy for the French banks to keep their surplus cash in French francs, we were not allowed to convert it into dollars. But I devised a scheme that solved the problem and would have mitigated the losses. By the end of 1993 I had made each bank use all its spare cash to store in its vaults large sums in US dollar travellers' cheques. Some francophone Meridien BIAO banks had in their vaults as much as $8 million in travellers' cheques, which would have given us a big enough profit to offset the effects of the devaluation, and much-needed liquidity in addition. Or so I thought, until I landed in Libreville, Gabon, a week or so after the official announcement.

The travellers' cheques had been sold the week before the devaluation was announced. There were none in the vaults. One of the French managers initially tried to present this as a major success on his part. He had made a 15 to 20% profit, he explained. I was thunderstruck and angry – he had made 50% loss, I shouted. He became aggressive and abusive. He told me that he was a respectable banker (as distinct from a Greek-Cypriot-turned-Zambian wheeler-dealer, I guess), and so long as he had the TCs in the bank he could not refuse to sell them. I checked his customers. They were Lebanese businessmen and some settler companies. He was not stupid and he knew why they were buying travellers' cheques, and he must have made a personal fortune out of it. And he was not the only one. I would soon discover that, with only a couple of exceptions, all the managers had done the same. And Burkina went one further: it refunded F CFA 750 million ($1.5 million) to a Lebanese trader for the devaluation loss he suffered on his deposits with the bank! But at least we did not have a controlling interest there, though we did have a 40% stake.

After Libreville I was due to visit Ndjamena, the capital of Chad, but the manager phoned to say that the authorities had refused us landing permission. And, yes, of course, he had sold the travellers' cheques before devaluation, he said, and at a very good profit. The same story – but I was determined to get to Ndjamena and vent my anger. I told him to get landing permission by the time I got there, but when overhead I discovered that we were not allowed to land obviously at his behest. I proceeded to Nairobi and from there back to Lusaka.

I have thought about the behaviour of the managers of the Meridien BIAO banks in French-speaking Africa ever since. Would they have behaved the same way if they had been working for BNP, or any other French institution? Or did they think that the opportunity was too good to miss and to hell with us, we were foreigners anyway? In my business career, spanning half a century, I have been taken for a ride by crooks of many nationalities, Anglo-Saxons, Indians, Cypriots, various Africans, Americans, etc. I can only say that none of them ever behaved as blatantly as some of the French managers of the Meridien BIAO banks in French-speaking Africa did in January 1994. (I would discover later that some of the Cypriots in our construction group deserved a close second.) And the problem with dishonest employees is that they do not just stop there. They have to create stories about you that put you in bad light, as if this would be justification for their own dishonesty. In our case, they started subverting us through the central banks and other governmental authorities. But that would come later.

In spite of all the problems that were springing up in my way every day, I was still determined to make the Meridien BIAO banking enterprise a success. After the collapse of BCCI and the scandals that unfolded as a result, the focus turned on Third World banks. We were small, and, as Stephanie Cooke had said in her article, our sums were trivial.

> ...Approximately $1.2 billion of depositors money, most of it in Africa. But more is at stake than money. The Sardanis venture is the first attempt to merge a pan-African network, under African control.

We were persuaded that we needed a domicile for the banking group. We were told that we needed a regulator that would undertake the consolidated supervision of all the banks in the group, and we decided to set about looking for one in order to stop the sneering that Meridien BIAO was a network and not a bank. Our natural home was Africa, of course, but most African countries operated very stringent exchange control regimes that would have made investment decisions cumbersome and almost impossible to implement. And no African central bank had the capability of coping with the work involved in supervising such a diverse and widespread group as ours. Except for South Africa, which was on the verge of democratic change, and I thought I would test the ground.

In Pretoria I was received by an officer of the banking supervision department, an Afrikaner. Before I even had a chance to state the purpose of my visit he said: 'I know who you are. You go around Africa and sign cheques in exchange for banking licences, and if you think you are going to do the same here you can forget it.' I did not expect to be the darling of South African whites, but such open hostility took me by surprise. By that time I had become so despondent with the BIAO venture that for a minute I considered that the best response would have been to give him a rundown of the thinking behind the merger of Meridien and BIAO and the woes that visited me as a result – but the dignity of Africa was at stake. I was not going to give this Afrikaner the pleasure of gloating over African 'incompetence' and 'unreliability' and whatever else he would conclude was the cause, in order to confirm his prejudices. So I explained to him that the success and acceptance of the group was entirely due to its philosophy – one that had evolved in order to best serve the continent: the deliberate choice of the local mass market of Africa instead of the multinational company and settler business sector, etc. and the preference for local management over expatriate. The incredulity in his eyes shone so strong that I soon brought the meeting to an end and left.

But the Reserve Bank of South Africa was not the only one that had views on black bankers and the indigenous market at that time. The deputy governor of the Reserve Bank of Botswana, another South African from Cape Town, had similar views but while the one in Pretoria was blunt, the one in Gabarone was openly patronising. When I explained to him that our philosophy was to appoint local management because it was more in tune with the market place he looked at me pityingly and said: 'We do not really approve causing conflict between people's family loyalties and professional duty. Tribal and clan loyalties are so strong in African societies,' he lectured, 'that they will inevitably force local managers into making the wrong decisions on loans, so we would rather have expatriates in such positions.' The attitude in Pretoria at that stage of South Africa's development did not really surprise me but I found the attitude in Gaborone, 25 years after independence lamentable.

I had not been allowed to visit South Africa for almost four decades, even though I always had the feeling that the South Africans took particular interest in keeping up with my movements. The feeling was reinforced in the mid-1980s when my office in Lusaka caught fire one night. We occupied the top floor of Kafue House, an eight-storey building in downtown Lusaka at the time. The amazing thing is that the fire was noticed at 2 a.m. by a passing motorist, who informed the fire brigade and the police. He was never identified. As the fire appeared to have just started not much damage was done, even within my office. It did not spread to other rooms. The police came to the conclusion that the fire had started from the air-conditioner, but the incident has puzzled me ever since. Downtown Lusaka is deserted at that time of the night. The office was located in a kind of cul-de-sac some 300 yards from the main road. As the damage was not significant (my desk remained intact), there could have been no flames by then so how could a passing motorist notice a little smoke rising from the eighth floor of a very long office block 300 yards from the main road at 2 a.m.? My conclusion was that the person who made the telephone call and the person who started the fire were one and the same. And the fire was not meant to damage, but just to warn. At that time some ANC friends occasionally spent weekends at Chaminuka, and in the sick mind of the South African spies who circulated freely in Lusaka in those days the visits may have been interpreted as conspiracy sessions.

When I was able to visit, in 1990, I found my early trips to Johannesburg very educative. The first thing that struck me was the inefficiency of the hotels. You could check in to the Hotel de l'Amitié in Bamako, or the Pullman in Ouagadougou, in five minutes, but at Johannesburg's Sandton Sun it would take you 20. The white girls at the reception took their time and would never interrupt telephone conversations, even when they were manifestly personal, in order to serve you. But what I found very revealing were the banking halls.

Not a single black teller or even back office staff. There may have been a handful of Indians and a sprinkling of coloureds but never any blacks. I shall discuss the slow progress of South Africa towards the creation of 'one nation' in a later chapter.

Our goal of consolidated supervision would remain elusive. We spent a lot of money in professional advice and travel trying to locate a suitable jurisdiction and we approached many authorities, but our efforts came to nothing. We did approach the New York banking authorities at one stage, and during one meeting an American official remarked: 'Do we really want to send our people to all those countries to check you out? And do you know how much this will cost you because, if we agree to do it, we shall charge you for it?' I always admired the Americans for cutting through verbiage and 'high-sounding' ideas and getting down to brass tacks. Thinking back on it now I think we should not have bothered. But we were brainwashed into it. We thought that we needed an overseas domicile in order to run a successful pan-African operation. We were wasting our time, though, trying to get the Western countries to cooperate. In their minds we were romantic fools, at best, and reality would catch up with us after we collapsed, and at worst we were a bunch of crooks who should be kept at bay. And, in any case, by that time they knew about our success in the market place, so why should they assist us to compete with their banks?

We were attempting all this after the BCCI scandal, when everybody blamed the Bank of England for not exercising closer supervision over it. BCCI had some 40 branches in Britain and could have been taken as a British bank so the criticism of the Bank of England had some justification. In our case the Bank of England was quite open about one reason it did not want to have anything to do with us: our place of business – Africa – scared it. It was not just the economic climate that worried them; it was also the fact that they would have to place considerable reliance on overseas supervisors, whom they obviously did not trust. (The minutes of the relevant meeting read: 'The Meridien Banking group consisted of a large number of banks in a variety of countries quite a number of which the Bank of England looked upon with suspicion in banking supervisory terms.')

Since then the consolidated supervision concept has been refined and I believe it is still kept under constant review. But, whatever the outcome, in the end it is the supervisor in the country of operation who has to remain vigilant. Years later I would discover that this was indeed the case. It was the Bank of Japan that penalised the Citigroup's Tokyo subsidiary for breaking Japanese rules in respect to selling products not allowed to private banking customers in

Japan, and the British Financial Services Authority that fined the same group $25 million over a controversial euro-zone deal. It was not the Fed or any other United States authority that discovered the infractions and imposed the sanctions.

With hindsight, I now know that we should not have bothered with Western presence or Western supervision. We should have remained an African network. Our banks in each country were locally incorporated; they were not branches. And in each individual country where we had a bank the local central bank had full supervisory power over it and exercised it with diligence in order to ensure that all the banks complied with the local rules. If we had concentrated on Africa and stayed out of the limelight we could still have operated with third-party foreign correspondent banks that would have competed for our business as our volumes increased. But we held the mistaken view that in order to provide better service we needed a toehold in the West. We thought that from a Western base it would have been easier to raise capital. But Western capital then was very wary of Africa, as indeed it is today.

Even though 1994 had started extremely badly on the international level, in the real world of Africa, where we belonged, Meridien BIAO was prospering and making great inroads against the established colonial banks.

The banking hall of the main Lusaka branch of Meridien BIAO Bank Zambia. Spacious, pleasant and efficient.

19. MERIDIEN BIAO: BANK OF THE PEOPLE

At grass-roots level, the Meridien BIAO operations in Africa were wildly successful. Most of our banks were moving from strength to strength, securing the number two or number three slots in the local rankings and their customer base and their deposits were expanding. The reason was simple. For a start, our products were tailored around the needs of African society and they appealed to the masses. The colonial banks had been established on the continent for decades and they had the handicap of being colonial. They did business with settlers and multinational companies and they did not care about the locals. They did not trust black customers and they considered them a nuisance: small deposits and small savings accounts, which they did not want and tried to discourage by setting high minimum balances for current accounts and low interest rates for savings accounts. And as they had no confidence in Africa they were against new ventures. Their stock advice in the 1980s was that more difficult times lay ahead and any new venture was bound to fail.

Our point of view was exactly the opposite. We believed that new investment in Africa would come from within, and always encouraged everybody who wanted to start up. Pioneers in this minor renaissance in Zambia and other Eastern African countries were long-established Indian families that had made their fortunes in trading and started turning their attention to industry. A young scion of an Indian family conceived the idea of a spinning mill that would process Zambian cotton into yarn for export. The advice of the bank where the family had had a business account for some 70 years was simple: 'Do not do it; you will lose the family money and you will be disgraced.' He came to us. Not only was the project eminently bankable, but the exchange control regulations at the time, which allowed foreign exchange earners to sell their export proceeds on the market, made it more so. The project turned out to be one of the more successful new industries in Zambia. On similar thinking, another bank tried to discourage the first safari lodge in the Luangwa Valley,

One of the millions of hard-working and cheerful peasants of Africa. This one, from Uganda, is carrying green bananas to the market on his bicycle. But his brothers, elsewhere, could be carrying charcoal, or vegetables, or chicken, or pigs, or goats, cycling daily many miles to the market and back, in order to earn a meagre living.

conceived by an internationally renowned wildlife conservationist. Again, we financed it and it is still one of the many successful lodges that have since filled the valley.

I do not know to what extent the attitude of the colonial banks towards the local market was being shaped by their head offices or by the local management. All senior managers were mainly metropolitan and they had no faith in the African countries where they had been attached. The few local managers had no input in decision-making. They were specially chosen because of their willingness to remain subordinate and never contradict their masters. At board level there was a sprinkling of prominent locals and for cosmetic reasons a local non-executive chairman – none of them chosen in order to get closer to the market place and its people. The choice was usually made from a corps of cocktail party floaters, preferably with some foreign education and Anglicised accents and the ability to echo the views of their patrons in profound-sounding affirmation. I was occasionally invited to lunches at banks in Zambia and I was always appalled at the quality of their senior local staff, most of them too old and under-educated. The discussions over lunch would invariably present a typically expatriate version of the local scene that I had difficulty in relating to the reality, but, to my surprise, none of the locals around the table would ever attempt to correct it.

We were different. Our senior management was overwhelmingly local, our cadres were young, well-educated, aggressive locals and our client profile was local too: the local businessman, the professional, the marketeer, the jobber, the small contractor, the guy who may never have had a bank account before. And, of course, the local entrepreneur, the promoter of new ventures, who gradually brought to us some of the old, established family businesses that wanted to break into new ventures.

Savings accounts in colonial banks were shunned? We encouraged them, streamlined the procedures and made them profitable. We gave savings depositors differently coloured chequebooks and the right to issue up to five cheques per month, in order to pay for their electricity, their water and their rent and withdraw cash, instead of cluttering up the banking halls in order to fulfil the complicated withdrawal procedures of our competitors. Current accounts in the colonial banks did not attract any interest, even though local interest rates were at stratospheric levels? We followed the example of American banks and paid modest interest on current accounts, so money that had remained under the mattress and never entered the banking system started trickling towards Meridien BIAO. We figured that, large and desirable as settler and multinational company deposits might be, the sum total of the money in the hands of the common man ought to be bigger. And we set about pioneering banking services and products for the average man in the street.

We had started product innovation in Zambia long before the BIAO merger. And after that we expanded the product development division by drawing into it marketing staff from elsewhere in the network, until we had a multinational group in Lusaka that represented the collective social culture of the countries we operated in. In the product development department, together with the Zambians, we had Liberians, and Malians, and Togolese, and Ivorians and Cameroonians, all working with my son Stelios, designing products suitable for the common man. We knew his way of life and his goals and his everyday concerns. We knew the anguish of not having enough money to pay for the children's school fees and uniforms, or the need to make up the shortfall at the beginning of each term.

A 60-second TV commercial encapsulated the Meridien philosophy. It was translated into French and was shown in all countries we operated. Its lyrics were:

Africa, Our World
A constantly changing world
A world that is growing
And Developing
With the help of Meridien BIAO, the Pan African Bank

But as in life, you should never stop growing
So Africa must continue to grow
To become a more prosperous place
Where our future generations can flourish

And along each step of the way Meridien BIAO will be there
Helping you with those moments
That are the foundations to building a better life
A better Africa
A better World

The commercial opened with a woman shopping in an African market, then driving away in her car. It covered all aspects of African progress – people picking crops, mechanical harvesting, buildings in progress, kids in a school playground, a graduation ceremony, new cars, new homes, people playing golf, breathtaking African landscape, etc. The accompanying African jingle became wildly successful.

We knew of the thirst for education and the aspiration for college education. We knew that lack of capital was the main obstacle to turning a good artisan into a contractor or a marketeer into a businessman. And we were convinced that that was the way for African societies to grow – from the bottom up. We created flexible products to deal with those needs and in the process we drew people into the banking system instead of shutting them out. We were not reinventing the wheel. The products we offered were not original. Stelios, who had worked in the United States for a decade, and his team were adapting American banking products to suit Africa's needs, and this is why Meridien BIAO became so successful. Despite our trials and tribulations at the international level, locally our banks were making great strides gaining market share in their individual countries. And, even though we were accused of not being bankers (because we did not have many whites at the top, I guess), the group brimmed with astute African bankers. The best-trained were those we took over with the Chase branches we bought in Cameroon and Liberia, and others who joined us from Citibank, attracted by our open-minded policies. Our view was that the very few American banks operating in Africa trained bankers; the colonial banks trained bank clerks.

The colonial bankers were livid. We were not bankers and were spoiling the market, they complained, which in their parlance meant that we disturbed the serenity of the colonial banking profession, which allowed them to play golf every Thursday afternoon and go home after 4:30 p.m. every day to play tennis or chess with their friends. Banking was easy before Meridien came on the scene. Banks would collect deposits and invest in treasury bills or government bonds, earning exorbitant interest rates, which in countries such as Zambia the government had to issue in order to raise more funds to retire the treasury bills and the bonds that it contracted when Chiluba and his then governor were 'sleeping, breathing and dreaming structural adjustment' and pushed interest rates to 200% per annum. And as our success testified, we were bankers – modern African bankers, free of colonial hang-ups. But in the crazed political climate of the post-Kaunda era in Zambia it would come to haunt us. If the colonial banks criticised Meridien they were surely right! They were British, after all, and they knew best.

First we overtook the British Standard Chartered Bank in Zambian market share. And then Stelios's team introduced in Zambia the Meridien Card, an electronic payment system that did away with cash, which at the time was circulating in ludicrously small denominations, the highest note in circulation being worth about one dollar because, in typical fashion, the Bank of Zambia was slow in catching up with the times and the highest currency note circulating in the market was the K1000, worth about 1 dollar. You needed large brown bags of notes in order to buy anything, never mind anything of value. The Meridien Card did away with all that. You could charge the card from your bank account and download it at a grocery store, a department store, a hotel, or wherever you needed to make a payment. It was a major coup. Even the London *Times* wrote about the Meridien Card with admiration under the title 'The smart card that is leaping ahead of western banking'. But the Meridien Card's function did not just end as an electronic purse. It was also used as a customer identification card, thus expediting service in the banking hall. If I remember correctly, we were able to reduce the time required to service the average customer to below a couple of minutes, a fraction of the time it took the other banks.

All these innovations propelled Meridien BIAO Zambia ahead of Barclays Bank into the number two bank in Zambia (the biggest bank was and is the government-owned Zambia National Commercial Bank) in terms of market share, Stelios announced to me proudly over the phone, some time in mid-1994. I congratulated him, and as a father I felt very proud of him, but as I put the phone down I wondered what retaliation we should expect. Barclays fancied itself as the last bastion of the empire, and after African independence its local chief executive bestowed upon himself the mantle of the colonial governor and thought of himself as the most important Briton around. Barclays would accept the position of number two to the Zambia National Commercial Bank, but it would not tolerate an upstart local bank pushing it into number three. And it was powerful with the Bank of England.

The discomfiture of Barclays with our success was reported in graphic detail in 1997, when a Mr Gary Marsh, Barclays' marketing manager, gave an interview to the *Times* of Zambia. Written by a Mr J. Kopulande under the title 'Marsh: the man who thwarted the Meridien BIAO threat', the article read:

> The existence of Meridien BIAO bank in the mid 90s did not only threaten the market share of the local banks but international banks as well. One of the international banks put on tenterhooks was Barclays Bank Zambia, which went to the extent of 'importing' an expert to combat the Meridien threat. BBZ recruited Gary Marsh from the United Kingdom to be head of marketing. 'They (BBZ) were looking for someone of my skills, my experience and my background to challenge what Meridien was doing', Mr. Marsh says.

BBZ wanted him to bring in some new products, new advertising campaigns, improve customer service and win back the market share the bank had lost. Meridien had been very successful on the retail side in the personal sector. They were offering better service than all the other banks at the time. The bank had quickly moved into second position behind the Zambia National Commercial Bank They had two very good branches, especially the main branch and they brought in the smart card at a time when no other banks had any cards. One of the major issues Mr. Marsh tackled vigorously was customer service. 'Quite frankly we were appalling; we were very poor at customer service in Zambia. All the other banks, except Meridien, were certainly different, but Barclays, without exception, we were poor', Mr. Marsh observes.

To turn it around he introduced a system of measuring customer service. A consultant was engaged in 1995 to undertake market research and make reports on a quarterly basis. 'What other banks in other African countries have done within Barclays is simply to take the Barclays model from the UK and impose it on their customers. This is wrong because the needs of the Zambian people are different and we quickly established that from the market,' he says… What troubled Barclay's customers most was queuing up and the long time it took to get their money. They also wanted new products introduced. Having 'tasted' the Meridien card they wanted cards and automatic teller machines, where cash is obtainable 24 hours a day…

So much for the myth about the competence or otherwise of the Meridien bankers; they were good enough to rattle Barclays so much that it had to import a UK expert to catch up. The simpler and more effective solution would, of course, have been to head-hunt some of our staff – but, no, they were Zambians and therefore not good enough for Barclays.

But I had good reason to fear the foreign competitors' reaction at higher levels. In 1992 the Bank of England had closed down the London-based Mount Banking Corporation, a Kenyan-Asian-owned bank whose depositors were, almost exclusively, Kenyan Asians resident overseas. *The Financial Times* of 6 October 1992 reported the news as follows:

The Bank of England took the highly unusual step of applying to the High Court on Saturday for a winding up petition… The company secretary and one of the solicitors to Mount Banking said last night that the petition was issued without notice and that the directors 'know of no grounds to explain the shutdown' of the bank. The Bank of England has powers under section 92 of the 1987 Banking Act to apply to the High Court for a winding-up petition as laid down in the 1986 Insolvency Act. In a statement issued at the weekend, it emphasised that it did not allege insolvency as one of the grounds for the petition and was acting in the interests of the depositors on 'just and equitable grounds'.

Mount banking also meets another requirement for authorization – the so called 'four eyes criterion,' in other words that there is more than one person controlling the business. Mount Banking has six directors. That leaves two other issues: whether a bank is conducting its business prudently and whether the directors and managers have exercised fit and proper control for the positions they occupy... The provisional liquidators said yesterday that they expected 'substantially all' the creditors to be repaid...

The mystery of the demise of the Mount Banking Corporation was never solved. Many years later, after a series of appeals, the case came up before the House of Lords and its decision was that there were no grounds for the action, but the decisions of the Bank of England were unchallengeable. In Kenya, Asians believed that the Bank of England acted on information supplied by foreign banks. It occurred to me that we might be due for similar treatment.

But our trailblazing did not end with the marketeer, the small businessman and the entrepreneur. We pioneered a direct payment system within Africa. Our network banks started opening letters of credit on each other directly, not through London or Paris, thus reducing intra-Africa payments to within a few days instead of weeks under the established system. We took the view that, as an African group, we would show faith in Africa's survival and assume that payments between our banks would flow, so we did away with the elaborate country credit risk evaluations carried out in Europe or America that hampered payments within the continent. And we soon discovered that this was appreciated, not only by the African traders but by the multinational companies themselves, so we started getting accounts from them as well. From monetising the money under the mattress, we moved to getting prestige accounts from multinationals, particularly oil majors that operated in more than one African country.

My worst fears about retaliation through the Bank of England materialised sooner that I anticipated. Up to 1990 I used to visit the Bank of England a couple of times a year, accompanied by the chief executive of Meridien. After BIAO came onto the scene the contacts became much more frequent. They revolved around the merger with BIAO, the functions of the London representative office, research on the possibility of British consolidated supervision, and then generally keeping the Bank of England up to date with our latest thinking and actions. But as 1994 wore on we started getting special attention. In a letter dated 6 July, a senior manager sent us the following ludicrously enigmatic, Hercule Poirot, type of letter:

> ...following our earlier helpful visit to see you we would find it most useful to understand in more detail precisely how MIB [Meridien International Bank – our Bahamian Bank] and MICC [Meridien International Credit Corporation – our credit company in London] function here in London particularly in relation to the LC business and any residual treasury type business here.
>
> We would, with your agreement, propose to send a small team led by Peter Phelan to look into these matters. They would find it most useful to meet with the relevant people in MIB/MICC here in London and they would propose to come to your office on Tuesday, 12 July. I know that you may not be available yourself until later in the week but I would hope that the bulk of the mapping could be done with the assistance of your colleagues. Peter would hope to see you when you are available.
>
> As I said this is essentially a fact finding mission to enable us to understand your London operations and the flow of funds associated with the business being undertaken here. We are doing it with your agreement and not after exercise of any formal powers under the Banking Act 1987...

From what I remember they spent quite a few days looking into the details of the London operation, and then left. They left as enigmatically as they arrived. No official conclusion, no comment, except what our staff gathered – that they did not find anything untoward. But after the launch of the Meridien Card, they would come again.

And by that time another bolt from the blue would strike us.

20. 'HOW COME NOBODY HAD GOTTEN SUSPICIOUS?'

For my share of the responsibility for failing to prevent the disastrous loss perpetrated by X I accept the blame, as I have already made clear – and you may judge that share for being anything from total to partial. I am very sorry indeed about the damage this has done to you and your family and indeed to mine and others.

That was the remorseful handwritten note that accompanied a seven-page memorandum I received from my deputy after a dealing room loss of $10 million was discovered at our London office. Like all such losses its magnitude was revealed by instalments; the first assessment was $4.5 million with the manager of our New York office, who was an expert in that field, initially hoping that we might get away with less. By the time we unwound the positions the loss rose to $10 million.

Danae and I were on our way for a week's holiday in Italy when the problem surfaced. She had had a mastectomy a few months before and at the time she was suffering from severe stomach pains. We were terrified that they might be due to metastasis, and when the results of the medical examination came in negative we decided to get away from it all for a week. I should not have given her the news, but she has the uncanny ability to sense when something is wrong, and I had been given the information as I was leaving the office and did not have time to regain my composure. She went straight to the heart of the matter: 'Will the business survive?' she asked. I said that I was very worried with this blow, coming on top of the CFA franc devaluation and everything else that was going wrong in many African countries at the time, particularly Angola, Liberia and Sierra Leone. But we both knew that I was going to fight to save the business, so it was 'chin up' and off on our holiday as planned.

Our London 'dealing room' had not been established for speculative trading in currencies. Its remit was limited to hedging the group currency exposures. As the group dealt in many currencies, British pounds, French francs, Deutsche marks and dollars, we needed to hedge our exposures in order to avoid losses on currency fluctuations. X, the man in charge, was an African who had been doing the same job for Meridien in West Africa. We brought him to London when we centralised the activity. He was a clever person and seemed to know his job well, but he had an overwhelming personality that dominated and intimidated everybody around him. Even though he was not supposed to speculate, his brief being simply to hedge our exposures, he seemed to have got hooked on exotic option combinations which were meant for speculative trading and not for hedging. The particular product that lost us all that money was called a 'butterfly option', which I did not understand and I cannot describe. He did not derive any personal benefit from the operation, but false accounting had been taking place over many months, which none of his two superiors (the manager of MICC and my deputy in London) detected, even though they were in control of the cash flow and had to make bigger and bigger sums available in premiums and margins because X had to keep increasing his trading positions to hide the losses incurred on them. The loss was, in fact, detected by the newly recruited manager of our New York office when he heard that X's Australian assistant was attending a course on exotic option combinations in New York. The Australian would later confess that he had become aware of the problem about six months before, but he did not report it because he thought that they would overcome it; and, inevitably, they got deeper and deeper into it.

I hesitate to say that I had suspected that something was wrong for many months, but I did so from completely superficial and inconsequential factors. I used to spend very little time in London, but when I was there I always went to the office before 7 a.m. I would work out of the boardroom, and at that time of the day anybody who felt inclined to see me could just drop in without appointment – my secretary would not arrive until 9 a.m. For some months preceding the discovery of the loss, X made sure to drop by two or three times during each of my London stays. He would tell me how wonderfully he was doing, how well he was controlling the dealing room and how much more he had learned since he came to London and how much money he was saving the group, etc. I came to the conclusion that something was worrying him; he had something to hide, and I said so to his superiors, who must have attributed this to the eastern Mediterranean side of my personality and ignored it. But I passed on another warning, which they should have taken seriously. On 30 June 1993 I reviewed the performance of the dealing room for the period 1 October 1992 to 31 May 1993, and, on 4 July, I sent the following memo to my number two:

I read the memo re the above. I do not pretend to understand it fully but it appears to me that the activity is much greater than it needs to be. Particularly in view of the fact that the LME copper is now quoted in dollars, I do not see the need for hedging on behalf of RST. That should reduce the activity substantially. I believe Harry (my second son who had been working in RST, in New York) has greater understanding of this and I shall ask him to communicate his comments directly to you.

And I did not stop there. I repeated my warnings at a senior staff meeting in New York in October 1993, and in London in November 1993 and January 1994. But I was talking to the wind. Even though the dealing room's cash demands grew bigger and bigger the two gentlemen in charge of dishing out the money still did not suspect anything untoward. All that is water under the bridge; the cash had gone, and what is left is my deputy's seven-page memorandum of 24 June 1994. Some paragraphs are remarkable:

> …Since the end of last fiscal year (September 30, 1993), I should have been alerted to the fact that something was wrong by the significant cash outflow in margin calls and option premiums. I was not alerted because I was not aware of this outflow. My monitoring of the group cash movements during this period was close and generally continuous but daily receipts into and payments from MIBL's accounts in London came to me only as net total movements… I believed the accuracy of the daily accounts; I did not imagine that such cash outgoings could themselves be losses or demonstrate the existence of losses not shown in the daily accounts… Should I, however, have suspected X of being dishonest or deluded or megalomaniac and done something about it? Obviously yes, and I am desperately unhappy and sorry that I did not… The serious questions about X started at the beginning of October (1993) since when, of course some two thirds of our present losses have been created. They arose from the gamble of the supposed Russian crisis taken by X and Y on 24th September way beyond their authority, which in a couple of days reversed $2.2 million of previous 'profit' and led to your aggressive questioning of X on his performance report for 1993, issued on 4 October (1993). His responses were combative but often woolly. We should have fired X then. I should have started to get scared at that time…

What was the use? My deputy had the problem of immersing himself in the minutiae and not giving himself time to think. He was the biggest 'paper factory' in the group. I did try to get him to snap out of it, but without success. Many a time I pointed out to him that some of the work he spent so much 'initiative-sapping' time on could be done by much lower-level staff costing a fraction of his earnings. Sometime in the mid-1980s, after I had read Primo Levi's book, *The Periodic Table*, I sent him a copy of the following extract:

> ....
>
> ...But in fact at that time I did not yet know the frightening anaesthetic power of company papers, their capacity to hobble, douse, and dull every leap of intuition and every spark of talent. It is well known to the scholarly that all secretions can be harmful or toxic: now under pathological conditions it is not rare that the paper, a company secretion, is reabsorbed to an excessive degree, and puts to sleep, paralyzes or actually kills the organism from which it has been exuded.

The missing line from the above quotation reads 'How come nobody had gotten suspicious?', and that is exactly what my mind was screaming. (I had omitted that line from my memo of the mid-1980s because it was not relevant then.) But that phrase was now screaming in me, and my mind kept repeating it time and again. How was it that the two supervisors of X (my own deputy, no less, and Y, one of the most senior London managers, whose father was a major shareholder) did not get suspicious? And how could my deputy seriously put forward such an array of lame excuses and expect me to accept them? But by the time of the $10 million dealing room loss he was too far gone to change. He was so totally devoted to paperwork that he would spend most of his time, including lunch hours, in his office dictating to his devoted secretary, relegating everything else to secondary importance. If he had given himself more time to think he would have put to the test the statement that he repeatedly makes in his memorandum ('I believed the accuracy of the daily accounts; I did not imagine that such cash outgoings could themselves be losses or demonstrate the existence of losses not shown in the daily accounts...'), and he would have come to the conclusion that something was indeed seriously wrong and would have taken steps to unravel it.

I responded on 27 June 1994 as follows:

> ...You come across as believing that what happened was an act of god. You say you are sorry for the losses but you do not really believe that you should bear any part of the blame. If everybody was doing his job properly it would not have happened. And you go into great lengths to justify why it was right and proper for you to assume that X and all the others were doing their job properly. But is it not the Chief Executive's responsibility to assume the opposite? And should you not have been alerted by the many warning signs that started surfacing from the performance and the repeated warnings from me?

Of course as the most hard working member of the management team, as you very often reminded us recently, you were very busy with your numerous administrative duties and volumes of correspondence that emanates from your office and did not have time to think and take note. But allocating time to thinking is the main duty of the CEO. As I said to you time and again the bureaucratic part of your work (which you love above all other) could be done by a £40,000 a year young lawyer whom you stubbornly refuse to recruit.

... You have to understand that you are the Chief Executive and not the ombudsman of the organization. We cannot afford to give the benefit of the doubt to incompetence, non performance or sabotage until a real disaster forces us to act. It is not my intention to carry on in this vein on paper ... Either you snap out of your present habits and routine and become a real Chief Executive or become the de facto company secretary. I must emphasise that in order to attain the former you need real determination for radical change of habit, attitude, approach and, dare I say it, secretary ...

Clever words and in some ways unfair; after so many years of working together I knew that my deputy could not change and I should have been more restrained. He sent me a deeply thought and dignified reply on 3 September. It was three pages long and ended as follows:

... Over the years I have seen many people fall out of the group. Truly I did not believe it would ever happen to me, despite one or two ominous shudders in the last few years. But recent events and some of our recent exchanges have brought me to a different view, albeit with great sadness and reluctance having devoted half my life to this enterprise and considering the many positive things we have achieved. My conclusion is that in planning the future of the group you should count me out rather than in. That being the case, if you wish me to leave now I would be prepared to do so, but in our present parlous state that may be inappropriate. Certainly I bear a heavy part of the responsibility for this state, but must ask that you do not repeat your recent assertion that the group has been driven into the ground by the option trading losses which I failed to prevent, for they are only one, and though a grievous one not even the largest of a number of things which have brought the group to its present position.

If you wish me to remain for a time I shall continue to serve the group with as much loyalty and energy as always and will seek every opportunity to maintain and improve morale. I shall also go on doing my best to reform myself in as many of the ways called for in your 27 June letter as I reasonably can, though I am unlikely to satisfy you in all areas. However as soon as you consider that we have got past our present very serious problems and can see a period of more stability, please will you arrange for me to step aside from the group ...

But the reality was dismal. The $10 million loss was a direct hit on our bottom line and a blow to our capital adequacy from which it would be difficult to recover, despite the remarkable successes of the Meridien banks in the market place. And as the news spread in the market place, so soon after the poison spread by the *Euromoney* article, it had a major impact on our bank lines and our depositors' confidence. But I was not going to throw in the towel. The group needed a thorough reorganisation and reorientation. But, first and foremost, it needed cash. We needed to sell assets and raise cash in a hurry and we needed to spin off divisions for the same purpose. I had been aware of this problem for some time now and an exercise was already on the way.

In 1991 we had prepared through a broker in Washington DC an offering of convertible preferred stock in order to raise $55 million for ITM. We had to postpone that offering as the negotiations for BIAO got under way, because the acquisition would have made such a profound change to the profile of ITM. We had hoped that the negotiations would be concluded before the end of our financial year on 30 September 1991, in which case we would have been able to approach the market with a more concrete image of the new group, but, as the reader knows, the negotiations dragged on and absorbed so much of our time and energy that the offering was put on the back burner.

Instead, in 1992, we decided to get out of some of our trading operations piecemeal, and, in line with our philosophy of promoting local enterprise, we chose to sell them to local businessmen. In some cases we organised management buyouts, with Meridien Bank providing the finance. In the bigger companies we maintained a shareholding of just under 20% in order to watch and guide, until the Meridien loans were fully repaid. In Zambia, where our trading activities under Chibote were the biggest and oldest in the group and included our biggest Caterpillar dealership and our biggest construction company, we sold to a prominent Zambian businessman and politician. I had known him from my days in the Industrial Development Corporation and we had helped him to start up in business back in 1971. In Malawi we did a similar exercise in the form of a management buyout by our senior Malawian staff. Smaller companies were invariably sold to their managers. Some money trickled in through these disposals but the sale of Chibote which represented the biggest value, of some $30 million, went wrong; the purchaser defaulted. Repayments became erratic, interest payments fell into arrears, and after repeated extensions Meridien International Bank had to repossess the shares in 1994.

At about the same time we lost the Caterpillar dealerships. In view of the civil wars in Angola and Liberia, the dealerships there were inactive. But with the changed economic climate in Zambia and Malawi and the advent of majority rule in South Africa, the dealerships in Zambia and Malawi had once again become attractive to Barlows (who sold us the Malawi dealership in the early 1970s), and Caterpillar – never particularly at ease with our political and economic views on Africa – would prefer to deal with them instead. We sold the Malawi and Zambia dealerships to Barlows in September 1994 and in the circumstances, we made a fair deal.

The erstwhile owner, the businessman and politician who had defaulted but whom I kept informed of developments because he had been assuring me that he was expecting large funds that would bring his MIBL account up-to-date and therefore able to repossess the Chibote group, went on the warpath. He wanted to use his political clout to summon the chairman of Caterpillar to Lusaka and threaten him that he would nationalise the dealership (he was still the powerful Minister of Defence at the time) if Caterpillar insisted on going ahead with the Barlows deal. I ignored him. First of all, what he was proposing to do was against my principles, but, more pragmatically, by that time I knew that he had an unrealistic view of his wealth and his importance. His cousin and President of Zambia would throw him out of his Cabinet soon afterwards.

Wade Adams was a profitable civil engineering contractor and we were advised that we could raise £25 million by floating it on the London market. We had embarked on the preparation for the flotation early in 1994 by asking our auditors to prepare audited accounts as at 31 March 1994. There seemed to be some interest in Africa by various investment funds at the time, but we would discover that this was focused mainly on shares quoted on various small African stock exchanges. Operations like ours that spread across many borders seemed to give investors cold feet. Interestingly, the merchant bank we were talking to about the flotation of Wade Adams would opt to finance a Zimbabwe–Zambia group, because it considered Zimbabwe more business-friendly and profitable at the time. And, not surprisingly, that group would come to grief within a few years, its Zimbabwe investments diving in value with the constant devaluations of the Zimbabwe dollar, a condition not unfamiliar to us.

As the need to reduce expenditure also became paramount, I had to embark upon a complete reorganisation of the group. Because of its geographical and linguistic spread, and in order to take account of regional sensibilities created by the advent of the BIAO merger, we had set up a regional supervisory office in Abidjan to parallel the one we had in Lusaka. And, because of the historical past of BIAO, we had also set up a Paris representative office. They were both very expensive and of little use. I decided to cut them down to three-people offices, in Abidjan in order to just retain the francophone West Africa connection, and in Paris to maintain liaison with the French multinationals that were trickling to our banks in Africa. The London office was the most expensive: hydrocephalic despite my best intentions, with too many people around and no clear-cut functions. And, worst of all, it had set itself in judgement of everybody else – the Africans, the Americans, the French, and it came to the conclusion that the people in London knew best. It did not occur to them that they were not producing any money, that the London employees owed their positions and their living to the people who worked in Africa.

But the biggest failure of the London office was that it never made inroads into the business world of Britain, and as a result we remained outsiders. That was primarily the fault of the man in charge – my deputy. An Oxford graduate with a first class degree, he did not utilise his credentials to network in the City but, as I said earlier, he applied his formidable education to generating paper instead. I must confess that everything that came from his desk was impeccable – the syntax, the grammar, the punctuation; everything was perfect, and his equally super-efficient secretary would be made to retype a letter if a couple of commas were missed out or placed wrongly. But perhaps our lack of penetration of the London financial circles had been my fault too. Personally I was always too engrossed in the day-to-day operations in Africa that generated the bulk of our income, believing that my presence was indispensable, and I spent very little time in London.

Maybe I should have brought on board someone more aggressive and able to project the group's considerable merits in operating successfully in Africa.

Part 3

The Final Blow

21. IGNORANCE AND PREJUDICE

What followed was a living nightmare out of the pages of Solzhenitsyn's *August 1914*. Like Samsonov, my feelings would move from the depth of despair to the peak of optimism, from confusion to perfectly clear thinking, from extreme emotional turbulence to unreal calm, gradually losing more ground and being progressively abandoned by many 'loyal and trusted' colleagues until I was the only one left to take the final blow. But, my feelings aside, I never gave up, I never stopped fighting to save the institution I had conceived and built as an instrument and an example for the development of African enterprise. And I did not for a moment believe that I would not succeed.

The first major battle started in August 1994, with our auditors (I shall call them 'Mitchells') expressing concern over the group's financial condition after the trading room loss. I set up a combined board and senior management meeting to hear their views in detail. 'Mitchells' made their presentation on 8 September 1994 and recommended that we appoint consultants to advise us what to do. Initially they said they should not themselves be the consultants, but would recommend an appropriate appointment. The board accepted the recommendation, but, in the meantime, 'Mitchells' changed their mind and decided that it would be appropriate for the consultancy division of their firm to do the work. They assured us that they operated a 'Chinese wall' between their audit and their consultancy divisions and that there was no possibility that the views of the one would influence the other. Naively we accepted the assurance in the interest of speed, and on 22 September 1994 on behalf of Meridien BIAO SA, Meridien International Bank Ltd, Meridien Corporation and ITM International SA – all the group holding companies – we accepted the proposals set out by the 'Mitchells' consultancy division.

The target was for phase I of the work, which was given the code name 'Meryl', to be done in four weeks with payment on account of £100,000 per week. The Meryl team carried out its work mainly in London, though it did pay a visit to New York, Johannesburg and Luanda in Angola. The team had no African experience. Nevertheless, it did not deem it necessary to visit any of our major African centres of operations, though it did meet some of our Lusaka executives in London. We would soon realise that the Meryl gentlemen did not just lack African experience; they were not business consultants but just another set of number crunchers. In my view they had no business nous and were not capable of offering business solutions. Instead of analysing the group operations in order to give us advice on a future course, they confined their interest to the figures they had obviously picked from the 'Mitchells' audit division and which they discussed with our accounts department. Sure, they did have some interviews with some group executives in London, but the people who ran the operations in Africa were ignored.

Two of them met me in New York and I gave them a rundown of the group, its genesis, its evolution and current operations in Africa, where the bulk of our income was generated. I explained the successes of the local banks, of which I was very proud, and analysed our problems in the francophone zone. But I am not sure they were listening. It seemed a very one-sided conversation and I did not get any hints that their minds were ticking or taking in what I was saying. I took them to lunch at a restaurant across the street and I was struck by the conversation over the lunch table. It was not a business lunch. The project at hand was ignored, they had no ideas to offer, no questions to ask, no relevant experiences to relate, and the lunch degenerated into story telling. One story was so incongruous that I remember it to this day. One of them talked about a bird that had got trapped inside his house and in the middle of the night was flying about making a lot of noise. He got out of bed and went downstairs to see what the noise was all about, but he had to retreat quickly because he thought the bird was going for his manhood. He had been stark naked, he explained with pride!

The Meryl team did not want to know what ITM and Meridien were doing. And it had no intention of finding out what we were doing in Africa, where 20,000 people were employed and hundreds of millions of dollars of income was generated. The team did not bother to visit a single one of our African operations to see what we did in the market place, or get a first-hand experience of what it was all about. It did not even visit Lusaka, where the group had started and where the biggest businesses were concentrated. It stuck to London, even though I made the point that, like New York, London was just a service centre. Lacking African background, or, perhaps more accurately, belonging to the school that believed that Africa is a lost cause and not wanting to learn otherwise, Meryl would inevitably draw the conclusion that everything in Africa, and by consequence the group, was worthless.

When we realised that they were not likely to make any contribution to our thinking we presented our plan to them. It was pretty radical.

For the Meridien BIAO banking network, we envisaged a reduction of our shareholding to 19% or complete exit from some of the most difficult banks. We had already reached an agreement subject to board approval with regard to Mali and were at an advanced stage of negotiations with regard to Togo, with a group of local bankers and shareholders to purchase the balance. We would grant them a franchise agreement that would allow them to keep the name Meridien BIAO, on condition that we would appoint at least one senior executive, who would ensure that group manuals, procedures, computer systems, credit policies, etc. would be adhered to and that the banks would remain subject to the discipline of the group central credit committee and inspectorate. The franchises would have to accept Meridien products relevant to their markets, such as the Meridien Card (by that time it was wildly successful in Zambia and ready to be launched in other parts of the region), and utilise the Meridien network for their international activities. These two deals would yield a profit of some $7 million and generate franchise fees of $1.2 per annum, but, more significantly, the group balance sheet would shrink by $190 million, greatly improving capital adequacy.

Our affiliate, Amedo, Kenya, had 22 branches selling Singer sewing machines and other domestic equipment it assembled. Sewing schools at most branches helped to create a loyal clientele.

We planned to apply the same scheme to other smaller or minority-held banks, such as Burundi, Equatorial Guinea, Gabon and Sierra Leone.

We also planned to exit Cameroon unless arbitration with the government achieved a positive result and a contemplated World Bank programme yielded actual funds for the government to reduce its arrears to the banking sector. (The reader will remember that the government of Cameroon owed Meridien BIAO Bank FCFA 81 billion, or some $160 million.) And we planned to sell our 40% shareholding in Meridien Equity Bank Nigeria, where the local shareholders had split into two groups and were fighting each other, and our relationship with the chairman and his group of local shareholders had irretrievably broken down. A fierce letter I wrote to the Nigerian chairman of the bank gives a flavour of the problems foreign minority shareholders face in a very individualistic environment, when the majority is dominated by a group of old-fashioned and stubborn patriarchs.

> You are very well aware that MEBN's problems commenced with your insistence to appoint R as Managing Director against my advice to the contrary. You will also recall that I felt strongly enough on this matter to invite you to New York for discussions… It is a fact that you only consented to the removal of R when you got into trouble following the distribution in early 1990 of anonymous circulars, which were highly embarrassing to yourself and certain director colleagues… The bank's performance has continued to suffer from the constant interference of local directors with day to day management duties. As a consequence of this interference, on the pretext of geographical balancing some bright young Nigerians were dismissed while others were so frustrated that they chose to resign. You and some of your colleagues were so short sighted that you kept salary scales at inadequate levels. I need not elaborate on the consequences of this intransigence. You and your colleagues established so many Board Committees that in the process you deprived professionals of their right to manage the bank. Instead of carrying out their duties they spent most of their time servicing your committees. I personally told you about the dangers of such interference by non executive directors…

In Zambia, Kenya and Tanzania we planned to inject the financial services companies that MIBL owned directly into the local banks and float the Tanzanian and Zambian banks on the local stock exchanges. Apart from reducing the 'nostro' accounts in those banks, it would diversify their income and increase their value. We also decided to liquidate the bank in Hamburg and concentrate the letter of credit business in MICCL, our London confirming house, which could do it more cheaply – a move that would release $6 million tied up in the capital of the Hamburg bank, which, apart from providing an illusion that we had a bank in the European Union, it did not actually do much in the way of banking. The above steps would generate a total of $39.2 million positive cash flow. And in order to strengthen the balance sheet we planned a valuation of all premises and other fixed assets in the CFA franc zone. With up to date valuations in hand, we intended to get rid of some commercial and residential properties and sell and lease back those we would still be using as banking premises, in order to generate cash.

Meridien International Bank Ltd our bank in the Bahamas, would sell its insurance subsidiaries, liquidate the cocoa book held in RST Resources, terminate the Zambia Airways aircraft leases that had been in arrears for a very long time, improve collections, etc., which would generate another $17.6 million cash.

At group administration level, we planned the drastic elimination of over-heads by closing down the offices in London, New York, Johannesburg, Los Angeles (where the Meridien Card and accounting systems had been developed) and Abidjan. We would concentrate the much-slimmed-down head office in Lusaka and give managers of large banks in Africa supervisory jurisdiction over smaller neighbouring banks, etc. That would reduce the overhead costs to the level of the fees that were being recovered from the network banks and eliminate the shortfall of $8 million per annum that prevailed.

After several preliminary presentations with widely varying conclusions the final Meryl report was issued on 22 November 1994. The work took longer to complete and cost £835,590, more than double the original estimate. The report made no mention of what needed to be done to bring the group to profitability. No new ideas and no suggestions on how our plan could be improved or which parts should be acted on first and which parts to follow.

For a start, their view was that that we did not have a hope in hell in obtaining a decent price for any African asset. And Meryl set about 'proving' its point with lame arguments, such as '"Credit Lyonnais" [a major French bank] is exiting several territories in Africa and therefore there may be competing sale target, (sic) which will affect realisable values'. That was in relation to our plan to exit Cameroon, where, in any case, we did not anticipate any cash effect. In relation to the CFA franc zone properties, the Meryl team was adamant that they were not worth more than half their previous year's value – a view that an auditor might try to justify, but certainly not a business consultant. Yet in Cameroon we were in the process of selling the two main bank premises to a property fund called Simerca for $15 million, almost equal to their pre-devaluation figure – a trend that was discernible right through the major economies of the CFA franc zone by that time. Meryl was not even prepared to accept that readily tradable imported fixed assets such as vehicles and

The Meridien BIAO Niger branch at Taboua, on the edge of the Sahara desert, was housed in a traditional building and serviced customers living in that remote area.

computers should retain their dollar value because, with the devaluation, new imports cost double the amount of CFA francs.

Thinking as liquidators rather than as business consultants they discounted every plan we proposed in order to raise cash. Their comment in the report on our proposal to float part of Meridien BIAO Zambia on the Lusaka Stock Exchange is a striking example:

> The Zambian Stock Exchange is not yet well established and currently has a market capitalization of only $130 million. There are currently only seven companies listed on the Zambian stock exchange including one bank (Standard Chartered). Whilst it is difficult to determine the market's appetite for MBIAO Zambia it is certain that the market's ability to digest a flotation is questionable.

An equally valid opposite argument would be that a newly established stock exchange would have a voracious appetite for shares, but this did not suit the Meryl argument.

And on the possible valuation of Meridien BIAO shares for flotation purposes the report said:

> Management have based their estimate of the bank's worth on a P/E ratio of 6... The P/E ratio used is a discounted average (8) for banks capitalised on Central African Exchanges which draws heavily on Barclays and Standard Chartered listings in more that one territory. *These banks have a better quality loan book and are internationally regulated* [my italics]. The P/E ratios for lesser known (local) banks are considerably lower than the average – between 2–6.

Never been to Zambia, never seen the workings of the Zambian Stock Exchange, completely ignorant of the market's strength, never assessed the market of Meridien in Zambia, which in their mind they classified as a 'lesser known local bank' (as the reader saw earlier, MBBZ was the second biggest bank in Zambia and very popular) and never reviewed its portfolio – or those of Barclays and Standard Chartered in Zambia, for that matter. But the all-British Meryl team knew best. The possibility that, as Zambians, we might know something about our country and the behaviour of the local market in which we operated successfully for decades did not enter their heads. And another thing that the Meryl team was quite sure about: Barclays and Standard Chartered were the best in Africa and their loan book is impeccable. (In 2004, after the bankruptcy of a major agricultural company in Zambia, when the two British banks were caught with exposures of over $20 million, this myth would be debunked.)

Amusingly (or should I say despairingly?), while Meryl discounted all the African assets on our balance sheet they had no dispute with the value we placed on our assets in Australia ($13.9 million) and the United States ($13.5 million). Their report ended on the following menacing note:

> A critical aspect of any way forward as suggested by management remains the issue of perceptions of the financial viability and stability of the Group (following the publication of the accounts) held by customers, the providers of third party bank facilities and minority shareholders in the banking network...

Unlike other business consultants I had known, who would take a scheme and find ways to improve it, the Meryl team had thrown in the towel.

After Meryl, various audit divisions lined up for more audit fees. First in line was 'Mitchells' Luxembourg. We needed consolidated accounts, they suggested, in order to comply with Luxembourg law. 'We had applied for an exemption through our Luxembourg company secretary; and your fees of £250,000 are exorbitant,' responded my deputy and the finance director. Then 'Mitchells' Luxembourg sent a four-page letter threatening hell and damnation if we did not go through with that audit. At that stage I decided to get in on the act. I sent them a letter that

> as an exercise in justifying with professional veneer why we should pay you £250,000 to consolidate the ITM accounts and an additional £1,500 per company dormant or disposed of your effort is superb, but we consider it dereliction of duty to do so.

They resigned as auditors. London followed. On 21 March 1995 they phoned saying that 'although the decision had not been easy' they wished to proceed with the group audit for a fee of £500,000. We relieved them of the agony. We said that the fee was exorbitant. They resigned on 12 April 2005. By that time the damage was beyond repair.

But, before that, the Bank of England would come snooping again.

22. MUDDYING THE WATERS

'Is it true that the Bank of England has closed us down in London?' That was my son Stelios speaking from Lusaka at 2 p.m. Lusaka time (7 a.m. New York time) on 19 December 1994. 'Nonsense,' I said. 'You'd better find out quickly, because Barclays Bank is informing all our major customers in Zambia,' was the response.

And it was true. I had just received the news from my deputy in London. He had been summoned to the Bank of England on the 13th and been told about it, but curiously he chose not to tell me until he received the confirmation letter. The letter dated 14 December 1994 informed him that the B of E had decided to take up the suggestion I made to them during a meeting on 25 November 1994 to withdraw from the UK. I had already made up my mind to close London anyway, and the closure was included in the plan presented to the Meryl team. But my deputy was upset that the London office had its Christmas party that evening and worried about informing the staff that day. As the B of E letter was quite accommodating, leaving it to us to make the arrangements and indicating that we could take some time about it, we agreed that we should say nothing to anybody until I returned to London early in January. That would give us plenty of time to make an announcement and put the departure in the best possible light. (As we would be moving the administration to Lusaka, it was my intention to present it as a 'returning home' move.) But Barclay's somehow, knew and was spreading the news in Zambia.

The latest bout of interest from the Bank of England started with a 'honeyed' letter to the London representative of MIBL, dated 16 November 1994.

> My thanks to you and your colleague for coming in at short notice to see Brian Quinn this morning. As agreed I am writing to confirm the main points arising from our discussion. We referred back to the informal visit to your office in July this year by a small fact-finding team from the Bank. While in several respects that visit was helpful to us, it has raised some further questions in our minds

regarding the nature and scope of the Meridien group's activities in London. There were two matters in particular which, we felt, require our further attention.

The letter proceeded to inform us that

> ...the July visit indicated possible deposit taking activity [and] did not fully assuage our concerns that the nature and scope of Meridien's activities in London might be such as to lead us to conclude that the mind and management of the Bahamas registered bank was effectively based in London.

The possible deposit-taking activity was a moot point and they could make an argument over it. But the 'mind and management' being in London angered me. By that time I was completely fed up: with our London office, its size and uncontrollable expenditure, its exaggerated view of its own importance, my deputy, the B of E investigations, the dealing room losses, the lot. And I was becoming more firm in my suspicions that this new investigation had nothing to do with our London operations, but was due to the success of the Meridien Card in Zambia. So when I met the Bank of England I told them that we would gladly leave London, provided they gave us enough time to organise our departure. Their latest verdict on the deposit-taking activity included in their letter of 14 December was:

> ...We remained of the view that the problem was a structural one arising from the way MIBL conducted its business. We recognised that the breaches had not been deliberate. [They did not pronounce on the 'mind and management,' but they were graciously taking up my offer to leave London and they] recognised that there would be logistical issues to address but wished to see this addressed as a matter of urgency. It would be for you to consider what detailed arrangements should be put in place to achieve all the above.

In the meantime the 'Chinese wall' that we were faithfully assured existed between the Meryl team and the audit division collapsed. Unbelievably and despite the assurances they gave us over the existence of a Chinese wall, the Meryl report was given to the audit division, which decided to circulate it as widely as possible, ignoring the consequences that such a move might have on the survival of the group. For a start, the audit division decided to release the report to all 'Mitchells' local affiliates, as well as the directors of the network companies, banks, creditors and regulators. It was only then that I discovered that the confidentiality agreement in relation to project Meryl prepared by our in-house lawyer in New York and sent to my deputy in London had not been signed. My deputy had determined that such an agreement was not necessary in Britain (on the grounds that everybody is a gentleman and 'a gentleman's word is his bond', I suppose).

A record of a conference call between our American lawyers, our London lawyers and our New York in-house Nigerian lawyer, held on 24 January 1995 to review the events since project Meryl was disseminated far and wide the month before, makes fascinating reading. Our American lawyer advocated a strong confrontation with 'Mitchells'. He took the view that the audit division had no right to see the Meryl report, never mind disseminate it far and wide. His advice was to dismiss 'Mitchells' as auditors and sue them. Our London lawyer agreed that the 'Mitchells' audit should not have had access to the Meryl report, which after all covered the affairs of the group holding companies. But in a typically compromising fashion he suggested that we should go along with the wishes of the audit division in order to keep its goodwill. And the dialogue continued:

London:

> Working with the group's management we persuaded 'Mitchells' and their UK Counsel that the scope of dissemination of a 'Mitchells' prepared summary of the report and the Group's Action plan should be limited to one nominated partner in the local 'Mitchells' offices in Africa who would communicate with one particular nominee of the local subsidiary. 'Mitchells' clarified that it would be left to the local audit firm to decide in accordance with local law what obligations they had to disclose the contents of the report. This is likely to result in wider dissemination of the report. In Tanzania and Kenya the 'Mitchells' offices want to provide the report to all directors and banks in those countries, and in Ghana the summaries had a wider distribution than hoped. But maintaining reasonable relations between the group and 'Mitchells' instead of dismissing them would allow the group to exercise greater control over their actions, *even though Andrew Sardanis told me that he does not think so* [my italics].

New York:

> In our view we are dealing with two separate groups in 'Mitchells' – the audit team and the management consulting team. The report we are discussing is a management consulting report, not an audit report. Does this distinction affect the duties of 'Mitchells' under the Companies Act?

London:

> In effect, information provided by the audit team was distilled in the form of the management report by 'Mitchells' consulting group [a very down to earth assessment of the truth, as I said in the previous chapter]. It was inappropriate for 'Mitchells' to take on this assignment but they did so under a written agreement with the relevant companies in the group.

In-house lawyer:

Did you advise the London office that it was not necessary to sign the confidentiality agreement preventing the 'Mitchells' consulting group from discussing the report with 'Mitchells' audit?

London:

I was not aware that such an agreement had been prepared and did not advise on UK law or practice on the issue of the necessity of signing a confidentiality agreement. *As regards the report my position is that it relates to the financial condition of the parent companies that commissioned the study and it is not information that the directors of the network banks need to be informed of.* [my italics]

New York:

'Mitchells' is now faced with a conflict of interest vis-à-vis the Group. It is clear that they are acting to preserve their interests rather than acting in the best interest of the Group. They should not have provided the report to their African affiliates.

London:

Unfortunately, the boards of the companies who commissioned the reports will be judged with hindsight in the event the decision is taken to terminate the relationship with 'Mitchells'.

New York:

The public perception will be that 'Mitchells' was fired because of the conclusions they reached in the report. But the Group must take the offensive. It has paid $1.5 million for a report which is now being used as a club to bludgeon the banking network if management does not comply with 'Mitchells' request to release the report widely. The consulting division is liable for releasing the report and the Group must take legal action to protect itself. There is a clear cut division between auditors and management consultants. The Group should take a two-step approach: (1) inform 'Mitchells' that the Group refuses to authorise further dissemination of the report and (2) work out the terms of their resignation.

London:

I suggest we ask them why they believe they should further disseminate the report.

New York:

Nothing will be achieved by asking the question. I recommend a more aggressive approach – the consulting division is liable for releasing the report and further dissemination of its conclusion will be improper and the Group will take legal action. We should make a clear distinction between the auditors and the management consultants. The Group should make 'Mitchells' feel nervous about the fact that management views the Meryl report differently from an audit report. 'Mitchells' had two separate assignments (audit and management consulting) – they muddied the waters by mixing the two.

But the above conversation took place five weeks after 'Mitchells' had circulated the Meryl report in Africa, albeit accompanied by a report prepared by us pointing out the glaring misconceptions of Meryl and a letter from the London partner in charge of our audit giving instructions as to who was entitled to see the report in their various local offices and who they should liaise with in our relevant local office. But, as the London lawyer pointed out, the 'Mitchells' local partners ignored the instructions and made their own decisions regarding circulation of the report.

As the London lawyer said, I was against the idea of allowing the circulation of the report. I knew that there is no such thing as confidentiality in Africa (in government, in everyday life, in legal practices, in accounting, in most professions). Gossip reigns supreme and there is very little understanding of how business functions. I also knew that the 'Mitchells' partners in Africa would take no notice of the letter sent by the partner in charge of our audit setting out the rules of its circulation and urging utmost confidentiality.

23. MISGUIDED INTERVENTION

If you can keep your head when all about you
Are losing theirs and blaming it on you,
If you can trust yourself when all men doubt you,
But make allowance for their doubting too...

As the reader will have gathered, Rudyard Kipling is not one of my idols in life, and I always found his unbridled imperialism objectionable, but I must confess that his poem 'If' strengthened me time and again during the turbulent months that followed.

While my deputy and the London staff together with our London lawyers were negotiating, in early December 1994, with 'Mitchells' over the simultaneous release of the Meryl report and our rebuttal, I decided to fly to Abidjan and Dakar to have discussions with BCEAO, the Central Bank of West Africa, and apprise them of the situation. By that time Alassane Ouattara, one of the fathers of the Meridien BIAO project, had left the region, having taken a position as deputy managing director of the International Monetary Fund in Washington, but I had always found his successor supportive. Our liquidity problems worsened during December 1994, exacerbated by withdrawals of deposits resulting from the *Euromoney* article and the rumours over the dealing room losses, which were intensifying in the market. At the same time the local central banks in his region started putting pressure for the repatriation of our subsidiaries' balances with MIBL. If this pressure continued the collapse of the group would become inevitable. I explained that panic within the group would be suicidal and made a presentation of the measures we had planned to put in place in order to raise cash, which I described in detail in Chapter 21. I estimated that, during the second half of 1995, our liquidity problems would be behind us. It was a difficult meeting, attended by many officers of BCEAO; the questioning was tough and uninhibited, with every point I raised analysed in detail until my interlocutors were satisfied that what I had presented was feasible. It was a relief to receive assurances of support from BCEAO, but when I returned to New York I was confronted with the demand of the Bank of England to close down our London operations and Barclays spreading the rumour in Lusaka.

The year 1995 could not have started more ominously. The Zambian press picked up the rumours spread by Barclays and followed the steady trickle of deposit withdrawals, every day carrying one item or another predicting the collapse of Meridien BIAO Bank in Zambia. I flew to Lusaka early in January to get a first-hand feel of the situation and stayed in the region for the rest of the month, flying in and out of Lusaka to visit all the major banks in the region – Nairobi, Douala, Yaoundé, Libreville, Dar es Salaam and Swaziland – while at the same time keeping a close eye on the Zambian situation. The liquidity pressures, grossly exaggerated in the market place, culminated in a slow run on MBBZ during the whole of January 1995. MBBZ's daily balances with the Bank of Zambia moved from K8 billion positive at the beginning of January to K4 billion negative by 1 February.

The local management of MBBZ was in daily contact with BOZ as events were unfolding, and I was kept informed. I met the governor and other officials of BOZ, and after considerable consultations I advised that MBBZ needed an injection of liquidity of the order of K10 billion in order to cover its position with BOZ and retain adequate funds to meet any future pressures. I recommended to the local management to try and obtain a loan of K10 billion from BOZ secured on Meridien Centre, a recently developed property in a prime area of Lusaka where the bank had its premises, and at the same time let office space to a number of top-class tenants. I met the governor and other officials, went to Dar es Salaam and Swaziland, and when I returned to Lusaka on 1 February I was informed that BOZ was prepared to lend only K4 billion. This was later increased to K5 billion.

I had asked for K10 billion million in order to have a cushion until the situation calmed down. Unlike commercial enterprises, banks' liabilities are deposits that can be withdrawn at any time, and if a panic run develops no bank anywhere can cope unless it can liquidate assets in a hurry or somebody comes to its rescue. But during February 1995 the situation worsened, with rumours springing up from all directions, including the Bank of Zambia itself – the common syndrome in Africa I spoke about earlier. The situation reached its nadir in the latter part of February. One Saturday a Dr Kani, in the banking supervision department of BOZ, leaked that the governor would be flying to Kasama, a northern town, to consult with President Chiluba and that the bank would be closed on Monday. There was a pandemonium of withdrawals the following Monday.

But the management made valiant efforts to improve the situation and recapture its share of the market. By the middle of March MBBZ had recouped K10 billion of the deposits it had lost, and by 15 March the overdraft with BOZ was reduced to K760 million This included a debit of K2.383 billion in the form of penalty interest, which was later cancelled (since then there has been a Zambian High Court decision cancelling penalty interest in the country). This would have brought the account to a credit of K1.623 billion.

All this was achieved despite open subversion from the two big banks, Barclays and Standard Chartered. At that time, there was an interbank market in Zambia where banks borrowed from each other to meet their daily obligations. MBBZ had been a major lender in the past, helping other banks including Barclays and Standard Chartered. But as soon as the MBBZ liquidity problems surfaced not only did they refuse to help, they advised their customers not to accept cheques drawn on Meridien. Worse still, they refused to accept MBBZ bankers' payments advising the relevant clients to settle their claims by drawing out cash. Yet, despite these obstacles, we were getting on top of the situation. But, unfortunately, on 16 March 1995 the then Minister of Finance decided to come to our 'rescue'. Though, as I say above, we had asked and received a loan secured on Meridien Centre from BOZ in early February, we had not asked for any help since. We did send a letter to the Bank of Zambia asking for the reversal of the 'penalty' interest, which it agreed to do, but that was operational routine. Yet, out of the blue, the minister made an announcement in Parliament that MBBZ would be restructured. The next day the governor of BOZ issued the following press statement:

> ...After extensive consultations a consensus has been reached aimed at removing any lingering uncertainties about the bank's future. Accordingly, under section 77 of the Banking and Financial Services act of 1994 the Bank of Zambia in consultation with the government is to appoint a new chairman, a joint managing director and a financial controller. The reconstituted board and management will assume responsibility for the affairs of the bank in the interim period. With immediate effect MBBZ has been de-linked from the rest of the Meridien global network. A group of local banks have agreed to cooperate in providing short term liquidity support while a long term solution of opening the bank to equity participation is being pursued...

For us it had been 'steady as she goes', admittedly with fingers crossed. But after the announcements all the confidence that had been so painstakingly regained was immediately lost. What followed was confusion compounded by more confusion. I returned to Zambia on 18 March and had a meeting with the minister. He confronted me with a choice between two Zambian candidates for the post of joint managing director, one with Citibank training and another without commercial banking experience and uncertain background. I chose the Citi banker who, I knew, was good, but the minister wanted to appoint the other one. I protested strongly, but he went ahead and appointed him anyway without even giving me the opportunity to interview him. He also appointed a retired former senior accountant of KPMG, Zambia, as chairman.

Between them, the new team had no business experience, never mind commercial banking experience. The chairman was a retired auditor and his approach to business problems was that of a liquidator. To make matters worse, the minister embarked upon an ill-conceived scheme to persuade other banks to provide a safety net for MBBZ. Naturally, Barclays and Standard were not prepared to participate, so they refused to attend. They assessed that we were on the edge of the precipice, and, even if they were not going to give us a push, they certainly would not give us a helping hand. Amazingly, MBBZ management was not even invited to the minister's meeting. It was not even asked to provide financial information.

The meeting took place during the weekend of 25/26 March, with only the smaller banks present, while I was in Cameroon. It was a harrowing time. I had gone to Cameroon and met the governor of BEAC, the Central Bank of the Central African States, on Friday 24 March. I made a presentation similar to the one I had made to BCEAO and sought BEAC's assistance over this period of difficult liquidity. I flew to Abidjan, had meetings on Saturday and returned to Yaoundé on Sunday to hear the governor's verdict on Monday. I knew I was not going to get anywhere, because the governor had been hostile to us all along. Earlier in the book I described the excessive borrowings of the governments of Cameroon and Gabon from our local banks (as well as from all commercial banks in those countries) and the governor's way of fobbing me off was to be bloody-minded and intransigent. As soon as I settled in the Hilton Hotel in Yaoundé, I had a call from Zambia. They told me the story. My immediate reaction was: 'We lost the bank. The government is bent on destroying it.'

On Monday morning, 27 March, MBBZ's managing director received from one of the bankers present a copy of a report circulated to the minister's meeting by the director of banking supervision. The report was entitled 'Analysis of Financial Affairs of MBBZ as at the end of February 1995'. It was uninformed, incomplete and full of inaccuracies, and drew the wrong conclusions. As a result it achieved the opposite effect. Not only did it scare the other banks away from giving support, it also gave them a document to use in order to canvas our customers. Reports prepared by the banking supervision are normally discussed with management, and corrected, and they are then presented officially to the Board of Directors of the relevant bank. They are confidential documents, which are never released to the public. The governor later apologised about the conduct of his director. He assured me that he had not authorised the distribution of the report, and that his director had done so without reference to him. But the damage could not be undone.

I returned from Cameroon in the evening of 27 March, and signed an agreement with BOZ regarding the course of action to be taken under the provisions of section 77 of the Banking and Financial Services Act. On my insistence the agreement provided for the appointment of an investment bank to carry out due diligence with a view to recapitalising the bank, or attracting outside investors. Meridien BIAO Zambia was a successful, well-managed bank with great potential. I was sure that with the right advisers it would have been able to attract interest from other banking groups that were eyeing Africa at the time, from Europe and South Africa. But the Bank of Zambia would ignore that part of the agreement and appoint KPMG South Africa to carry out the task (the high fee-earning liquidation approach, no doubt recommended by the new chairman, the ex-KPMG senior partner in Zambia). What was galling was that KPMG Johannesburg was chosen, compounding the high fees with extravagant travelling expenses, with the team carrying out the task travelling weekly between Johannesburg and Lusaka and staying in the topmost hotel. MBBZ would eventually be placed in liquidation and many myths would be created about the government exposure. It is important therefore that I place on record the numbers before the government intervention.

As I said earlier, on 15 March MBBZ's overdraft with the Bank of Zambia had been reduced to K760 million This included a debit of K2.383 billion in the form of penalty interest, which BOZ agreed to waive but which in any case was later nullified by a High Court decision. Without this debit the account would have been in credit to K1.623 billion.

In addition there were two loan accounts: loan account no. 1 for K5 billion, secured on the Meridien Centre, and loan A/C No 2 for K4,512,300,000, secured by government bonds with a face value of K5.852 billion (5.(point) 852), but whose real value including interest would have been, according to my calculations, nearer 9 billion.[1] Since I have no record as to when these bonds were bought by MBBZ I assume that they were bought at the time when its liquidity was good – i.e. the early part of 1994 or even 1993. In such a case I must assume that their real value was at least 50% higher than the face value, if not more. If I assume ballpark interest rate of 100% p.a. and duration of six months, their real value would have been K 8.778 billion.

On this basis the account of MBBZ with BOZ as at 15 March 1995, if the bonds were sold at that date, would have been as follows:

Value of GRZ bonds	K8,778,000,000
Penalty interest cancelled	K2,383,000,000
Total	K11,161,000,000
Overdraft and loans as per BOZ statement	K(10,273,331,449)
Credit balance	K887,668,551

In other words, if the bonds were sold, the account would have been in credit to K887,668,551, and the Meridien Centre mortgage would have been repaid.

And we had two outstanding loans in our favour, due to Meridien International Bank in the Bahamas: $5.5 million by Zambia Airways for the unpaid balance of the loan for two ATR-42 planes Meridien financed in 1987; and $3.3 million by Zambia Railways, for the unpaid balance of the loan for 15 locomotives it took out in 1992.

We had got on top of the situation and we were in the process of floating the Meridien Centre, which would have given MBBZ the liquidity it needed to carry on. But, after we lost control and the bank eventually collapsed in August 1995, I was shocked to learn that its position with BOZ was K63.52 negative. And, in the minds of many people, we are considered responsible, even though it is the government-appointed team that received the funds.

The government-appointed management team created havoc from day one. They came in as the new tsars, not as joint managers. They cast aside the long-serving managing director and refused to consult the senior management. I offered to make myself available for advice, but my offer was never taken up. I attended the first meeting of the new board, and realised that the new management had its own agenda, which had nothing to do with saving the bank. I was never invited to any other meeting. The customers abandoned the bank in droves, some of them reporting that they had been asked for bribes in order to have their facilities renewed. The inevitable result was the collapse that followed. What is strange was that BOZ continued to advance large sums of money to the new management of MBBZ. Surely it should have seen the exorbitant demands for cash as an indication that the new management was incompetent.

Two facets of Tanzanian agriculture: rice processing at Kapunga factory, built by Wade Adams, and a Masai boy herding his family's cattle in the foreground.

Within a few days of taking over MBBZ, the government announced the creation of ZAMBANK by merging MBBZ with the Zambia National Commercial Bank (ZANACO), the biggest bank in Zambia, which it owned 100%. I could not fathom the motives for such a merger. ZANACO was notorious for its huge, underprovided loan portfolio to parastatals, politicians and MMD faithful. Everybody knew that, if proper provisions were made, ZANACO would become insolvent. And merging two banks in trouble hardly seemed a sensible idea. The first to protest against the merger was the polemic independent newspaper *The Post*, and its cry was taken up by many Members of Parliament and the general public. The merger was aborted, but after the demise of MBBZ its government-appointed managing director went on to greater glory: the government appointed him as managing director of ZANACO instead of giving him the sack. He did not last very long, though. He was dismissed on allegations that he had granted an unauthorised unsecured loan of $3 million to a friend.

I was not able to fathom the government's agenda. But I would get a hint about its motivation a year later.

24. AKASHIMI[1]

President Chiluba has exposed a plot by a leader of an opposition party and a fallen bank to fan political violence in Zambia using $39 million which was transferred from the Bahamas to South Africa for easy access. The colossal sums of money were siphoned from Zambia to the Bahamas and now there were frantic efforts to relay the funds to South Africa for easy withdrawals. Mr Chiluba disclosed, when he toured the bombed 'TIMES' offices in Ndola yesterday, that leaders of a party were now hopping from Lusaka to Johannesburg every week to finalise the clandestine deal. He said the Government knew who the perpetrators were and warned the culprits would be cornered soon. He called on Zambians to remain calm and not be intimidated. The President wondered why the good editorial comments of the 'TIMES' could annoy someone to an extent that one could think of blowing up the offices... The President said it was surprising that the government in the second republic could allow a bank to siphon such large amounts out of the country. On the recent assenting of the contentious Constitution [Amendment] bill Mr Chiluba said that evil hearted people had now stuck their heads out and it was now easy to deal with them.

The above was carried by the *Times of Zambia*, one of the government-owned newspapers, on 6 June 1996 under the title 'Fallen bank diverted $39 m to cause chaos'. The unnamed leader of the political party was Kenneth Kaunda; the Constitutional Amendment bill was specially enacted to deprive Kaunda of his Zambian nationality and prevent him from standing against Chiluba in the forthcoming presidential elections, and the unnamed fallen bank was obviously Andrew Sardanis's Meridien BIAO. And, in line with Chiluba's policy of destroying everything that Kaunda had started, from ZCCM to Zambian Airways, to the clothing industry, to the parastatal sector, Meridien in Zambia (which Chiluba probably imagined belonged to Kaunda) had been crushed.

Myth-making is an ancient African tradition that carries weight because it disseminates history. It has been used for generations to pass on the history of the family, the village, the clan and the tribe. And it has been used to educate the young in the ways of their elders. But this venerable tradition has, in modern times, been appropriated in the urban areas and it is used to spread gossip, to malign and to destroy. And 'leaders' such as Chiluba would use it without shame or restraint in order to justify their own misdeeds, cover up their dubious activities, or shape public opinion in their favour. This is a problem that anybody of prominence has to contend with in Africa in general, but perhaps, more so in Zambia – and it applies as much to business as to politics and social life. The myth of the $39 million to create political violence in Zambia was yet another example of Chiluba's naïve manipulation of what he cynically considered the gullibility of the masses. But I do not think that many people believed him and the story was never repeated.

But Chiluba would find an opportunity to create a more 'appropriate' myth against Kaunda and arrest him a year or so later. A Major Chiti, nicknaming himself 'Captain Solo' from the television series, attempted a coup against Chiluba on 28 October 1997. The coup failed and Chiti and his accomplices were arrested within a couple of days. But the aborted coup gave Chiluba the opportunity to embark upon a witch-hunt against some high-level political 'enemies'. He accused Kaunda and three other prominent politicians, Roger Chongwe, Princess Nakatindi and Dean Mung'omba, of complicity. Kaunda and Chongwe (they had been shot at by the police and were slightly wounded a couple of months earlier when, in the same vehicle, they were leaving a political rally) were away from the country at the time of the coup. Chongwe chose not to return until years later, when there was a change of government. But Kaunda returned the day before Christmas.

At 4 a.m. on Christmas morning his house was surrounded by armed paramilitaries, and after some hours of searches and arguments with his lawyers he was bundled into a truck and taken to the Lusaka remand prison, charged with masterminding the coup. He shared a cell with 19 people for two nights and late in the afternoon of the third day he was flown by helicopter to the maximum-security prison in Kabwe, a small town some 140 km north of Lusaka. There he was given a cell and a bed. I do not know where the other two were taken, but I do know that they both suffered major health problems during their imprisonment. Mung'omba contracted tuberculosis, from which he died in 2005. (Chiluba had the audacity to attend his Catholic funeral, at which he took communion even though he is a born-again evangelical – behaviour that caused indignation around the country.) The whole country knew that Kaunda as well as the others would not possibly have been involved in the aborted coup. But charges were trumped up by the Attorney-General's office nonetheless.

Kaunda is a veteran fighter and a very tough one. Upon entering prison he promptly went on hunger strike, a weapon he had used time and again in the past. He declared that he would take no food or water until he was sent home. I have known Kaunda, a Gandhi disciple, to fast for weeks, and I was wondering how Chiluba would be able to get out of this very tight corner he had boxed himself into. But he managed it, with the help of President Nyerere of Tanzania.

Nyerere was one of the most intelligent, articulate, well-meaning Presidents in Africa, who will go down in history as the architect of the decolonisation of his country, both politically and mentally. I met him often in the 1960s, after UDI (Rhodesia's Unilateral Declaration of Independence), when we were organising Zambia's supply routes from the north, and I last met him in 1994, in the northern Tanzanian town of Arusha, when I had the onerous task of introducing Chiluba as the keynote speaker to an African Business Round Table dinner. We were sitting next to each other and spent the evening talking about the past and passing asides on the proceedings. At one stage he asked me: 'Andrew, do you regret what you and Ken did at Mulungushi?' [The Mulungushi and Matero reforms of 1968 and 1969, at which the government of Zambia took a controlling interest in a number of major companies and the mining industry, about which I wrote extensively in *Africa: Another Side of the Coin*.] 'I would do it all over again,' I responded. 'I would do Arusha again too,' he said [meaning the Arusha economic reforms he promulgated in 1967]. 'The Tanzanians are now Tanzanians, even if some of them do not yet know it.'

I said that at that meeting I had the onerous task of introducing the keynote speaker, who was the darling of the West at the time. As I explained in *Africa: Another Side of the Coin*, I never had any time for Chiluba, whom I considered an opportunist and a hare-brained one at that. But as I was a prominent member of the Round Table and a Zambian, and the board in its wisdom decided to invite him, it fell upon me to introduce him. I hated the task. I did not want to join in the universal acclamation Chiluba was receiving those days. Rereading my speech, I do not think I did a bad job. I praised the changes, but I avoided praising him for them. I said:

President Chiluba is part of what one would call the second generation of African leaders who came to power after the second wind of change started sweeping across the Continent a few years ago. For most Africans, especially those of us in business, this new wind ushered a new ray of hope that our Continent is now permanently moving from state intervention and control to free market regimes. We all pray that the mistakes of the past will not be repeated. Africa lost more than two decades of economic progress by putting too much premium on politics at the expense of the economy.

Substantial credit must be given to the business sector for its resilience. There were times in the past decade when most entrepreneurs would have given up. But thanks to the African spirit of enterprise we soldiered on. And there could be no better proof of this spirit than the gathering this evening. We have come from all four corners of our Continent to demonstrate our collective resolve and commitment to the acceleration of the economic development and social progress on our Continent, regardless of the obstacles we face. We are all aware of our responsibilities to this Continent. Our governments cannot on their own create the necessary jobs, the schools, the hospitals and related basics of development. These goals can only be achieved through economic growth. To achieve economic growth we need to attract substantial amounts in private investment, both domestic and foreign. In fact I believe it is the domestic investment spearheaded by the African businessmen that will attract foreign investment. It is up to all of us to generate viable and profitable projects and seek foreign partners and financing.

But our governments must help out by providing political stability and consistency in their economic policies. I would like to emphasise the word consistency. Even a small temporary deviation from free market policies disturbs investors and makes them lose confidence in our commitment to reforms. And we must remember that we do not have a good reputation in this field. I promised myself to be short but I had to take advantage of the presence of one of the champions of the enabling environment for private sector development in Africa – President Frederick Chiluba. On his assumption of office he had the courage to grasp the nettle and introduce sweeping reforms to the Zambia economy.

The most recent steps taken in our march towards regaining economic prosperity were the opening of the Lusaka Stock Exchange and the complete abolition of exchange controls. Both these measures will go a long way towards attracting investment and I commend them to all our governments in Africa. I hope that even more business oriented decisions will be taken at the OAU summit in Tunis. I understand from press reports that history will be made there, with the return of South Africa to the concert of nations.

I wish to take this opportunity to add my voice to those who have already welcomed our colleagues from South Africa among us here tonight. Together we shall create a better tomorrow for our Continent. As the saying goes, in unity lies strength. Your country has the technical expertise and the financial sophistication and we have the resources and a highly profitable collective purchasing power.

But back to KK's hunger strike. Nyerere in his goodness flew from Dar es Salaam with his wife Maria and visited Kaunda in jail. His approach was simple but compelling: 'Ken, you are going to eat, or Maria and I are staying here to starve with you.' And Ken obliged, while Chiluba was shamed into sending him home, albeit after declaring his home a 'private jail'. I am still debating in my mind whether Nyerere's charitable intervention was appropriate. He did it out of concern for the health of his friend. But in the process he got Chiluba out of a tight corner. Kaunda is tough and would have survived the hunger strike. But Chiluba would have been mortally wounded politically.

I do not think Chiluba expected it but the 'private jail' turned into a shrine: lots of sympathisers milling outside and many prominent people and friends paying their respects. I tried to visit a few times. The policemen on guard duty always had an excuse why I could not go in: he had other visitors; he was resting; the senior officer who had to grant authority could not be contacted; and 'come in the afternoon' or 'come tomorrow'. But, as I am white and they assumed I would not understand, they warned each other in Chinyanja that 'this old man must not go through'. After a few attempts I gave up.

Kaunda would be released many months later on a 'nolle prosequi'. This has now become the routine process of setting free people who should not have been arrested in the first place. What is sad is that prominent lawyers in the country's legal department are prepared to do the President's bidding without protest. And the Law Association of Zambia seems to consider it an acceptable routine and does not raise any objections.

But myth creation is not the preserve of Africans. White professionals from South Africa can be equally good at it. A $90 million Meridien myth was created by the KPMG Johannesburg liquidators, who desperately needed something spectacular to appease public opinion that started turning against their wasteful liquidation of MBBZ. They had been engaged, instead of investment bankers, by the Bank of Zambia to carry out the 'due diligence' that the Minister of Finance committed himself to on my insistence, in the agreement we had signed in March 1995 for joint management of Meridien BIAO Zambia. I have never seen their report and I was never interviewed when it was being prepared. No MBBZ senior executive was ever asked any questions. But KPMG Zambia, the official liquidators, in a letter to the creditors wrote:

Investigations have shown transfers in excess of US$90 million to Meridien International Bank Ltd in the Bahamas. Any future recoveries will be tracing the personal assets of the ultimate beneficiaries of these transfers. It will be imperative to have access to the books and records of MIBL. The success of this exercise will depend on the Bahamas banking laws and the cooperation of the MIBL liquidator.

No details were given on how this figure was arrived at and over what period of time this huge sum of money was transferred, except for the deadly innuendo: 'Any future recoveries will be tracing the personal assets of the ultimate beneficiaries of these transfers.' And a whole mythology has been built around this innuendo, with a new myth emerging every couple of years.

I confronted the Zambian liquidator. He told me that he quoted that paragraph from the report he received from Johannesburg. I put it to him that the statement was deliberately inserted to mislead. Unless the transfers occurred after March 1995, when we lost control of MBBZ, the $90 million would represent the total foreign exchange business of MBBZ over a period of a couple of years. He told me it was the latter. In that case the purpose of the transfers was in the course of business and the comment had no place in the letter to the creditors. 'Foreign exchange business', at the time, was the amount of foreign currency a bank bought from the Bank of Zambia for its customers' needs. Generally these were to cover customers' foreign obligations, such as opening letters of credit or paying for imports, or other services obtained from outside the country, for the remittance of dividends, management fees, consultancy fees, etc., etc. As these transactions were consummated at the MIBL end, the credit was extinguished.

And I would get an unexpected confirmation of this from the Bahamian liquidator of MIBL in 2006. On 5 January, I received an email from her regarding a visit to Zambia she was preparing for her assistant. Inadvertently she attached the two briefs she prepared for him. One is titled 'Matters to resolve in Zambia'. It is three pages long and under the heading 'Claims by MBBZ' (Meridien BIAO Bank Zambia) it says:

MBBZ has a deferred claim in the liquidation of $112,998,660 of which $90 million is a fraud claim. This part of the claim appears to be completely invalid as it relates to amounts already credited to the account of MBBZ, so by claiming fraud they are claiming the same amount twice. BOZ appears to have taken over the liquidation of MBBZ personally, so this should be discussed with the person responsible. The other part of the claim appears to be substantially in agreement with MIBL's books (check this) but MBBZ may have received benefits from assets of an ITMZ subsidiary. Certain properties of Chibote Ltd and possibly other ITMZ subsidiaries were transferred to MBBZ and it is not clear what the consideration received was for these assets (AT to review ITMZ file to clarify what is known about this and the additional information required). Consideration needs to be given to whether MBBZ has received a benefit from MIBL assets for which MIBL received no benefit. [*The reader will find out more about the transferred properties and their fate in Chapter 31.*]

The above notwithstanding, the specific transactions would have been documented in detail in the books of MBBZ and BOZ (because all foreign transactions were routed through BOZ in those days) and the liquidators did not need to investigate them in the Bahamas. They would find the beneficiaries by just checking their local records. But they knew that, if they invoked the Bahamas, its banking secrecy laws would shield them against ever having to produce the answer – hence the sentence 'The success of this exercise will depend on the Bahamas banking laws and the cooperation of the MIBL liquidator'. They knew that in the Bahamas their lie could never be checked.

So much for the $90 million saga. But many myths continue to be created over it. The most recent was another statement through the press by a minister in the administration that succeeded Chiluba's and promptly commenced prosecution against him for plunder. According to that minister's version, the money was transferred to the Bahamas and was collected in cash by Chiluba's director of security. This myth has taken root and is widely believed to be true. Nobody asks how does one collect $90 million in cash (which bank would disburse it and where can you travel with such a huge and bulky loot?). But MBBZ either supplied Kaunda $39 million for political violence or Chiluba $90 million for pocket money. The two should be mutually exclusive and of course neither is real.

But the *coup de grâce* came from Swaziland, one of the tiny countries of Africa, wedged between Mozambique and South Africa.

25. A GROSS ANACHRONISM

The Lion (ingwenyama) and the Elephant (indlovu) appear together in Swazi cosmology as most powerful and dominant animals... The King is titled and addressed as Ngwenyama and his mother as Ndlovukazi (she-elephant). The lion is characterized by bravery, strength and cleverness but is also generous and aware of others' needs. It is a great meat eater but only kills for food... The Ngwenyama as king has qualities of the lion, king of animals and the Ndlovukazi as his mother has the qualities of the great she-elephant. The elephant is the largest of all the animals, it is also the strongest, but no one has ever seen a lion and an elephant fight. They are both strong and fearless but do not attack without reason. (From *Swazi Culture* by S.J. Malan, 1985)

One can say, with a bit of a licence, that the lion and the she-elephant form the cornerstone of Swazi life. Swaziland is probably the most quaint country in Africa. It is not only conservative; in some ways it is antediluvian. The capital, Mbabane, is a modern town with shopping malls and all the facilities that go with a reasonably prosperous capital. One would not detect in the people who go about their daily business the deep conservatism that prevails. Sartorially (in national celebrations and official functions) the country seems to still be in the middle of the eighteenth century, with a way of thinking to match. I was taken aback when I first visited Swaziland and was received by a very senior government official at his office. When the elevator door opened, I saw standing in front of me a barefoot man who wore a kind of 'wrap' around his loins that did not reach his knees and left most of his right thigh exposed. The top was a kind of waistcoat worn without a shirt. The officials, almost all with the surname Dlamini, the King's clan, which accounts for a quarter of the country's population, take pride in their national dress and wear it on all official occasions domestically and abroad. I remember the attention the Swazi Minister of Finance attracted in Bangkok, wearing his national dress for the official opening of the World Bank meetings in 1991. His picture was on the front page of most newspapers. By contrast, matrons are more decently dressed and their dresses are very colourful. On the other hand maidens performing the annual reed dance barely cover their loins.

Swaziland had been a British protectorate until it was granted independence in 1968 under a constitution handed down by Britain, which provided a limited monarchy and an elected Parliament. But King Sobhuza tore up that constitution five years later and restored the traditional system of government, in which all power remains in the hands of the King. He abolished Parliament and outlawed political parties, even though some years later he introduced an advisory legislature, but maintained the ban on political parties. He was reputed to have had 70 wives and his sons ran into the hundreds.

The current Ngwenyama (the King), one of Sobhuza's youngest sons, succeeded to the throne in 1983 while he was still a pupil at a British public school. He shares power with his mother, the Ndlovukazi. Despite his Western upbringing the King seems to have taken his traditional role very seriously. He attends the annual umhalanga (reed dance – a kind of 'bonding' ceremony for teenage girls, which includes a special dance for him by bare-breasted maidens) and he chooses a new wife every year. So far he has 13. The incongruity of the ancient and modern is most striking at major state and international events where the Ngwenyama, the Ndlovukazi and the Nkosikazi (King's wives) are present. I cannot think of any other country in the world where a speaker has to begin with 'Your Majesty' for the King, 'Your Majesty' for the Queen Mother and 'Your Royal Highnesses' for the royal wives. At one conference I attended the 10 beautiful and very fashionably dressed Nkosikazi were sitting together at a special table, while the King and his mother were sitting at another. There have been strong mutterings against the reed dance and the King's marital pursuits in recent years. Young girls nowadays have boyfriends who object to the King's medieval droit de seigneur. But the Ngwenyama does not seem to notice.

Decision-making is the King's prerogative and all members of the Cabinet are simply his advisers under the constitution. I do not know how much leeway in decision-making he gives them, but I have been told that when they are summoned to his presence they have to approach on their knees and make sure that they never turn their backs on him, even though some of them are advanced in age, very mature and cosmopolitan. And because political parties are banned the trade unions seem to have taken on the mantle. Strikes are frequent, not only over labour matters but over the constitution and other political demands. I have not detected any inclination for change amongst the King and his establishment.

Meridien BIAO Swaziland, which we bought directly from BIAO before the merger with Meridien was even contemplated, was a good bank, small but profitable, and was developing very nicely until a well-meaning septuagenarian

A labour-intensive but effective packing facility of pineapple and grapefruit adjacent to the plantation, belonging to one of Meridien BIAO's customers in Swaziland.

governor of the central bank persuaded our local management to take over the portfolio of BCCI Swaziland after the international demise of BCCI. And again we made the mistake we had made in Cameroon: we agreed to clean the portfolio as we went along, a promise that would not be honoured by the governor's successor.

The successor was a nice enough young man. From what I remember, he had been working for the World Bank before he was appointed governor. He was well-meaning, but as this was his first executive appointment he was unsure of himself and placed great reliance on the advice he was getting from local whites. A South African accountant and KPMG partner who became very influential must have read about the difficulties of our group and targeted a possible liquidation with a huge fee potential. He must have decided to 'help' the process along and used the governor. Meridien BIAO Bank Swaziland had a maturing deposit with MIBL amounting to $5 million (if I remember correctly) which MIBL would not be able to repay on maturity, because of the heavy withdrawals it was experiencing at the beginning of 1995. I had visited the governor on 31 January 1995, and explained our difficulties and the measures we were taking to raise cash. I made the same presentation to him that I had made to the governor of BCEAO the previous month. He seemed understanding and willing to agree to a postponement. Or so I thought when I left Mbabane. But in the middle of March he petitioned the High Court of the Bahamas for the winding up of MIBL.

I met him again on 31 March, in Johannesburg. He had a very large entourage, which included the KPMG partner and an attorney from a Swaziland practice. He confronted me with a transfer form, asking me to surrender our 55% shareholding in Meridien BIAO Bank Swaziland to the central bank for one emalangeni (the Swazi currency unit). I protested at being confronted with a lawyer and an accountant when I was expecting the governor and his officers only, and had not therefore arranged for professional advisers to be present. But the KPMG representative assured me that they would be prepared to postpone the High Court petition to give MIBL time to meet its obligation. As the governor did not raise any objection to that statement I took it to be a quid pro quo and signed the transfer.

The African Development Bank was, sensibly, anxious to avoid the domino effect that assaults on individual banks would cause, and had hoped to arrange a meeting of all the central bank governors of all the countries in which the bank had operations, in order to see if they could coordinate action. It was hoping to have such a meeting in Abuja, during its annual general meeting in the middle of May. But I soon realised that the Swazi application was proceeding. I phoned the governor on 11 April and he assured me that he had no objection to the postponement. I was again 'mistaken' as is obvious from my letter of 12 April, which reads:

> When we spoke on the phone yesterday in relation to your court petition against MIBL I understood that you would have no objection to a postponement. I gained the same understanding from your advisors when we spoke in Johannesburg on March 31, 1995. I communicated this to our Bahamian lawyers and they in turn communicated with your Bahamian lawyers who on receiving instructions from Swaziland refused the postponement. Can I have clarification of your position please?

His response the following day was not exactly that I am a liar or a dimwit but the polite society equivalent:

> I did not give you any undertaking relating to the liquidation petition of MIBL and your impression is regrettably a misunderstanding. Again the impression you gained in Johannesburg is also unfounded…

As the reader will have gathered throughout this book, I am not prone to wishful thinking and I do understand what I am being told. But the young governor says I did misunderstand him and his advisers twice. I rather think that his decisions were reversed by his minders.

The director of banking supervision in the Bahamas suggested a course of action that might achieve the critical postponement we were looking for. He suggested that the Central Bank of the Bahamas should suspend the licence of MIBL for a period of 90 days under section 9 of the Bank and Trust Companies Regulations Act. To do so it would have to impose stringent conditions during the 90-day period, which would include the complete cessation of all banking transactions (no receipt of new deposits under any circumstances and an absolute moratorium on payments to all depositors or other creditors, no payments of expenses of any kind outside the Bahamas). That would give time for MIBL to collect monies due to it and make maximum efforts to dispose of other realisable assets.

My deputy, who had flown to the Bahamas for the case, sent a letter along those lines on 21 April at the suggestion of the director, but, somehow, it was not acted upon. I received no explanation why. On 25 April the High Court of the Bahamas appointed two partners of KPMG Bahamas as liquidators of Meridien International Bank. And on 26 April, a Mr Robert Cloete and a Mr Arthur Fandam, the lawyer and the accountant from Swaziland marched into our London office carrying a letter (undated) from the newly appointed liquidators authorising them 'to act on our behalf for the purposes of obtaining information from yourselves in connection with Meridien International Bank'.

They had no role to perform for the liquidator. They were in transit from the Bahamas to Swaziland and they just wanted to snoop. I threw them out, but I knew that the end for me and the group had come.

26. THE CURTAIN FALLS

> The Board of Directors of Meridien BIAO sa met in Paris on 25 April 1995 to discuss the situation of the Group as it has developed over the last few weeks. The Board received reports from the various general managers of the network banks regarding the characteristics of their individual markets and suggestions on how to handle the situation. During the meeting the Board was informed that following the action initiated by the Central Bank of Swaziland, the High Court of the Bahamas had placed Meridien International Bank Ltd. in liquidation. In view of this, Mr. Andrew Sardanis who has been the Chairman of both Meridien International Bank Ltd. and Meridien BIAO sa, offered his resignation as Chairman of the Board of Meridien BIAO sa.

By that time I was almost alone. Only some Zambians and a sprinkling of other African colleagues remained supportive. Nearly all senior London colleagues jumped ship in indecent haste. 'It is OK for you,' they said; 'you are not British and you do not live here.' The fact that they had a large share of responsibility in the collapse (the $10 million dealing room loss being the latest) did not seem to enter their heads. Most important for them were their terminal benefits (they got very generous terms from my deputy) and we had a very generous pension scheme fully funded. My deputy was the first to resign, though I must immediately add that he very honourably stayed around to the end. Rereading the letter he sent me on 6 January 1995 I confess that I find it touching.

> ... With the forthcoming concentration in Lusaka of the entire management of the banking group, my post comes to an end. I recognise that a considerable amount of work will need to be done over a number of months... Thus I do believe that it is sensible to set a time limit of 31 March to my position in the Group so this letter can be regarded as the statutory twelve weeks notice required to that date [punctilious to the end]. If my memory serves me correctly it will be during March that I will complete 30 years working for you of which more than 23 have been in this group. [When I first walked into his office in the Industrial

197

Development Corporation of Zambia in 1965 and asked him whether he was planning to give me his resignation like everybody else was doing, his question was: 'How many years can you guarantee me a job.' 'At least five,' I answered.] It has been a time full of interest and variety, with many achievements and plenty of disappointments, and has often been great fun, but I think it is perhaps long enough...

He did stay up to the end of April, though, and handled the Bahamas court hearing, and attended the swansong board meeting too. The most pitiful departure was that of the only remaining East African Indian. He had become British and had achieved middle-class respectability, with his wife serving as a magistrate in Surrey. He resigned in February and left immediately in case our problems developed into a scandal that would affect his wife's position, he said. Intellectually he was one of the the best accountants I came across. But standing up to be counted was not one of his attributes.

I do not have a clear recollection of what went on in Paris. We were all staying in the same hotel. I do remember the French managers who had come from Africa having drinks away from everybody else when I arrived the evening before the meeting, and I do remember some French-speaking West African colleagues showering me with advice: whom to solicit support from, whom to brief in advance of the meeting, etc. But supplication is not in my repertory. I was touched by their concern, but I was determined to let things run their course. In any case, due to the time difference, the verdict of the Bahamian court had not as yet been made. The next day, the 'case for the prosecution' was handled by the BOAD (West African Development Bank) representative, supported by the one from ADB. Like good bureaucrats, they wanted to wash their hands on the record. Witnesses for the prosecution: the French managers of the network. In attendance: our London lawyer, to explain to the members of the board their rights and obligations. The French managers hit hard and without restraint. Meridien was blamed for everything. All the banks would have been successful and profitable if only they had been left alone. No mention that they were bankrupt before we got involved, that their portfolios were lousy and got worse, because they always caved in to government, parastatal or local shareholder demands for more loans, thus piling more non-performing loans on the huge mountain of existing ones; and no mention of the disgraceful sale of the many millions of dollars of travellers' cheques a few days before the CFA franc devaluation.

I have already described the problems of the francophone banks in previous chapters. But, to recap for the reader, I copy below an amazingly accurate summary of the BIAO problems that appeared in the London publication *African Analysis* at the time:

> When Meridien Bank took over the ailing Banque Internationale pour l'Afrique Occidentale in 1991 with the minority shareholding support of the African Development Bank and Banque Ouest Africaine de Développement, the deal represented a historic business breakthrough. Meridien's Zambian-based founder, Andrew Sardanis had now created a unique pan-African banking group with thorough coverage of both Anglophone and Francophone markets. And one of West Africa's most venerable institutions had been saved from disintegration or closure. Four years later, Meridien BIAO wrestles with a daunting array of financial and management difficulties across the Francophone markets. It is in dispute with several governments and since 1991 has had to inject $41 million in extra finance into local banks within the network. In at least one country it has been put under pressure to sell its shares to a businessman linked to a prominent politician; in others it has been hit by government's failure to service loans.
>
> Under franc zone bank laws a major shareholder in a bank – known as actionnaire de reference – can be told by regulators to inject extra funds. The takeover made Meridien BIAO an actionnaire de reference in many local BIAO offshoots, even where its stake was below 50% per cent. Meridien had promised the west and central African franc zone banking commissions that it would inject agreed sums of CFA franc capital into a number of troubled offshoots and most payments were made soon after the takeover. The January 1994 CFA franc devaluation has halved the hard currency of any subsequent payments.
>
> In July 1994, BIAO Niger needed new capital. The banking commission insisted this was injected as a condition of granting Meridien BIAO a much sought after banking license in Benin. But responding to capital injection orders from supranational banking commissions has sometimes brought Meridien BIAO into conflicts with individual governments anxious to keep local BIAO operations under majority local ownership. Local shareholders have sometimes refused to inject the parallel capital sums that would maintain their share of total equity. Meridien BIAO's stake has therefore risen and in Togo is now 81%. In two countries Meridien has been forced to provide extra money as temporary shareholder loans, to avoid taking the extra shares and thus upsetting a national government. Meanwhile, in Burkina Faso Meridien BIAO has also come under pressure to sell its 40% in Banque Internationale du Burkina. The technical cooperation agreement between the group and the local bank is due to be terminated.
>
> BIAO Mali has been ravaged by local shareholders believing their shares gave them the right to unlimited credit and the bank is now in a serious crisis.

Meridien BIAO group provided extra funds and has now ended up with 52% stake – but the authorities in Bamako would like local shareholder control restored. The group has now decided that in view of this it will cut back to 19%, which will end its obligation to provide any fresh bailout. In Guinea, which is outside the franc zone talks over recapitalisation of the Banque Internationale pour l'Afrique en Guinée (BIAG) dragged on for two years before Meridien concluded that it was no longer worth pursuing and ceded its stake to the government for a symbolic one franc two years ago. Since then the government has talked with a number of banks, including reportedly Citibank, Credit Commerciale de France and recently, La Belgolaise. No replacement international shareholder has yet been signed.

In Cameroon the entire banking industry has been hit by the failure of the government to service loan obligations. Meridien BIAO has injected $7.5 million in new capital sufficient to keep the Cameroon operations turning over quietly. In all investments by Meridien BIAO in its offshoots in the franc Zone since the original takeover have amounted to $41 million.

As soon as the information that Meridien International Bank had been put into liquidation came through I offered my resignation as chairman of the board. As I no longer had any status in the Meridien International Bank I did not feel that I could any longer represent its stake in Meriden BIAO. In my farewell speech, I said that I still believed in the idea of a pan-African bank, and added that maybe Meridien BIAO was ahead of its time. But for African private enterprise to develop, it is necessary to have an African network that understands Africa's needs and is ready to take risks on the indigenous people of Africa, something the major international banks that operate in Africa do not do and will not be prepared to do for years to come. They are geared towards the multinational companies and they will not take risks on local enterprise.

The board selected an interim management committee composed of the representatives of the ADB, BOAD and the managing director of Meridien BIAO Cameroon, the biggest bank in the network. He was the best possible choice to run the network. He was French but spoke very good English and had worked in both anglophone and francophone Africa. The ADB representative, a Cameroonian, saw his position on the interim committee as an opening for future glory. He appointed himself a kind of interim spokesman-cum-chairman, and for the next few days he was giving press conferences, pontificating on what went wrong and explaining how he would fix it and bring the network back to its old glory. Until he was cut down to size by the ADB legal department, which sent him a rude minute telling him to shut up because his statements could be construed as a commitment by the ADB to fund the rescue. I cannot even remember if he was allowed to attend the final board meeting in Paris, on 19 May 1995, which decided to put Meridien BIAO SA into liquidation. What I do remember is that the ADB lawyer was calling the shots at that meeting. KPMG were there lobbying and cajoling to get the assignment. We did make the decision to put Meridien BIAO SA into liquidation, but KPMG were not recommended.

27. THE VULTURES

I have come to the conclusion that on your appointment as liquidators of MIBL you determined to take over the liquidation of the entire ITM group and you have concentrated your efforts to that end in order to maximize your fees. I have reviewed the entire correspondence and minutes of meetings between us and all of them revolve around this subject. Never have you or anyone else spent any time discussing the business of MIBL. Any mention of MIBL was incidental to your main aim: to take over the liquidation of ITM. On being appointed liquidators you dismissed immediately all members of its [MIBL's] staff except one and you embarked upon reinventing the wheel on your own. This may well generate more fees for you but is it in the best interest of the creditors? I was in Lusaka most of the month of May and your Mr. T and his team were also there, all of us working in Meridien Centre. If any one had bothered to come and see me you would have known a lot more about the agreement with BOZ and ITMHZ, and a great many other issues. However, your aim at the time was to obtain the assignment for due diligence on MBBZ, another opportunity for fees. Now that the liquidation of Meridien BIAO and ITM are in process [KPMG did not get either] it is time to concentrate on your main assignment. As I said to you at the beginning I am very willing to cooperate. But it takes two to do it.

Thus I wrote on 15 July 1995, to the London partner of KPMG, who seemed to be directing the MIBL liquidation process. Their quest for the liquidation of the whole group had surfaced from day one. The KPMG Bahamas partners came to London in early May, and on the 4th May they took our financial director to Luxembourg to 'educate' him on the procedures available to deal with companies in financial difficulties. They saw me the following day: 'They raised concern,' according to the minutes of the meeting, 'about ITM's directors' exposure if decisions on ITM were delayed.' I told them that 'that was my problem and my view was that they had a serious conflict of interest. They triggered the liquidation of the Bank in Swaziland by their advice to the Central

Bank to the long term detriment of MIBL's shareholders and creditors and they were appointed liquidators of MIBL in the Bahamas through a letter of support from the interim chairman of Meridien BIAO Zambia, a former KPMG senior partner.' I also told them that they had not shown adequate independence to protect the interests of all creditors so far. But they were persistent.

Until the middle of July, when they lost both the liquidations of Meridien BIAO and ITM, they had two partners full-time on the job, and they used every trick in the book to persuade me, intimidate me, cajole me and coerce me into giving them the assignment. The minutes of meetings and exchanges between us over that period would make a libretto for a Gilbert and Sullivan operetta. They played the role of the good cop/bad cop to perfection. One was concerned that I might get into trouble with the law if I did not follow their advice. The other was threatening to petition immediately to put ITM in bankruptcy. My patience snapped on 4 July 1995. We had sold our London apartment and had to vacate it that day. Leaving the emotional strain aside, we were busy packing and they knew about it. Yet at 2 p.m. they phoned to ask for an urgent meeting. I reluctantly conceded at 4 p.m. I left Danae on her own and went to the office on time. They arrived at 4:30. It was the 'bad cop's' turn. The minutes read:

> ... he wished to discuss the course of events over the next 48 hours in the light of KPMG's legal obligation to recover money from ITM for the benefit of MIBL creditors. He was aware that disposals were in process in relation to Wade Adams with completion possible by the end of July at which time part of the sales proceeds would be received...

Would I confirm that a bankruptcy of ITM would seriously jeopardise the sale, he asked. Back over the ground we had been over again and again; he knew the answer, I said, and I quoted a Greek saying: 'Say something better than silence or keep your mouth shut.' That was the last time I spoke to that bully.

It was inevitable that the fall of Meridien would have a domino effect on the whole group: first on Meridien BIAO, and later on ITM itself. That was the intention of KPMG anyway. But they were not successful in securing the liquidations of the last two. A Luxembourg liquidator was appointed. He did use KPMG Luxembourg from time to time and I met one of the partners, who unlike the others I had met, was businesslike and sensible. The Luxembourg liquidator's approach was completely different. He was interested in what I had to say and took copious notes of my views. By that time I had made considerable progress in the sale of Wade Adams's African operations to a large Swedish/Danish construction group. I handed him all the files and I understand he later concluded the sale himself. I had also reached an advanced stage for a quasi-management buyout of the Wade Adams's Dubai operations, but the liquidator wanted to renegotiate because the managers involved were Cypriots (if he had known my views of them he would not have worried). I do not know if he ended up with a better deal.

I was never able to fathom the behaviour of KPMG Bahamas. A couple of senior partners (both British) spent some time in Zambia, but when they lost the liquidation assignment for the rest of the group they seemed to be in an indecent haste to get out. They resold the Chibote group for a derisory price ($2.4 million, I understand) to the same businessman/politician who had defaulted in the first place. He has also defaulted on them since, but they have not bothered to pursue him. The original Chibote group ended up in a state of disintegration, losing one asset after another to its creditors, amongst them the biggest farm in the group (15,000 acres). And the construction company, at one time the biggest in Zambia, is moribund.

But the most unusual decision they made was to attempt to sell Meriden Financial Services (MFS) for the paltry sum of $20,000, to a group that called itself Emerging Markets Zambia Ltd (EMZ). It was led by an American who had been the manager of MFS and its parent. He formed the EMZ group in association with another employee of the company, of Kenyan origin, and some Zambian executives of MFS, as well as a British/Indian group. They had in fact started operating under the EMZ name, using the MFS offices, vehicles and other assets and cash, a few months before. I was livid. I procured a counter-offer of $30,000 (equally laughable), but when the board sat the liquidators presented a second offer from EMZ for $31,000. The offer was signed by the Kenyan on behalf of the American who used the title 'managing director of EMZ'. Both of them were still employed by and receiving salary from MFS. They lived in MFS rented houses, fully furnished by MFS, and were running large cars owned by MFS. In view of my objections the EMZ offer was rejected, but the 'dual managing director' was not dismissed, as I demanded. He was suspended on half-pay until 'he had the opportunity to explain himself'!

To add insult to injury, at the end of the board meeting I was told that Andrew Kearns, a lawyer (he has since been disbarred) representing the liquidators sent a message to the American: 'Tell him not to worry. MFS will be his.' I was then convinced that something underhand was going on. EMZ had already got Meridien Leasing from the liquidators of Meridien BIAO Zambia for next to nothing. I went to court and asked for an injunction to stop the sale. It was granted on 12 October 1995. At the time of writing MFS still has over

$31,000 in its bank account, after it had paid off all its employees, even though none of its fixed assets, such as staff vehicles, household furniture, etc., were recovered as a result of the behaviour of the Bahamian liquidators.

Danae and I returned to Zambia on 7 September 1995, after a harrowing summer. I seemed to be constantly in the air, flying between New York and Los Angeles and London and Luxembourg and Frankfurt and Copenhagen, seeing lawyers and accountants and liquidators and staff, some of them Africans who had been stranded in foreign countries as a result of the collapse. The biggest strain was passing through London. For some reason, the immigration authorities at Heathrow airport had been briefed to give me a hard time every time I passed through. It had started in about March 1995; they would give me the treatment of those who are suspected of being illegal immigrants. After tapping my name on the computer, the immigration officer would show me to a chair and ask me to wait, and I would move to a group of waiting youngsters, mainly from the Middle East and South Asia. After an hour or so they would call me, stamp my passport, give me the usual six-month stay and say nothing. But, on 16 May 1995, they went one step further. They issued me with a 'Notice to a person required to submit to further examination'. The 'Notice' did not make much sense to me. It read:

> You have arrived at this port from Luxembourg by ship/aircraft LUXAIR 403 on 16/5/1995 and are a person to whom paragraph 2 of Schedule 2 to the Act applies. You have been examined by an immigration officer* and you may also be examined by a Medical Inspector**. You are hereby required to submit to a further examination by an immigration officer***.

After an hour's waiting the further examination was carried out by a very polite and embarrassed girl, who after glancing at her computer for a long time, and looking at the grey-haired man in blue business suit sitting in front of her, told me that she could not understand why she had to do this and advised me to get a lawyer to sort it out. I did not, and it took another year or so before I could pass through Heathrow normally again, even though by that time Zambians started needing visas for the UK and I had a two-year multiple entry visa stamped in my passport issued to me by the British consulate in Lusaka. But by that time I had got used to the charade, and I factored it into my timetable and treated it as a joke.

In the meantime, rumours that we would never return to Zambia appeared so often in the Zambian press that I had to issue strong denials time and again. Some of our friends in London and New York were worried about our fate and advised us to delay our return for a few months, but none of the members of the family ever wavered on this issue: as soon as I finished with liquidators and lawyers we would be back. There was one Zambian who tried to scare me about returning: the businessman/politician (and at that time still the Minister of Defence) who had defaulted on the purchase of the Chibote group from us, but had just re-purchased it from the liquidator for peanuts, as I described earlier. He called me to his suite at the Dorchester Hotel in London to warn me that, much as he would like to protect me, the police were uncontrollable in high-profile cases and he was worried about what might happen to me if I returned. I might be arrested and humiliated, and even tortured – 'the routine in such circumstances,' he said. I came to the conclusion that he had something to hide, and it was not my personal safety he was concerned about but my presence in Zambia. And, sure enough, it was my reaction to his agreement with the liquidator that worried him.

Home, at last – jet-lagged and tired and traumatised; the staff looking anxiously at us and at each other, the cook who had been with us since 1966 unable to control himself and bursting into tears. We did not want to see or talk to anybody. We did not want to even talk to each other. We just wanted to sit on the deck overlooking the meadow that had been the Chitoka lake, but had dried up after three years of drought, until we could digest what had happened to us and come to terms with it. But the press arrived at the Chaminuka gate. Two very persistent youngsters, Anthony and Chilombo, wanted an interview. I did not have the strength to face it. I told the staff to tell the guard not to let them in. The guard did not, even though they tried to persuade him that he owed no allegiance to us: we were foreigners and would soon go and leave him without a job, they told him. But he knew better and did not yield. The bitter irony in all this was that Chilombo's family, one of the most prominent in Chavuma, was amongst the first I made friends with in the 1950s, when I lived in the North Western Province. And I was the best man at her aunt Winnie's wedding to my friend Leonard Chinjavata at Chavuma in 1962, the first wedding Danae attended, about a month after she had arrived in the country. Youngsters can be unwittingly cruel, but that comment when we were feeling so low hurt most.

We had a week of rest. But, on 13 September, I had a police 'call-out'. I went there the next day with my lawyer and friend Edward Shamwana. After a couple of hours 'fishing' (impeccably polite and professional), the police charged me with 'inviting people to take part in an unauthorised scheme, under Sect. 74 (a) (b) of the Securities and Exchange Commission Act No. 38–1993'. I had no idea what they were talking about. The banks in the Group were making their own decisions and issuing products suitable for their markets in association with the group marketing department. I was never involved. I learned later that a Meridien Zambia bond had fallen between two stools, having been issued just before a new act was promulgated. I was to appear before the resident magistrate of Lusaka on 20 November 1995. The day beforehand, I received a message from Edward not to go to the court directly, but to pass through his office first. I arrived there early in the morning with a very distressed Danae and my son Harry, who happened to be in Zambia at the time, but Edward received a telephone call that the case had been postponed *sine die*. They kept my passport for a couple of years, though they always released it when I needed to travel.

In the meantime, the liquidation of Meriden BIAO Zambia was turning into a disaster.

28. A WASTED EFFORT

Home, familiar surroundings, people who love you and care for you and the serenity and tranquillity of Chaminuka had a healing effect on our minds, even though the problems remained. The press and some hard-core settlers apart, the ordinary people did not view us with hostility. There were those who would stop us in the street and tell us to 'be strong', a very touching admonition. Others would remind us of something good we did in the past, as if it could be balanced against the disaster. And there were those who would lament the passing of Meridien, 'the bank that cared for the people', they said. Many would stop me in the street and say: 'I had money in Meridien, but if it opens tomorrow I shall be the first customer.' Others were indignant with the liquidation process. For some unfathomable reason, KMPG South Africa resurfaced. Accountants from Johannesburg would breeze in and out of Lusaka at tremendous cost. Arrive Monday or Tuesday from Johannesburg, return Thursday or Friday. It was a scandal but I swallowed hard and told myself that I should not get involved. But early in January 1996 I received a call from the Attorney-General. He was also perturbed about what was happening and asked me if I could do something about it. 'Could, for example, Meridien be reopened?' He asked me to think about it and send him a letter.

On 11 January 1996 I wrote:

> It is now eight months since Meridien BIAO Zambia was placed in receivership and five months since liquidation. During this period a number of professional accounting firms were appointed to perform various functions (KPMG South Africa – Due diligence, Price Waterhouse Zambia – Receivers, KPMG Zambia and South Africa – Liquidators), at what must have been inevitably substantial costs. I am aware that liquidation tends to be a very slow process but I am worried that in the case of MBBZ it is extraordinarily so. I am also very worried that assets have been disposed of at derisory prices to the detriment of depositors and other creditors. I particularly have in mind the disposal of Meridien Leasing

which had an extraordinarily successful and profitable history and was sold way below its true worth.

Looking at the banking scene in general, the situation also looks grim. The demise of MBBZ was followed by that of other indigenous banks and the flight of deposits to the local subsidiaries of the three foreign banks, thus re-establishing their dominance over the financial sector. One might see nothing wrong with that trend but I am afraid I get a lot of complaints that since the closure of MBBZ local businessmen cannot get a hearing from foreign banks, never mind favourable consideration of their financial needs. I receive such complaints, even from depositors of MBBZ who assure me that regardless of what happened they would return to MBBZ if it were to reopen its doors again. I may be the wrong person to say it but the emergence of Meridien BIAO group changed the banking environment in Africa. [I was not the only one to say it. The Price Waterhouse Zambia *Newsletter* of January 1996 says: 'Meridien grew rapidly because of its innovative banking products and perceived superior customer service.'] With particular reference to Zambia MBBZ changed the banking scene from one of stagnation to a truly competitive market place. It now appears that the old set up of three foreign banks catering for multinationals and only the very major local companies has returned... I have not seen the accounts of MBBZ since February 1995. A lot of events have taken place since then and no doubt the accounts look quite different now. However, I still believe that it is not in the interest of anybody, least of all the depositors, to liquidate MBBZ piecemeal. Maximum value will be got only from refinancing and reopening it. I feel confident from approaches I have been getting that there is serious interest in reopening MBBZ and I have been urged to undertake it.

The purpose of this letter is to enquire whether the government would welcome such initiative. If it does I would be only too pleased to prepare a financial plan for the restructuring and try to put together a group of interested parties. I would like to assure you that there is no selfish or ulterior motive behind this approach. My only aim is to reopen the bank in the interest of the depositors and other creditors and re-establish its role in the promotion of local enterprise. I would like to guide it in its initial period towards providing good service and making profits in order to repay past obligations but financial participation by me is not an imperative condition in this initiative... I would need access to the liquidators and their cooperation in order to review the current financial position of the bank and determine the best method of proceeding... Should this be acceptable the liquidators must also be advised to cease disposal of the bank's assets during the period of review.

I had a meeting with the Attorney-General to discuss the letter and he suggested that I also write to the President along the same lines. He also asked me to see the Minister of Finance and prepare an outline plan for discussion between them. They both emphasised that the plan should provide for 'no more than three or four shareholders'. I protested that it was too soon for a plan. I needed to see the books of the bank first. But, against my better judgement, I sent him the following on 31 January:

I refer to my letter of 11 January and our meeting of 29 January on the subject of reopening MBBZ. You asked for more details of the plan, which I provide as follows:

A group of serious investors both local and foreign are prepared to invest up to $5 million in order to reopen the bank, provided that after investigations they are satisfied of its viability. I have been asked to lead the group and carry out the necessary investigations and prepare a suitable scheme. Even though I am not familiar with the financials of MBBZ I believe that the funds available are adequate (in view of the probable substantial contraction of its balance sheet) provided a suitable agreement is reached with the creditors and depositors.

The biggest creditor is the government through the Bank of Zambia followed by the PTA Bank. Considering the likely pay-out from the current liquidation, if it is allowed to proceed in its current fashion, I believe it would be in the interest of both institutions to agree to a reasonable rescheduling and/or restructuring of their loans in order to obtain maximum value. I also believe that the World Bank and the IMF will go along with such a scheme, provided the terms are sensible and I am ready to prepare a suitable presentation in due course. A number of large depositors may be prepared to participate in the scheme by agreeing to convert their deposits into capital in the form of either ordinary or preferred stock. The aim will be to pay out smaller depositors in full as soon as possible but I envisage that even these depositors should be offered the alternative of participating in the capital of the Bank should they choose to do so. If there is positive response to the above MBBZ should become a public company quoted on the Lusaka Stock Exchange. Naturally in order to prepare a detailed scheme one needs access to the books of MBBZ...
If the investigations reveal that a scheme is feasible and the potential investors agree to proceed the following would be necessary:

1. Preliminary discussions with GRZ/BOZ, the PTA Bank and some of the large depositors...

2. Preliminary discussions with BOZ regarding the amounts and method of payment of the small depositors

3. Assuming 1 and 2 above prove successful, preparation of a detailed plan with the assistance of an international investment bank for submission to the interested parties.

As regards timetable I believe the following is possible:

1. Investigations and preliminary discussions with creditors and major depositors: 2–3 weeks

2. Approval from investors, appointment of advisors and preparation of detailed plan: 2–3 weeks

3. Final negotiations: 2 weeks

4. Implementation, meetings with depositors, publicity and completion of legal formalities: 6 weeks

I did not provide an estimate for recruitment of staff because, from my continuing contacts, I believed that the loyalty of Meridien employees was so high that the task would be completed simultaneously with the above steps. In other words, MBBZ could reopen as early as mid-May, or at the latest by 1 June 1996...

I received the following astonishing reply from the Attorney-General dated 7 February:

I received your letter of 31 January 1996, which I passed on the Minister of Finance and the Chief of Staff at State House. I must mention that the proposals are far from being realistic as approved and I have a distinctive impression that an attempt could be made to engage in some rather innovative financial engineering and nothing much. This is because it is clear that there would be no meaningful capitalization of the bank and therefore these efforts are not likely to be fruitful.

I interpreted his comments about 'innovative financial engineering' as the part of the plan that provided for the restructuring of MBBZ as a public company. It did not suit them. They had emphasised three or four shareholders time and again. I did not know who they had in mind, but I had strong suspicions that it meant that 'three or four shareholders' had already been selected, and in that case I did not want to be involved. But the letter could not remain unanswered. On 14 February, I had the last word:

...I must confess I am not sure I understand the comment 'the proposals are far from realistic as approved and I have a distinctive impression that an attempt could be made to engage in some rather innovative financial engineering and nothing more'. The first part of the above sentence refers to approval of proposals and I am at a loss to understand who approved what. The second part contains the insinuation that the plan for the restructuring of MBBZ is somehow underhand... My motivation was the realisation that the assets of MBBZ were disposed of at giveaway prices and depositors and creditors would in the end receive very little. As a result I took the view and continue to do so that offering them shares in addition to cash would be the right and fair thing to do. This method would give them the opportunity of either receiving dividends or of disposing of their shares at a more advantageous price in the future. In taking this line I was fully aware that MBBZ would end up as a public company and that this would be against the wishes you expressed during our meeting that the shareholding should be limited to three or four parties only...

I did not add that I was not prepared to work for 'the three or four principals you have in mind', because my purpose of helping the depositors would not be achieved. On 14 February I received a letter from his boss. Chiluba wrote:

I refer to your letter of January 17 in respect of your intention to reopen MBBZ and suggest that any proposals to that effect be processed through the pertinent authority [Bank of Zambia] ...In the past schemes of such seriousness, which have been politically leveraged, have been a source of problems... It is my sincere hope that the losses incurred by the depositors and government be redressed.

That really made me mad. I responded:

...You make two statements, which are completely unfair but more importantly patently wrong. The first is my 'intention to reopen MBBZ' and the second is a reference to 'politically leveraged' schemes... My letter did not indicate my intention to reopen MBBZ... I was ready to lead an effort to resuscitate MBBZ with or without my participation. I did not write to you in order to obtain political leverage. I wrote after discussion with the Attorney General and out of the realisation that the MBBZ issue is politically sensitive and no progress can be made without political clearance. I was always aware that substantive discussions would need to take place not only with BOZ but the International Financial Institutions and professional advisors. In fact all the details are spelled out in my letter to the Attorney General of January 31 [which, according to the Attorney General's letter, it had been passed on to the State House Chief of Staff] I was also aware that my interest could be completely misunderstood but I considered it a risk worth taking. Now I know that my worst fears have materialized...

And that marks the inglorious end of my business career.

29. BUT LIFE CARRIES ON

I said in the epilogue of *Africa: Another Side of the Coin*:

> The security and permanence of my childhood did not follow me in later years.
> My life has been hectic and eventful, sometimes easy, sometimes difficult, more
> often difficult than easy. But I always coped. I always believed in what I was
> doing, and, arrogantly perhaps, believed that I followed the right course. I was
> always at peace with myself and in turbulent times, I had a wealth of experiences
> and memories to soothe me and sustain me: from Karavas and my childhood,
> from Balovale and Kabompo, from friends and family. I could always ruminate
> on the peaceful image of the valley and the sea and the Byzantine chant from the
> church of Haghia Eirene. Or the soft light and the stillness of a wet afternoon on
> the Kabompo River, when the rays of the setting sun strike the trees horizontally
> and give them a golden glow. And the blue smoke from the cooking fires rising
> slowly to the sky in the early evening and the kids of the village playing and
> shouting and laughing.

And, after the debacle, life in Chaminuka, which had started off as a nostalgic
reconstruction of my days in the North Western Province, had all the idyllic
ingredients of the village. We shared it with the five members of the staff and
their families. And we enjoyed the mornings and the evenings; the morning star
and the morning breeze, the birds that herald the sunrise and the cries and the
laughter of the kids as they left for school; and the stillness of the early evening
as the sun went down, and the quiet that followed when the kids were called
home for supper and the sounds of the birds died down, and the crickets and
the frogs and the hyenas and all the other night creatures that bring the African
night to life took over. But the days were long and the turbulence in our hearts
made them endless. We had always lived a hectic life. And I was still in my
mid-sixties and Danae was 10 years younger. We needed something to do; to fill
our days in order to enjoy the hours of rest. I had always been a busy person and
happily coped with 12-hour days and seven-day weeks. I could not just sit back

and do nothing. And, more importantly, we needed the income. Chaminuka is a big property and an expensive place to run and needs constant attention. Without funds it would quickly turn to ruins. We had to make it meet its costs and earn us a living or we might have to sell it.

We had always been reclusive and Danae and I were quite happy to be alone. We had always been very good friends to ourselves and to each other and our circle was very limited and our friends very few. Chaminuka had been a 'well-kept secret' in Zambia, open only to family and close friends. So much so that many myths had been created around it: opulence, marble, Persian rugs – the 'descriptions' of it that reached me from time to time would fit Mobutu's Versailles in Gbadolite, which I described in Chapter 13. (In the 1980s, a visiting friend told me that when he mentioned to his country's ambassador that he was staying at Chaminuka he got the response: 'You mean you are staying at the palace!') So it was with trepidation that we decided to open it to the public. We worried how we could cope with strangers around the house, checking the way we had set it up, and looking at everything we had lovingly collected over the years and making comments and asking questions. (In the early years one visitor said to me 'You've got plenty of things here don't you?', as if he was speaking to a spoiled kid who had plenty of toys he did not deserve.)

And we did have a lot of interesting… 'things'. We had been collecting Zambian modern art for nearly half a century and the artistic fraternity had all been close friends. Afterwards, with our travels to West Africa and other parts of the continent, we built a sizeable collection of traditional art as well. And we had conceived and developed the first private wildlife reserve in Zambia, which had matured over the years and made it a joy to tour, and see how the giraffe and the zebra, and the eland and the kudu, and the wildebeest and the sable and all the other animals of the Zambian bush had settled in and adapted and made the Chaminuka Park their natural habitat as if they had been there for centuries. The birds were equally 'at home' in the park: the fish eagle and the kingfisher, and the secretary bird and the ibis, and the egrets and the ducks and the geese and all the migratory birds that visit the lakes for rest and recuperation during their long annual sojourns from the Antarctic to the Russian steppes and back. The park has pristine Miombo woodland, one of the rare pieces of land that survives untouched around Lusaka, and savannah and fields, which we are in the process of rehabilitating. We plant trees, all local species (no jacarandas or bougainvillea or pines or gum trees), which will take 35 years and more to grow; and Danae and I joke that, at our age, we shall never live to see that. But we keep on planting, nevertheless.

And we know Africa. Apart from Zambia, where we have lived since 1950 and have an umbilical connection, over decades of travelling we have built up a wealth of knowledge of the countries we visited (all the countries south of the Sahara, with the exception of Guinea-Bissau, Lesotho and the Horn of Africa countries). We know their history and their traditions and have views on their development, their way of life, their politics and their future.

All this combined to break the ice and make the visitors love the place and make us comfortable with them. We discovered that, after all, we like meeting people and talking to them and learning about them and answering their questions, and teaching them about Zambia and its early years and its early leaders, and Africa and its problems and what caused them, and birds and wildlife and local art, and the weather and the seasons and everything that is local and interesting.

We opened Chaminuka as a lodge in 1998 with the eight family bedrooms – our two sons, Stelios and Harry, were both working abroad at the time. But, soon enough, that turned out to be too small. And, as most of the original members of the staff retired, we converted the five staff cottages into 10 additional suites, which allowed us to host conferences, making visitors more regular and increasing the occupancy that enabled us to recruit more staff. Before we knew it, Chaminuka had become a popular tourist resort, and as demand was still on the increase at the end of 2005 we decided to add 12 more suites, always making sure that the original concept does not change and the village character of the place remains. Garages became conference rooms and offices and Stelios returned home and took charge of the place, assisted by the many young people who are running it, most of them from the surrounding area. And it is a joy to watch Chaminuka grow, instead of declining with the years, like the two old people who fathered it.

The two old people (Danae and I) may be declining with age, but they are not decaying. Chaminuka is keeping us busy and alert, and it inspires us. And we are proud to 'preside' over it (like a headmaster and headmistress, I used to say in the early days, but now I have been promoted to 'shikulu', grandfather – an honorific of respect that applies to men of my age). And we do seem to be the grandparents of the Chaminuka community, which has now grown to some 700 and is a microcosm of Zambia, a mixture from all the tribes, with many kids of all ages and churches and schools and its own soccer team, which competes with those of the farms in the area.

And the visitors? I used to say: 'I know everybody in Zambia over the age of 60 but I know nobody under that.' But we are now discovering the younger generations. They come to Chaminuka with their families. The children – town kids – know nothing about wildlife. And we enjoy testing their knowledge after they come back from the park. They spotted the elephants and the giraffes and the zebras and the lions and the hyenas, they proclaim proudly. But when we ask 'what else?' all we get back is: antelopes. They cannot identify more than two or three species from the 20 or so in the park and they get embarrassed, and we have great fun with their embarrassment.

But most visitors come for conferences and we are getting to know the younger generations of Zambian professionals, the yardstick of the progress that Zambia's society has made since I arrived in 1950. They represent all sectors of the society: business, NGOs, professional bodies, government departments, churches, medical teams, etc. And it is a joy to see them work into the night and talk to them during their breaks. It makes us happy to see that through them society is progressing and maturing, and able to tackle its problems as it goes forward. And it has strengthened our conviction that, with them around, the country is in safe hands.

And the foreign visitors? There are business visitors who want to get away from Lusaka over weekends, or tourists who come for the wildlife and the birds of Zambia – one of the most diverse in the region. They have different interests but they are all thirsty for local information, and it is fascinating to see their different focuses and a pleasure to give them information about the country and its people, its development and its business sector, and help them see that Africa is not dying, that on the contrary it is making fast progress and catching up with the rest of the world – an easier point to make on the spot, with all the evidence around, than from a distance.

And it is flattering to hear the praises of Chaminuka, especially from local visitors, who take to it intuitively and admire its local character and the almost exclusive use of local materials for its construction, and the local art that speaks so much of their everyday life. And, of course, from the foreign visitors, who also find it a unique piece of Africa and marvel at the skills and achievements of both the local and traditional artists, and the stories and the aspects of everyday life that African art highlights. And of the friendly hospitality they get from our staff, which is a natural characteristic of the Zambian people.

I guess it would be customary to say that all this praise humbles us. But it would not be true. It makes us proud because everything about Chaminuka, from the concept, to the design, to the execution, its collections and its way of life is our creation and we feel that if we achieved nothing else in life, we have at least managed to put together this synopsis of Africa, which will nurture us and sustain us as long as we live.

But our interests have not narrowed to Chaminuka. We still care about what goes on around us, and keep informed and follow developments on the continent and the region and at home, in Zambia. Some I have already covered in this book. But I still have a few words to say about the region, and about political developments in Zambia since the advent of 'multi-party democracy'.

Part 4

More Challenges in the Southern Region

30. SOUTH AFRICA: FREE AND IN BONDAGE

...Out of the experience of an extraordinary human disaster that lasted too long must be born a society of which all humanity must be proud. Our daily deeds as ordinary South Africans must produce an actual South African reality that will reinforce humanity's belief in justice, strengthen its confidence in the nobility of the human soul and sustain all our hopes for a glorious life for all... To my compatriots I have no hesitation in saying that each one of us is as intimately attached to the soil of this beautiful country as are the famous jacaranda trees of Pretoria and the mimosa trees of the bushveld. Each time one of us touches the soil of this land we feel a sense of personal renewal. The national mood changes as the seasons change. We are moved by a sense of joy and exhilaration when the grass turns green and the flowers bloom. The spiritual and physical oneness we all share with this common homeland explains the depth of the pain we all carried in our hearts as we saw our country tear itself apart in a terrible conflict and as we saw it spurned, outlawed and isolated by the peoples of the world precisely because it had become the universal base of the pernicious ideology and practice of racial oppression...

So said Mandela in his inauguration speech on 5 May 1994, the day that ushered in majority rule to South Africa and that will remain the most emotional day of my life.

I never expected majority rule in South Africa to come about as swiftly and peacefully as it did. I was anticipating a protracted civil war at least twice as long as Zimbabwe's and Namibia's. But the cold war had ended and the South African apartheid regime could no longer sell itself to the Western powers as a bastion against communism and the freedom fighters as communist agents. And, to be fair to F.W. de Klerk, the last white President, he proved pragmatic enough to grasp that this new reality weakened the whites' hold on power and their ability to withstand the sanctions against their country, which were spreading and weakening its economy. And South African business assisted him

221

by taking a down-to-earth view that it had more to lose from economic isolation and the best option would be to negotiate a settlement.

So far, South Africa has proved a successful democracy; so much so that Thabo Mbeki, who succeeded Mandela, was able to proclaim with some satisfaction during his second inauguration, 10 years after 'independence',

> ...Despite the fact that we are a mere 10 years removed from the period of racist dictatorship it is today impossible to imagine a South Africa that is not democratic. Nobody in our country today views democracy as a threat to their interests and their future. This includes our national racial and political minorities. This is because we have sought to design and implement an inclusive democratic system rather than one driven by social and political exclusion.

But the economic system is not yet inclusive. The business scene is overwhelmingly white, not only in ownership but in executive and middle-level employment. The government did pioneer a scheme for Black Economic Empowerment (BEE) but what this has achieved is only a sprinkling of black tycoons. Some view it as tokenism, black-controlled companies accounting for only 3% of the value of the Johannesburg Stock Exchange. But employment practices are pivotal to the transformation process. I do not know the degree of the involvement of the black owners in the management of the companies they control, and I cannot say if the black-owned groups have actually changed employment practices, which in the country as a whole are still overwhelmingly biased in favour of whites – up to 2005 blacks still formed less than 10% of senior management in South Africa. In my view South Africa needs a much more radical approach, and employment practices are the crux of the matter.

The government is not short of gratuitous advice. Every time I go to South Africa and read the *Business Day* I marvel at the variety of self-serving suggestions on economic policy offered by various economic gurus, business bodies, chairmen of companies, etc. I remember, on the eve of the budget, a couple of years after majority rule, somebody telling the Minister of Finance, through the columns of *Business Day*, that if he did not keep the budget deficit below the equivalent of 1.5% of GDP economic Armageddon would follow. That was at the time when most countries in the European Union were struggling to bring theirs down to 3% – a target they did not succeed in holding for very long. But the European Union is not emerging from centuries of dictatorship (as far as the black people of South Africa are concerned) and lopsided development that needs to be tackled with vigour. For, unless this is done, there will be widespread dissatisfaction and unrest, and, sometime in the not too distant future, irrepressible demand for equity. No sensible person would blame South Africa for a moderate budget deficit, as long as it is used to accelerate the transformation.

But South Africa's businessmen (not unlike their Rhodesian cousins) seem oblivious to the long term and care only for today: more foreign investment through the Johannesburg Stock Exchange, which will increase the price of their shares. If such investment is slow in materialising they blame the government and the uncertainty it creates in its quest to tilt the balance in favour of black enterprise. So they shower the government with schemes it must adopt to achieve that aim. The most outlandish came under the name of the 'Brenthurst Initiative', in August 2003. The *Financial Times* reported it as follows:

> South Africa's richest industrial family has floated a scheme to award companies tax breaks for helping to speed the country's post-apartheid transformation. Nicky Oppenheimer, grandson of the founder of De Beers and Anglo American, yesterday put forward an initiative that would lower companies' tax rates on the basis of their performance in such areas as black ownership, employment equity, skills development and procurement.
>
> This is aimed at solving the South African problem: 'how do you grow and transform at the same time?' Mr Oppenheimer said yesterday, sporting a black tie emblazoned with multicoloured South African flags. The Oppenheimers own 45% of De Beers and Mr Oppenheimer is a non executive director of Anglo American, the mining group. The family has dubbed the proposal the Brenthurst Initiative, after its Johannesburg estate where it presented the plan yesterday to about 140 guests, including government ministers, trade unionists and President Thabo Mbeki. In proposing the plan, the Oppenheimers are grasping the nettle of South Africa's thorniest public policy debate.
>
> Johannesburg stocks have been hit over the past year amid uncertainty about government guidelines on 'black economic empowerment' aimed at shifting business ownership and practices in mining finance and other sectors. Companies complain of draconian and fickle government regulation... Some black political and union leaders, meanwhile, say white-controlled companies are doing too little to transform their management and business practices. Many black South Africans are ambivalent about big business and it remains unclear how the Oppenheimers' proposal will be received. 'There is a traditional distrust between white business and the government so it might not fly' said Reg Rumnie...

Naturally, it did not fly. The *Financial Times* concluded its report:

> The family said it had presented the president with details of the plan in late 2002. 'My belief is that President Mbeki has bought into the idea of transformation and growth and realises that without both these elements South

Africa will have problems down the road,' Mr Oppenheimer said. The president's spokesman refused to comment.

Nobody would doubt that transformation and growth had been in the President's mind for ever. The question must be whether his priorities in this regard are the same as those of big business. I do not know the thinking of the South African government, but maybe it came to the conclusion that it would be adding salt to the wound if it made the taxpayers (even the poorest are taxed at the rate of 14% VAT on their purchases) pay business giants to do their duty of spreading the economic cake wider and training black people, a duty that they happily performed for the whites but chose to ignore for the blacks, over generations.

But it is going to be difficult to break the stranglehold that big business has on South Africa. It is a very like-minded incestuous body that speaks with one voice, and nobody will want to rock the boat. This diagnosis is not mine. I read it in 1992 in an article published in the *Financial Times* by Sir Alan Walters, Margaret Thatcher's economic guru and vice-chairman of AIG at the time, and George Guise, ex-director of Consolidated Goldfields, both well versed in the South African business establishment. I found it very perceptive and very witty. Its title was 'Feather beds in South Africa's boardrooms'. It said:

South Africa is a continental anomaly. A third world country with the tribalism, the violence, the excessive public spending, overregulation, overweening bureaucracy, state owned behemoths, the protection and politicisation of much economic activity. But superimposed on these is a convincing presence of the first world in the form of the great mining and manufacturing corporations. The English speaking South Africans have dominated this private business sector just as Afrikaners have been predominant in government employment while blacks have provided the labour. An oversimplification? A caricature? Perhaps but it conveys the essence of South Africa for most of this century [the twentieth century; it is 1992 and they are speaking of the government of F. W. de Klerk] ...

As in any dirigiste socialist country (and, with its high ratio of government involvement and interference in economic life South Africa must be so classed), the economy is dominated by very large corporations. In South Africa fewer than 10 conglomerates dominate the first world industrial sector. They have pyramidal or interlocking shareholdings, which lock out their external shareholders from any influence over management and protect their management from any true accountability to shareholders. As is well documented, conglomeration, especially with monopoly power and protection against intruders leads to much inefficiency. The rate of return on capital in the many peripheral activities is low. This is reflected in the fact that for most of these conglomerates the share price is less than the value of their component assets...

Many reasons explain these feather beds in the boardrooms. The most important is that everyone is in a feather bed with everyone else. Large blocks of shares are held by corporations in the same group as well as by controlled pension and insurance funds. It is virtually impossible for any outsider to mount a takeover bid against the interlocked interests of the five conglomerates, which account for more than three-quarters of the market capitalisation of the Johannesburg Stock Exchange...

And the solution? Walters and Guise suggest:

The main task of a reforming government must be to insist on the disentanglement of the crossholdings of the conglomerates and the opening up of South Africa for foreign as well as domestic corporate raiders. The first step is so simple. It is for the regulatory authorities of government and the stock exchange to cease the restrictive practice of protecting entrenched management groups from their disenfranchised private shareholders...

This article was written in 1992, by highly intelligent insiders. I do not know how much the cross-shareholding of South African companies has changed since then. But the complaints that South Africa is not getting adequate foreign investment and that the Johannesburg Stock Exchange is being hit time and again persist. And, though business attributes this to the uncertainty over government guidelines on local participation, maybe the government's contribution to the uncertainty is only a part of the problem. The main problem may still be the feather-bedding that Walters and Guise highlighted in 1992.

How does one solve it? In my view, by introducing antitrust legislation of the type all major economies have these days. Apart from feather-bedding there are companies in South Africa that have near-monopoly positions in many sectors of the economy. A law that would force companies to divest down to 30% of a sector would have a cathartic effect on the market. Foreign investment would stream to South Africa from both East and West. And, more importantly, it would bring with it new work practices unburdened by the legacy of apartheid. This is what will lead to greater black participation in business. The surest route to black capitalism is through executive positions. Black executives who make their way to the higher echelons of the corporate ladder will without doubt identify opportunities for acquisition or start-up ventures, and because of their experience and their reputation they will have no problem in procuring finance for them. And the black executives' chances of climbing up the corporate ladder will be higher under new investors without apartheid hang-ups.

What has been achieved so far in Black Economic Empowerment is an insignificant change at the top. And the legislation that 26% of mining shares should be in black hands by 2009 will not achieve the fundamental change to the profile of employment that is urgently needed. Businessmen are sufficiently inventive in devising ways to bypass the spirit of BEE. The De Beers scheme is just one example.

On 8 November 2005 De Beers announced what it called a 'ground breaking, broad based Black Economic Empowerment transaction' in respect of their South African operation, which it grouped under De Beers Consolidated Mines Ltd (DBCM). The announcement was made jointly with Ponahalo (emergence) Investment Holdings, which is being described as a 'new generation BEE company with an exceptional combination of complementary business, professional, community leadership, and investment skills that was specifically established to acquire an equity interest in DBCM'.

The interesting part is the structure of the deal. It is split into two halves. One half will be owned by two employee trusts: the 'Key Employee Trust' (15%) and the 'Equal Allocation Trust', described as 'the De Beers Family', representing over 18,000 'current and future employees and pensioners' (35%). The other half will be owned by a company composed as follows: three individuals, holding 18%, 13% and 8%; a company owned by four women, holding 16%; and by three additional trusts, for 'Disadvantaged Women' (17.5%), 'Community Beneficiaries' (17.5%) and 'Disabled Persons' (10%). These trusts will get their shares gratis. The method of financing the rest of the shares had not been announced by the time this book went to the printers. Ponahalo will appoint three directors to the board of DBCM. But can the three directors of a company with such diverse shareholding make any difference to the governance of DBCM? The answer must be that it has been specifically designed not to be able to do so.

South Africa is doing well and, despite grumblings, everybody acknowledges that the government is doing a good job with the economy. But one can never be too fast on the transformation front. The predicament of Zimbabwe is very close and nobody in South Africa, least of all big business, would want it repeated in their country.

But how has Zambia fared since the demise of the one-party state?

31. TEN WASTED YEARS

Zambian Presidents enjoy a honeymoon period with the donor countries lasting a whole first term of five years. That was certainly the case with Chiluba, who succeeded Kaunda in 1991, and was their darling until 1996. The scales fell from their eyes when he undemocratically declared Kaunda, the founder of the country, a foreigner in order to prevent him from standing against him in the 1996 presidential election. As a result UNIP (Kaunda's party) made the decision not to contest the parliamentary elections, and Chiluba, much to his delight, ended up with an overwhelming majority in Parliament. He tried to use his majority to change the constitution in order to stand for a third term, but to everybody's surprise he did not succeed. The outcry was so strong that he suddenly declared that he did not really want to stand, and withdrew. How his successor was chosen and how he was elected I shall cover later. I first want to highlight some major aspects of his presidency.

His main platform during the 1991 election campaign was the privatisation of the parastatal sector. He started with great vigour. A hundred or so companies were privatised in a hurry, some of them going to party faithful and others to local residents, all of them on credit terms, much against the advice of the first members of the Zambia Privatisation Agency, which was established to carry out the task. Many of those businesses had to be repossessed when the new owners proved unable to run them or keep up the payments. By the end of the decade most of the smaller commercial and industrial companies due for privatisation were sold.

But none of the major state companies, Zambia State Insurance, Zambia National Commercial Bank, Zamtel and Zesco (the telecommunications and electricity companies), Nitrogen Chemicals, Kafue Textiles, Tazama pipelines, National Oil Company, etc., were put on the market during the Chiluba era. Some of those companies were the milch cows for his party, the MMD (paying for conferences, election campaigns, etc.), as well as his government. (When I asked a Zamtel engineer when he expected his company to be put on the market, his answer was a very emphatic 'never'. 'The government owes us so much in unpaid telephone bills, it cannot possibly privatise us because it will need to pay for its telephone calls after that,' he explained. I drew the conclusion that one of the reasons telephone costs are so high in the country is because the public have to make up for the unpaid government bills.)

No progress was made on the privatisation of the mines until Chiluba's second term, despite increasing pressures from the multilateral institutions and the donor countries. The reasons were partly the same as those for the other big companies, but ZCCM had an additional attraction. Chiluba was able to give directions on metal sales, and even before the end of his administration one major scam surfaced. He had granted exclusivity on all cobalt sales to an Israeli company, Metal Resources Group (MRG). An audit, initiated by the donor countries, that was carried out in 2001 revealed that MRG was buying the cobalt at a fraction of its international price and making huge profits. The audit calculated 'discrepancies' on the MRG contracts amounting to $60,067,898.

To counter the pressures for faster action on the mine privatisation front from the donor countries, Chiluba very skilfully managed to create a semblance of activity that would result in no progress until the very end of his term. One of his tactics was to bypass the Zambian Privatisation Agency by appointing, in March 1997, a new team named 'the GRZ/ZCCM Privatisation Negotiating Team (PNT)', under the chairmanship of Francis Kaunda (the erstwhile ZCCM chairman whom he had unceremoniously dismissed in 1991, before he even took the oath of office). It was ironic that the World Bank was taken in and agreed to fund Kaunda's salary, even though it was obvious in Zambia that his appointment had been announced in order to delay the process and not to accelerate it – a feat he achieved very skilfully.

While some details of the purchase price became public, the exact details of the agreements and the concessions given to the new mine owners did not. I tried to obtain the agreements from the government for the purpose of this book but I struck a wall of silence. I was told that the agreements are private and cannot be made public. I asked how government agreements involving the sale of national assets could be termed 'private'. They were entered into on behalf of the Zambian people and the Zambian people are entitled to know the terms, I observed, and pointed out that the 1969 nationalisation agreements were approved by Parliament. But the senior civil servants I spoke to seemed to genuinely believe that if the private party involved in an agreement made with the government does not want it disclosed then the government should oblige. Sad but true. And I had a similar response from an opposition Member of Parliament I tried to enlist for help. The reply was: 'Andrew, you know they will never release those agreements.' So there you have it: if the government does not want to do something the loyal opposition must acquiesce. After that I lowered my sights. I wrote to the Attorney-General on 2 November 1995, asking for just the Anglo American agreements: acquisition of Konkola and termination. I am still waiting for a reply.

It was more difficult and time-consuming, but I did manage to get comprehensive information from various other sources.

The first new investor in mining was First Quantum Minerals (FQM) of Canada, which bought the Bwana Mkubwa surface tailings for $26 million in 1997. Production amounted to 10,000 tons of copper per annum until 2003, when First Quantum acquired the Lonshi copper deposit in the Democratic Republic of the Congo, 35 km across the border. The combined operation was initially producing 30,000 tons per annum at a cost of 44 cents per pound, one of the lowest in the world.

Two small mines were privatised by the end of 1997: Luanshya/Baluba and Chibuluma South. Bids for Luanshya/Baluba had been received and evaluated, and the Zambian Privatisation Agency had started detailed negotiations with First Quantum before the PNT came on the scene. But the PNT had a different agenda. It demanded revised bids, as a result of which Luanshya was awarded to the Roan Antelope Mining Corporation (Ramcoz), a new Zambian company owned by an Indian metal trader, Gokul Binani, whom Francis Kaunda knew from his days as chairman of ZCCM. The details of Binani's winning bid (with First Quantum's in brackets) were: cash $35 ($34) million, new equity investment $21.7 ($20) million, commitment for new investment $69 ($70.4) million, contingent investment $103 ($26.3) million, ZCCM participation 15% (17.5%). A 'neck-to-neck' outcome, except for the very nebulous $103 million 'contingent investment' that Binani stuck to the tail of his offer.

First Quantum was furious with the award. In a strongly worded letter to Francis Kaunda, its chairman wrote:

> …To its extreme surprise on 17 June 1997 FQM was asked to submit a revised bid at only two days' notice. FQM duly complied with this request, despite the unreasonably short notice, even though a re-bidding exercise was clearly inconsistent with all discussions FQM was having with ZCCM, ZPA and NM Rothschild. FQM does not accept, after this effort and consistency of behaviour on its behalf that ZCCM had grounds to announce another party as the

purchaser without first establishing that there were irreconcilable differences in negotiations with FQM.

Of concern to us are reports that Binani appears to have received details of our bids and had knowledge of private correspondence between FQM and ZCCM and their advisers... If what we are hearing about the bidding process is true then the board of FQM may be obliged to seek legal advice to establish what formal recourse it may take to protect its position and obtain legal remedies. We would emphasise that any perception that the privatisation process has not been conducted with transparency, consistency and correctness will be alarming to the international financial markets... (From *Selling the Family Silver*, by Francis Kaunda)

The above notwithstanding, First Quantum went on to become one of the major mining companies in Zambia. In addition to the expansion at Bwana Mkubwa it went on to develop the Kansanshi copper and gold deposit, which is expected to produce 145,000 tons of copper and some 80,000 ounces of gold per annum, while Ramcoz went into receivership in November 2000.

Liquidity problems at Luanshya mine surfaced soon after the Ramcoz takeover, amid rumours that the copper proceeds were not being received regularly. But the government bent over backwards to keep it going, ordering Zesco to supply electricity despite huge unpaid bills, and ordering the Zambia National Commercial Bank (ZANACO) to grant additional facilities ignoring huge arrears. At one stage the government even contemplated diverting a World Bank facility intended for mineworkers' retrenchment to Ramcoz. In *Selling the Family Silver* Francis Kaunda describes it thus:

> ...Mines Minister lent a sympathetic ear to Ramcoz over their problems and tried to get the government to help by approaching his colleague at the Ministry of Finance to extend a World Bank facility on ZCCM retrenchment to Maamba Collieries and the Luanshya/Baluba Mine...

But the Finance Minister of the time wisely put a stop to it (I wonder what the World Bank and the mineworkers' union would have had to say if such a scandalous attempt had succeeded?). And the government's justification of such extraordinary generosity? The need to keep the mine operating and the workers employed. But in the end ZANACO decided that enough was enough and appointed a receiver.

Chibuluma South was purchased by the Metorex consortium of two small South African mining companies and a securities firm. The cash consideration, according to *Selling the Family Silver*, was $17.5 million with a commitment for future capital expenditure of $34 million.

Both Ramcoz and Chibuluma were granted more or less similar tax concessions (the concessions would become more generous in later deals as a result of the bloody-minded bargaining of the Anglo American Corporation for the Konkola complex). For Ramcoz and Chibuluma, the most generous concession appears to be that each mine was deemed to be a new mine under the 1975 Act, which allows a 100% deduction of capital expenditure in the year it is incurred, presumably inclusive of the acquisition costs as well as all subsequent investments. Carry-forward losses were permitted for a period of 10 years, but there was no concession on the income tax rate, as far as I was able to ascertain – an academic point because, with the generous deductions granted, income tax would not become payable during the so called 'taxation stability' period of 15 years. The mineral royalty was reduced from 3% to 2% of revenue (minus transport and smelting and refining costs), deductible against income tax. Other concessions included exemption from import duties above 5% for capital items and 20% for all other goods and materials, and, more significantly, VAT exemption for a period of 15 years, with arrangements that input VAT (the VAT that mines pay when they buy goods locally) be refunded by government the month following the submission of a claim. As there are no exchange controls in Zambia the two companies were allowed to operate bank accounts domestically and abroad, and the government gave an undertaking that if exchange controls were introduced in the future the companies would be exempt up to the end of the 15-year taxation stability period. In fact, all concessions mentioned above were granted for a 15-year period.

It was not until 31 March 2000 that the mining privatisation process was completed, with the simultaneous signing of agreements for the two biggest mining complexes: with Mopani Copper Mines (MCM) for the Mufulira and Nkana mines, and Konkola Copper Mines (KCM) for the huge Konkola complex, which included the Nchanga open pit, the Nchanga underground mine, the Konkola underground mine, the Nchanga tailings dump, the Chingola refractory ores, the Nchanga leach plant, the Nkana smelter and refinery and the Nampundwe pyrite mine near Lusaka, as well as Konkola Deep, a very large copper deposit that with an investment of several hundred million dollars will become the biggest mine in Zambia, producing over 200,000 tons of copper a year for 30 years. (KCM would announce, in November 2005, that the project would go ahead with an initial investment of $400 million.)

The Mufulira and Nkana mines and related assets were sold to Mopani Copper Mines, majority-owned (73.1%) by Glencore International AG, a Swiss metal trading company, at the price of $20 million cash and $23 million in deferred payments, $159 million new investment commitment and an additional 'conditional investment' commitment of some $200 million (*Selling the Family Silver*).

As I said earlier, the government had had to turn to the Anglo American Corporation, because it had nowhere else to turn, after it had rejected the Kafue Consortium's bid for the Konkola complex two years earlier. As a result, the country lost the opportunity of dealing with a very respectable group of willing buyers (the Kafue Consortium included some of the biggest names in the mining world: Anglovaal Minerals (Avmin) of South Africa, Noranda of Canada and Phelps Dodge of the United States) and ended up negotiating with Anglo American from a position of weakness. Anglo American knew that the government had no other option and it used its advantage to the hilt. It set impossible conditions that needed to be fulfilled before going forward, it dragged its feet for a couple of years, and ended up with a bargain both in terms of price and unbelievable concessions, which made KCM non-taxable for 20 years.

The Anglo American offer, made through its Bermuda-based subsidiary ZCI (Zambia Copper Investments), was very complex and full of caveats and demands for changes in existing legislation, but, in summary, it appears that Konkola Copper Mines Ltd was sold for a total of $60 million payable as $30 million cash and the balance over six annual instalments commencing in January 2006 (in other words full payment would not be completed until 2011), with a follow-up investment of $300 million. (The actual purchase price was $90 million, but against that the government had to buy the ZCI shares in ZCCM for $30 million.) By comparison, the Kafue Consortium's offer had been $150 million cash with a follow-up investment of $1 billion. But, more importantly, it would not have included all the fancy concessions that the government had to make under pressure from Anglo.

The rejection of the Kafue Consortium's bid mystified the country, but it was a cunning delaying tactic that gave Chiluba control of the biggest mine for a couple more years. The donor countries, however, were up in arms and withheld the disbursement of promised aid until the two big mines were sold – pressure of which Anglo American was fully aware, and which further weakened the government's negotiating position.

It is important to highlight the inclusion of the tailings dumps and the Chingola refractory ores in the package. These are residues of decades of mining and, by the then available technology, inefficient metallurgical processing that contain some 380,000 tons of copper. With technological developments these residues can now be treated at very low cost, because they are lying on the surface. Anglo was aware of this bonanza. In 1999 it paid $130 million to buy the Kolwezi tailings in the Democratic Republic of Congo. And, as I mentioned earlier, Bwana Mkubwa, another similar operation in Zambia, is one of the lowest-cost producers in the world because of them.

Apart from giving Konkola away, the government of Zambia made the following tax and other concessions: flat income tax rate of 25% (instead of 35%) for a period of 20 years; KCM to be treated as a new mine under the 1975 Act; carry-forward losses for a period of 20 years; no withholding tax on dividends, royalties, interest and management fees paid to KCM shareholders, affiliates or third parties; royalties of 0.6% (instead of 3%) on the gross revenue of minerals produced (less transport and smelting and refining costs), deductible against income tax; exemption from rural electrification levy and excise duty on electrical energy; no customs and excise duty on all capital goods and only 15% (instead of 25%) on all materials; and total exemption from VAT with input VAT refundable within 10 days of submission of claim. In addition, the government of Zambia bound itself not to impose new taxes and not to increase the ones mentioned in the agreement for a period of 20 years. As regards the treatment of the foreign exchange earned from copper sales, KCM was granted similar concessions to those granted to Ramcoz and Chibuluma, with some additional privileges. The most important was that it only needed to remit to Zambia foreign earnings in order to meet local commitments if it did not already have kwacha available to meet such commitments. And for this purpose it was allowed to borrow kwacha locally up to 5% of the value of its annual sales revenues, which at mid-2006 revenues and rates would translate K225 billion – a privilege that has no doubt been transferred to Vedanta, Anglo's successor, about which I write in detail in the next chapter.

But the concession that affected the miners' lives most was the one relating to 'social assets and municipal infrastructural services'. While under an agreement with the Mineworkers Union (MUZ) KCM agreed to 'the provision or procurement of certain medical and recreational services and access to other recreational facilities', the government took over the provision of municipal infrastructural services in areas where KCM would operate. These included: water, sewerage, solid waste, domestic electricity supply, street lighting, storm drainage, roads, markets and cemeteries. By tradition in Zambia and many other parts of the world, the mine owners build housing for their employees and run the townships, including the maintenance of all services, schools and hospitals. No housing needed to be built in Zambia, but Anglo American baulked at the expense of running the townships. With a nod from the IMF and the World Bank, which, I believe, offered to make some initial contribution, the government was landed with the task. This was later passed on to the local councils, which do not have the financial resources to cope. As a result, the townships are neglected and the miners are angry.

The verdict about the mining privatisation process must be that it was botched, and intentionally so. Chiluba wanted to milk the mines for as long as possible and employed many tricks to delay the privatisation process. In the end the mines were sold at giveaway prices and some of the new owners lacked the expertise to operate them. Two were metal traders: one has since failed; the other was later cited by the Volker inquiry for complicity in the Iraq oil-for-food programme. The safety record of the industry, which was an example in southern Africa, has deteriorated, with a major accident reported almost weekly, some involving serious loss of life (an explosion at a new explosives factory killed 52 people in early 2005).

Anglo American Corporation handed Konkola back to the government early in 2002 and withdrew in indecent haste. The professed reason was not convincing: the price of copper was too low at 73 cents per pound, against a break-even requirement of 80 cents. (The price at the end of 2005 was $2 per lb. and in 2006 was averaging about $3.50 per lb.)

There are many cases of plunder pending against Chiluba, and as they are all before the courts I shall remain silent about that aspect of his administration. But other aspects need to be mentioned. I described earlier the arrest and incarceration of Kenneth Kaunda and other prominent politicians on trumped-up charges relating to an aborted coup. Chiluba seemed paranoid on that front. Before the coup many other imagined conspiracies were 'exposed', the first one early in 1993, which gave him the opportunity to reintroduce a 'state of emergency' (another campaign promise reneged on) and incarcerate 26 opposition politicians. This would become another hallmark of his administration: opposition politicians regularly arrested, incarcerated, sent to trial and acquitted mostly on 'nolle prosequi' motions from the Attorney-General, who must have known at the beginning that he did not have the evidence to prosecute.

A number of assassinations, a phenomenon never experienced in Zambia before, remain unsolved: Baldwin Nkumbula an ex-MMD minister who resigned citing growing corruption in the MMD, died in a car accident under very suspicious circumstances; a lawyer who was investigating a case of fraud; a senior MMD official who was due to give evidence against the government the next day; Ronald Penza, the ex-Minister of Finance a few months after his dismissal from the Cabinet; and many others. But the most famous amongst them is the assassination of Wezi Kaunda, the former President's third son and the most politically active amongst his children. He was dragged from his car as he stopped to open his front gate on the evening of 3 November 1999, and shot four times. The assailants, who did not hurt his wife, escaped with the car. The police called it a car hijacking, but even car hijackers must have the common sense not to go for prominent people outside their gates. Most people believe it was a political assassination. The doctors at the University Teaching Hospital fought valiantly to save his life, and after an operation lasting many hours they declared that Wezi would survive. But he died from an internal haemorrhage at 6 a.m. the next day. The family believes that somebody interfered with the tubes during the night. His father says: 'My son was assassinated twice.'

I visited Chiluba for the last time on the day of Wezi's funeral. I had received a call from State House the previous day setting up an appointment for 11 a.m. I said I could not make it because I was going to the funeral. They came back and suggested 6 p.m. Chiluba was very gracious this time – he obviously needed a favour. By that time he had dropped from his Cabinet his cousin, the businessman/politician who had bought the Chibote group from us, lost it after a default, and then bought it again from the liquidator. (The reader will remember that MIBL repossessed Chibote when the loan became delinquent.)

When MBBZ got into problems, MIBL transferred a large number of Chibote properties to it in order to strengthen its balance sheet and reduce the 'nostro' account. But after the collapse the cousin managed to get the properties back through a High Court Commissioner's order in Kitwe, a Zambian copperbelt town. The Bank of Zambia was appealing and Chiluba was trying to enlist my support: 'Are you prepared to give evidence for the Bank of Zambia?' he asked. I said that I would welcome the opportunity to tell the story in court. 'You can rest assured that it shall be nothing but the truth,' I added. He praised my public spirit and added: 'My cousin says he is one of your acolytes; it is a pity he did not learn to tell the truth.' (The duplicity of Chiluba had no bounds; now that he thought he needed a favour from me he was ready to flatter, ignoring the accusations he had made about me over the years. On departure he escorted me all the way to the entrance of State House.)

Before the end of the visit Chiluba had one more point to make. He was very shocked and distressed about Wezi's murder, he said. He wanted me to convey this to the family and to reassure them that he would leave no stone unturned in order to solve it. He would be calling the British High Commissioner to ask for assistance from Scotland Yard, he said. But the murder was never solved.

The properties saga came to an ignominious end in January 2004. After an inordinate number of postponements, the trial eventually started at the end of November 2003. Only the 'cousin' and one of his cronies managed to give evidence during the allotted session. The case was postponed to February 2004, when my evidence was expected. In mid-January I phoned the lawyer representing the Bank of Zambia to check the dates. He informed me that the case had been settled out of court. I was stunned, and so was the lawyer. The case was going extremely well in favour of the Bank of Zambia and I had no doubt that after my evidence the properties would revert to BOZ and the 'cousin' would have to refund the rents that he had been collecting over the years (there were some 60 properties, industrial, commercial and residential). I later learned that the settlement terms were extremely generous to the 'cousin', being valued at some $2.5 million in properties and cash, plus the retention of the rents he had collected from all the properties over the 10-year period.

The deterioration of the economy during his 10-year tenure testifies to Chiluba's incompetence. He adhered blindly to the economic policies dictated by the multilateral institutions and the donor countries without questioning their suitability and their effects on Zambia. He seemed to take perverse pleasure in destroying structures instead of rectifying faults and solving problems. The agricultural marketing institutions that had been in existence for more than half a century were closed down abruptly, before alternatives had been put in place and without any thought that this might affect agricultural production. Fertiliser distribution was suspended without any thought as to the effects on the income of the peasants or the production of maize, the country's staple food. In fact, any progress made in agriculture was made by and for the benefit of the commercial sector, dominated by large international companies and long-established settlers. Peasant agriculture contracted during Chiluba's period in office.

Foreign imports flooded in from South Africa and other countries, destroying the small industrial base that had been so painstakingly built over nearly three decades of independence. Second-hand clothing was allowed duty free into the country, thus destroying 200 or so clothing factories and tens of thousands of jobs. Total formal employment fell by about 200,000 during his period in office and per capita income deteriorated by 15%, with the number of people living below the poverty line rising to 73% of the population. (This masks a horrible imbalance between urban and rural areas: while the urban average was 56%, the average for the rural population was 83%.) And school enrolment fell by 15% during Chiluba's period.

Zambia Airways was closed down with no regard to the effects on the tourist industry. It had been established in 1965 and had a 30-year history of reliable service and name recognition amongst the international travel industry. It did have problems, such as extravagant management and high over-employment, but, instead of addressing them, the government decided to close it down. The result was an abrupt interruption to the flow of visitors, because Zambia no longer had direct international flights and visitors had to be routed via Harare or Johannesburg. Tourism took many years to revive, and even though statistics show a large increase in the number of visitors the biggest proportion of those are business visits relating to the mining sector. I have already written about Chiluba's high interest rates policy, which destroyed many businesses and stifled domestic private investment after 1993.

But his downfall came about because he underestimated the intelligence of the Zambian people. He schemed to change the constitution in order to run for a third term. He did so clandestinely. First he went though a series of underhand manoeuvres. He issued an edict that no MMD official was allowed to campaign for the presidency until he said so. After that he announced that he did not want to stand for a third term but if the people wanted him to he would consider it. Then he started a vigorous campaign through a number of cronies to win support. Amusingly, he asked one of the televangelist stations in the United States to pray for him; a cynical explanation that I heard at the time was that he believed American witchcraft to be stronger than African. Then he manipulated his party's conference to elect his own surrogates on the MMD central committee. And, suddenly, it all collapsed. There was such an outcry from the institutions, the churches, the professionals and the country at large that he ran scared and announced that he had never really intended to stand. With only a few months before the election his party ended up without a candidate and very little time to find one.

Chiluba, then, conjured up a new scheme in a hurry. He would have a puppet whom he could manipulate from the back seat. Didn't Nyerere do the same in Tanzania? Like Nyerere, Chiluba would remain the president of the MMD, and from that position he would exercise power over the President of the country. He did not realise that what Nyerere was exercising was not power but persuasion, because he had the intellect, education, selfless public spirit and sheer gravitas – qualities conspicuously absent from Chiluba. And Nyerere never did anything for personal gain, which was always Chiluba's prime motive.

Eventually Chiluba stumbled on Levy Patrick Mwanawasa, a lawyer from Ndola, the capital of the Copperbelt Province of Zambia, as the repository of his ambitions. He had been his Vice-President for a couple of years in his first administration, and then left (on a matter of principle, Mwanawasa would say, but much, much later). The immediate job at hand was to win the election, to market the candidate, to make him popular and electable. It was a difficult task. Mwanawasa was not a crowd-puller. He was not a natural speaker and he was not comfortable on the hustings. But the opposition was split into four, which made the job of winning the election easier, especially with the weight of the government and its resources in support.

It made for a very confused and entertaining campaign. The candidates did not care about campaign platforms and defined policies in order to win the electorate. They were throwing verbal arrows at each other. This inspired Hugh Russell (a pen-name, I found out later) to write a series of hilarious articles in the London *Spectator*. Russell came to the conclusion that none of the candidates was good enough and proposed Vera Chiluba as an alternative. I shall copy one of the many snippets about her, because I found it very funny. It starts with Chiluba and his wife Vera arriving for a banquet at Buckingham Palace.

> ... It was as they say a glittering occasion. But as he went to take his seat beside the Queen, President Fred realised that much of the glitter was provided by the extensive range of cutlery at each place setting. He could handle it. But Vera, who had previously been his house servant and still lacked some sophistication, would be lost. And distressed. Worse, Vera was seated several places away somewhere to the south of the Duke of Edinburgh; far too far away for Fred to whisper advice in her ear. He must help her, President Fred decided, but how?
>
> Inspiration came. Turning to the Queen, the President asked politely if, as a committed Christian, he might be permitted to say grace. And, furthermore, might he say it in his native tongue, the language known as Bemba? Royal assent was graciously given. President Fred rose to his feet and delivered his grace. Roughly speaking it translated thus: 'For what we are about to receive... Vera, listen. The round spoon is for the soup, the funny shaped knife is for the fish and the spoon at the top is for the pudding... may the Lord make us truly thankful. Amen.'

Mwanawasa did win the election, with 29.2% of the vote, against his nearest rival, who polled 27%, but his party, the MMD, did not win a majority in Parliament. He secured it later when he appointed many members of opposition parties as ministers and deputy ministers. They ignored the provision in the Zambian constitution and did not resign to re-contest their seats. They claimed that they did not cross the floor; they merely decided to participate in the Mwanawasa government in the national interest while still remaining loyal members of their party. Even after some had been expelled by their parties and had no alternative but to bow out, they managed, with court injunctions and lawsuits, to hold on to their seats, and with adjournments, etc., they did so until Parliament was dissolved for the new elections in September 2006.

But Chiluba did not get to be the puppeteer he schemed to be. Quite the opposite. Early on after his election his chosen successor went to Parliament and succeeded in getting Chiluba's immunity removed. He has since charged him with a number of cases of plunder, which come up before the court from time to time and keep the country entertained.

And where is the Mwanawasa administration going?

32. QUO VADIT?

Mwanawasa branded his administration as the 'new deal government' (I am not quite sure what this meant to convey). But he later introduced new labels: 'the anti-corruption government', 'the government of laws', etc., all of which made him the darling of the West. (Nothing special about that – Mwanawasa was still in his first term.) And his government had one major economic success. It managed to attain the benchmarks required of heavily indebted poor countries (Highly Indebted Poor Countries [HIPC] status), and Zambia qualified for foreign debt forgiveness in 2005, albeit after the IMF benevolently accepted 'commercialisation' in place of the privitisation it had demanded for certain large parastatals. More about this strange concept later.

It could also boast of some success in agriculture, where, with the help of reasonable rainfall, maize production increased and made Zambia self-sufficient in food for a couple of years. But then the rains failed again and the 2004/5 harvest was very poor. Zambia had to import maize again – back to the normal cycle. There was some influx of Rhodesian farmers in the first couple of years of the twenty-first century (courtesy of Robert Mugabe's land redistribution policies in next-door Zimbabwe), which was hailed internationally as the agricultural salvation of Zambia. It was not. Most Rhodesians were actually tobacco farmers and their contribution to the increase in maize production is exaggerated. In fact, the complaint locally is that, though they promised one acre of maize for each acre of tobacco, they turned to wheat instead because they found it more profitable. The problem is that both tobacco and wheat are irrigated crops and there are concerns about overusing meagre water resources.

Contrary to general belief, Zambia does not have abundant water supply for agriculture. It does have two large river catchments: the Zambezi, which covers 75% of the country (and includes the Kafue and the Luangwa tributaries), and the Congo (which includes the Chambeshi and the Luapula rivers). As the Water Board of Zambia highlights, the northern part of the country has a